MONEY MANAGEMENT FOR THE FAITHFUL

MONEY MANAGEMENT FOR THE FAITHFUL

SCOTT CARTER

CFI
An imprint of Cedar Fort, Inc.
Springville, Utah

This is not an official publication of The Church of Jesus Christ of Latter-day Saints. The opinions and views expressed herein belong solely to the author and do not necessarily represent the opinions or views of Cedar Fort, Inc. Permission for the use of sources, graphics, and photos is also solely the responsibility of the author.

Paperback ISBN 13: 978-1-4621-4598-0
Ebook ISBN 13: 978-1-4621-4657-4

Published by CFI, an imprint of Cedar Fort, Inc.
2373 W. 700 S., Suite 100, Springville, UT 84663
Distributed by Cedar Fort, Inc., www.cedarfort.com

Library of Congress Registration Number: 2023942346

Cover design by Nada Orlic
Cover design © 2023 Cedar Fort, Inc.
Edited by Liz Kazandzhy
Typeset by Liz Kazandzhy

Printed in the United States of America

10 9 8 7 6 5 4 3 2 1

Printed on acid-free paper

Dedicated to friends who have passed through the veil before me:
Jim Hughes, Kelly Paine, Darrin Buttle, Karen Lewis,
Perry Merrill, Tom Tate, and Mike Alex

Contents

Acknowledgments

A GRATEFUL SALUTE TO ALL THOSE WHO HAVE INFLUENCED MY LIFE, and a short reason why:

- Jesus Christ: His Atonement. Now all things are possible.
- Paul Dunn: Since men and women are to have joy. Early in life, I observed Paul exhibit joy in all places he taught.
- Victor Davis Hanson: His knowledge of history grips me. All presidents should seek his counsel.
- President Gordon B. Hinckley: The rock and at times fun.
- Elder Jeffrey R. Holland: Humble and bore a testimony that always gripped me.
- Kim Johnson and Pat Tate: These ladies showed an interest in me and encouraged me to be great while I was growing up.
- President Abraham Lincoln: No mortal suffered so much for so many who brought about freedom for so many. He also put forward what the founding fathers could not.
- Harvey Mackay: For his business wisdom in the shortest of many stories.
- Elder Neal A. Maxwell: He and I connected when he admitted to struggling with an English class. From then on, I listened intently to his masterful speeches. In a single sentence, he can preach a sermon.

- President Thomas S. Monson: If you could have a third grandfather, he would be mine. He truly loved us all.
- Dr. Jordan Peterson: Against popular opinion, Dr. Peterson speaks the truth so very clearly that it is liberating.
- Jim Perrault: Teenage friend. Companion on many occasions.
- Ayn Rand: She promotes the young entrepreneurs of our day, and she gave me an eternal glimpse of the telestial kingdom. In the end, her characters live happily alone while striving to work their will for their benefit alone.
- Fred Rogers (AKA Mr. Rogers): He taught me that the most important person was the person directly in front of you.
- Jim Rohn: First motivational speaker I discovered who encouraged me to set my life's course on a path of success for myself, my family, and others.
- The Prophet Joseph Smith: An imperfect person called to restore the seemingly impossible.

I thank my Father in Heaven for these individuals who nurtured me during important crossroads in my life. Who are yours?

All my profits will benefit the Humanitarian Fund program.

Preface

The gospel and our personal finances, I believe, go together hand in glove.

One day as I perused the shelves dedicated to self-help financial books at my local Deseret Book, I discovered how lacking the available material was that linked sound money advice with known gospel principles. As a person who built his career around money matters, I was surprised at that fact. Isn't the gospel the cornerstone of everything in our lives? Why should finance be any different?

Right then and there, I decided to write that book myself. After all, I have experience in both areas.

Even among the members of The Church of Jesus Christ of Latter-day Saints, finances seem to be a taboo subject. We don't talk much about finances among our family and friends. It can be embarrassing or appear as though we are prying, and often our left hand doesn't know what our right hand is doing . . . but in a bad way. In my professional career, I often find that one spouse knows the money and the other does not.

So to help get past all of that, I thought of a few questions we need to ask ourselves when we start a faithful financial journey:

- How much money do you need while completing your time on God's good earth?

- Will you have enough money to satisfy your needs and your wants?
- Do you want millions of dollars? Do you want the responsibility that goes along with having millions of dollars?
- If you suddenly came into a fortune, how would that change your life?
- Is seeking a fortune congruous with God's plan for you?
- What do you want to accomplish in your life? Is it possible to have enough money for those needs and wants?

I believe it *is* possible to dial in very closely to the amount of money you will need without getting overly wrapped up in continuously pursuing more money just for the sake of having it. Isn't more money best? Not at the exclusion of what is most important.

To dial that in, we need to look at numbers. Luckily we live in a world where technology allows us to peer into our financial futures and help figure out what we need to do today.

What's called the "Monte Carlo approach" takes into consideration all your income streams, assets, liabilities, financial needs, and wants.[1] The supercomputers of today will number-crunch a thousand possible outcomes over your future lifetime and present your probability of successfully achieving your financial dreams. What this means to you is that you can now hone in on what is important in your life, not just the pursuit of yet another million dollars for an unknown reason. How much money do you need? Having sufficient for your needs is the answer! The Monte Carlo approach to financial preparedness can drastically help you.

Financial preparedness also involves investing. I know that seems intimidating to some, but trust me, it's also a gospel principle.

For me, investing means you believe in the future. I think the Lord sees things the same way. As I witness a newborn coming into the world, I think to myself that God is investing in our collective futures. He still believes in us and our potential for better tomorrows.

You will too.

Believe.

1. Will Kenton, "Monte Carlo Simulation: History, How it Works, and 4 Key Steps," Investopedia, last modified Mar. 26, 2023, https://www.investopedia.com/terms/m/montecarlosimulation.asp.

Some choose to fear the future. If fear is your focus, you will never find peace. I say save for college, purchase life insurance, and invest for your retirement—because knowing you are prepared will give you peace. Live as though the Second Coming of Jesus Christ is tomorrow, yet plan for a long and happy future.

And following gospel truths, even when it comes to money, will reap benefits far beyond your bank account balance.

Over my life, I have valued the gospel and have stayed close to it. I intend to use gospel principles throughout this financial guide. I will draw from leaders and authors I respect and those who have demonstrated such great wisdom worthy of passing on. I cannot do it all myself, and I will not even try to "out-do" the best of the best.

For instance, while serving a mission, I had the privilege to hear from Elder Robert L. Backman. The 1984 Summer Olympics were all the conversation then, and his talk, entitled "Swifter, Higher, Stronger," struck a chord within me.[2] His words inspired me to set goals so I could achieve more out of my life.

Similarly, in 2007 I listened to Elder Dallin H. Oaks, then a member of the Quorum of the Twelve Apostles, give a talk entitled "Good, Better, Best."[3] That sermon resonated with me as it did with many in the Church. I still hear others referencing that magnificent talk from time to time. This speech in particular inspired an important framework I'll be using throughout this book: Good, Better, Best, and Awful. Why awful? Jim Rohn, another key figure in my life, once said it was unfortunate that people who failed in their endeavors were never invited to go around giving seminars. We can all learn what *not* to do from these individuals. So to present both sides of life's many experiences, I want to include awful failures too, as Jim Rohn suggested.

This is a collection of known principled techniques, skills, and a bit of restored gospel to help you determine what choices you need to make today so that you can create your very best financial future. Use the techniques, skills, tips, and suggestions to evaluate where you are and where you want to be.

Mortality without gospel truths is to suffer through life. I choose not to suffer through life. Men and women are that they might have

2. Robert L. Backman, "Swifter, Higher, Stronger," *Liahona*, July 1982.

3. Dallin H Oaks, "Good, Better, Best," *Ensign* or *Liahona*, Nov. 2007, 104–108.

joy (see 2 Nephi 2:25). Joy is choosing to be a disciple living the covenant life and, therefore, a complete mortal existence. This is the closest you'll ever get to Matthew 5:48: "Be ye therefore perfect, even as your Father which is in heaven is perfect."

Now get ready—because we're going on a journey that will open your eyes about how much the Lord loves each of us and how much He cares about our financial security and the peace that it affords.

Introduction

Whether you're twenty-eight years old or fifty-eight years old, what is written here will expand your understanding of the relationship between finances and the gospel.

The principles contained are often small and simple, but that's the point.

It is by the small and simple things that all great and marvelous works are created (see Alma 37:6–7). God has revealed how He works among His children. If you believe in Bible stories, recall David slaying Goliath—a small and simple young man, but how profound his impact! This example teaches us that God can work through a simple young man to bring about great things.

Again, consider that a simple and mostly uneducated fourteen-year-old boy searched for God's gospel while in upstate New York. Joseph Smith learned about the history of a people who lived in the Americas anciently, and they left a record engraved on metal plates. Those plates were entrusted to Joseph and translated in only a few months' time. Only a small handful of Saints gathered on April 6, 1830, to organize the Church of Jesus Christ in these latter days. From small and simple things, the gospel flourishes worldwide, now millions strong.

By small and simple things, you too can accomplish your great mission. You can read through and apply what this study guide has to offer and financially succeed in your righteous desires.

Read on. I think you will enjoy what you discover.

1

In the Beginning

If you live in North America, you live better than most kings and queens of Europe ever lived. You probably have access to relatively clean running water, generous amounts of food in all their varieties, decent health care, education, and police protection. If done right, you may retire somewhere around sixty-six years old and be on a paid vacation for the rest of your life. The US has about 330 million people.[4] Imagine about 300 million kings and queens. Who is blessed in these latter days? Certainly you and me.

That being said, there are still billions of people who are not as richly blessed.

The most effective way I know to correct many of the worldwide social problems we face today is to lift the standard of living of all God's children everywhere. Starving people destroy nature to eke out a living, while prosperous people are more concerned about Mother Earth and strive to conserve nature. Poverty, starvation, climate change, deforestation, wildlife endangerment, pollution, and other problems facing society are better corrected and maintained by increasing the standard of living for all God's children.

4. "2020 Census Apportionment Results," United States Census Bureau, Apr. 26, 2021, https://www.census.gov/data/tables/2020/dec/2020-apportionment-data.html.

But you can't effectively help others until you have the resources to help yourself. Once you embark on improving your own life, *then* you can venture out to take on social problems in your community. From there, go as far afield as you want in making the world a better place.

That's the goal, right? Live our lives in such a way that our presence here in mortality makes the world better. Finances are actually a big part of that. Money is a resource that allows us to bless the lives of others. The Lord gave each of us five talents, or two talents, or maybe one talent. Accept these talents God has given you—whether it's five, two, or one—and return more to Him (see Matthew 25:14–17).

The way we do that is by managing our resources effectively. Lucky for us, God gave us principles that can be applied as easily to money as they can to our spiritual well-being. That is the goal over the next 200+ pages: to get all of us to a firm understanding of how the gospel applies to our personal financial well-being.

And it all starts in the same way it did even before God said, "Let there be light"—with a plan.

I have planned out my life for decades. Now, I know what you're probably thinking, "How could you have planned out your life?" I didn't just sit down and say, "This is how life is going to unfold," and then it happened that way. I made plans based on what I wanted and how I thought life would go, but those plans were never static.

Over time these plans have adjusted with mentoring, environment, interests, maturity, understanding, and new experiences. If you do not earnestly plan your life, your life will continue on its course, and you may never arrive where you want to end up. But if you make an honest effort at planning and applying, you will arrive in a good place.

If you're not a big planner, don't worry. We'll go over different strategies that will simplify this process and help take away some of the intimidation you may be feeling. Also, if you don't want to go through the process alone, consider meeting with a financial advisor. We all need mentors and coaches at different stages in our lives. Finances are no different. Don't be afraid to ask for help! With the guidance of a trusted financial advisor, you will know where you are and where you're heading, and you can avoid the fear that comes with being unprepared.

During our journey through this guide, I will often share my professional opinion. I will be careful not to judge harshly. We are taught to judge in matters of lesser mortal importance; God reserves the right to judge matters pertaining to those of an eternal nature. Judge, but make a righteous judgment.[5]

I intend to couple my knowledge with the teachings I find in The Church of Jesus Christ of Latter-day Saints as they pertain to money and success.

As we progress on this financial trek, please do not compare yourself to anyone else. Our experiences in life differ significantly, and I believe it is a mistake to compare one person or circumstance with another. Take Moroni as an example. In the book of Ether, Moroni read the Jaredite record and transcribed portions for the benefit of future readers in these latter days (see Ether 12: 23–41). Moroni was concerned that his weakness in writing would be mocked. For Moroni, this was a moment of self-awareness. Moroni's weakness was not so much his writing ability but rather comparing his writing skills to those of Ether.

We are all different by design, and that's a good thing. We have unique talents and divine purposes for those talents. We have an individual mandate. God had a plan for Ether, a plan for Moroni, and a plan for Joseph Smith, and He has a plan for you and me. Let us not confuse God's plan for us with our perceived shortcomings compared to other people in our lives. Dr. Jordan Peterson said, "Compare yourself to who you were yesterday, not to who someone else is today."[6]

When you read this guide, consider for yourself what could be good for you, even better for you, and finally, what would be best for you. Grade yourself, and do not compare your progress to others. Certainly learn from others—their successes and failures—but don't judge yourself because you didn't know something that someone else did. This may be a fine line, but you can separate yourself from others without beating yourself up. I have included examples of good

5. To delve deeper into this subject, see the work of Dr. Lili De Hoyos Anderson, including her podcast *Choosing Glory*. She has spoken extensively on why and how we need to judge people and circumstances correctly.

6. Jordan B. Peterson, *12 Rules for Life: An Antidote to Chaos* (London: Penguin Books, 2019), 85.

experiences all the way to awful experiences. I believe we can learn from those people who have made serious, life-altering mistakes. The Bible tells stories about men and women whose examples you'll definitely want to follow and plenty whose examples you'll want to avoid at all costs.

Good, better, best, and awful. You can judge for yourself which one most closely fits where you are today. Then choose for yourself if you want to move toward the best or anything in-between.

Waste Not Thy Time

Time is all we have, and while it may seem abundant, it isn't limitless.

Let your mind ponder on the concept that time is money. I know we think of that phrase as something a businessperson would say to justify ending a conversation with an annoying employee, but let me be clear, it is 100 percent a true statement.

I'll repeat it again: time is money.

Church leaders of experience and wisdom have voiced concerns that people today spend too many hours each day playing video games, scrolling through social media, or binge-watching enormous amounts of television.[7] There's nothing inherently wrong with these pastimes when used in moderation, but they too easily devour our most precious resource: time. We trade that time away, and often we are no better because of it. What do we get in return? Maybe a bit of entertainment? Is it worth hours and hours of our lives that we can't get back?

That's a question each of us must answer for ourselves.

We've been counseled to enjoy screen time prudently. Use good judgment with your time and mind. Time is a terrible commodity to lose. Ask yourself what you have to show for a week's worth of screen time. More to the point of this conversation: what have you done with your last week, month, or year as it pertains to your personal development? Time is money. In my profession, I believe this is absolutely true (and I'll dive more into that later). Trade your time wisely. Discipline is key to everyone's success, so work to develop your discipline.

7. See Gordon B Hinckley, "Rise to the Stature of the Divine Within You," *Ensign*, Nov. 1989, 94–98.

In my younger years, I played one of the newest video games called Halo. Later in life, and as the elders quorum president, our presidency occasionally hosted Halo video game nights. We networked several computers and monitors and had a varied group of young elders and older elders playing against each other. We had an absolute blast, and I make no apologies for the camaraderie we enjoyed. So have some fun and laugh together—because that's important too—but then get back to smart and productive work.

Within these pages, we will explore investments, debts in all their varieties, life insurances, wills and trusts, higher educational planning, the purpose of wealth, the law of tithing, provident living principles, gifting, and much more. I will highlight people who succeeded and those who failed in an awful way. Drawing from both examples will inform your decisions. If you find yourself in an awful place, perhaps you will claw your way to a good place. Later you may migrate to a better place, and then perhaps to your best place. After reading this guide, you may come away with a feeling that you are good with investments, better with debt, awful in the area of a legal will, better with life insurance, and good with planning for higher education. Using this guide, you will embark on upgrading the areas of your life that need strengthening while shoring up the areas where you already excel.

A Few Thoughts before We Begin

At the end of each chapter, I have written a section called "Something for the Kids" to help apply the principles of that chapter to children. If you have kids, don't leave them out of your financial discussions and preparation. We do a disservice to our children when we avoid talking about sensitive subjects like money. Bring them in and teach them as you learn some of these principles.

I was quite young when I first began investing. I know you might think that's weird, but I'm a financial guy who loves all this stuff. My point is you should not wait until your children are grown before starting them on a path of sound financial understanding. If you have kids at home, share these portions at the end of the chapters with them, and they will benefit also. Perhaps some time at home evening may be in order?

We're going to be talking a lot about money, obviously, so you need to prepare yourself for having mature discussions about your personal finances and where you may fall short in your skill set. Enter these possibly uncomfortable waters prayerfully. The Lord wants you to succeed, but to do that, we often need to take a hard look at ourselves and realize where we are not doing what needs to be done in order to achieve our life goals, all the while understanding His will for our lives.

It may be painful at times, but you can do it.

We'll briefly discuss job advancement and how to earn more money, if that's what you want. That being the case, I would give you this counsel right now: choose a career over a job. A career is something that motivates you to get up in the morning and invigorates you—a simple "job" doesn't do that.

I have some personal experience in this arena.

My first employment opportunity after graduating from college was with an aerospace company. After the newness wore off, I found myself staring down my next forty years more than a little troubled with the prospect of working there. If you walk into work every Monday morning immediately wishing Friday would come, be warned: this is not a recipe for a rewarding life. From such turn away.

Although my job there was comfortable, in 1999 I entered the office of the human resource representative at that aerospace company. I asked to see the "golden parachute" being offered by my employer should I decide to leave.

I took it.

I left a comfortable "job" and pursued the career I have today. I do not regret the risk I took while making that change. Stepping out of our comfort zone in any aspect of our lives can be very difficult. But the right move is worth it. Whether it's Monday, Friday, or any day between, I enjoy what I do for my livelihood. I hope the same can be said for you.

And it doesn't matter what that career is. I'm interested in investments; someone else may be in software design; another person may be a soap manufacturer. The guy that started Waste Management,

Inc., began by picking up other people's garbage.[8] He became a very wealthy person. Now other people pick up his trash for him!

The moral of the story is that you can be the best at anything and make a very good living for yourself. Be the best gardener, the best plumber, the best hairstylist, the best doctor, or the best educator. Your community is looking for the person with the best skills. And the best are always paid well.

Let me end this introduction with this excerpt from a talk by President Thomas S. Monson, one of the best storytellers I've ever listened to:

> The Apostle Paul described life as a race. He said, "Know ye not that they which run in a race run all, but one receiveth the prize? So run, that ye may obtain."
>
> The writer of the book of Ecclesiastes also wrote of this subject, saying, "The race is not to the swift, nor the battle to the strong." Actually, the prize belongs to him who endures to the end.
>
> In the private sanctuary of one's own conscience lies that spirit, that determination, to press onward and to measure up to the stature of true potential. But the way is rugged, and the course is strenuous. So discovered John Helander from Göteborg, Sweden. John was a young adult. He had the same yearnings for the blessings of success as do all. But John is handicapped, in that it is difficult for him to coordinate his motions.
>
> At an activity of young people in Kungsbacka, Sweden, John took part in an 800-meter running race. He had no chance to win. Rather, his was the possibility of being humiliated, mocked, derided, and scorned. Perhaps John remembered another who lived long ago and far away. Wasn't He mocked? Wasn't He derided? Wasn't He scorned? But He prevailed. He won His race. Maybe John could win his.
>
> What a race it is! Struggling, surging, pressing, the runners bolt far beyond John. There is wonderment among the spectators. Who is this runner who lags so far behind? The participants, on their second lap of this two-lap race, pass John while he is but halfway

8. See Steve Wine and Terry Spencer, "Chicago-born Wayne Huizenga dies at 80; built his fortune through Waste Management and Blockbuster Video," *Chicago Tribune*, Mar. 23, 2018, https://www.chicagotribune.com/business/ct-biz-wayne-huizenga-dies-20180323-story.html.

> through the first lap. Tension mounts as the runners press toward the tape. Who will win? Who will place second? Then comes the final burst of speed; the tape is broken. The crowd cheers; the winner is proclaimed.
>
> The race is over—or is it? Who is this contestant who continues to run when the race is ended? He crosses the finish line on but his first lap. Doesn't he know he has lost? Ever onward he struggles, the only participant now on the track. This is his race. This must be his victory. No one among the vast throng of spectators leaves. Every eye is on this valiant runner. He makes the final turn and moves toward the finish line. There is awe; there is admiration. Every spectator sees himself running his own race of life. As John approaches the finish line, the audience, as one, rises to its feet. There is a loud applause of acclaim. Stumbling, falling, exhausted but victorious, John Helander breaks the newly tightened tape. The cheering echoes for miles. And just maybe, if the ear is carefully attuned, that Great Scorekeeper—even the Lord—can be heard to say, "Well done, thou good and faithful servant."[9]

I definitely couldn't have said it better than that. We're all in our own race. We're all in different places financially and in our understanding. This isn't the time to compare, lament, or quit. The gospel holds the answers we need, and with prayer as our compass, we will overcome the obstacles and discover that our money journey isn't one we need to take alone. The Lord knows what we need before we ask, but it's up to each of us to follow the principles He's laid out if we want to truly succeed.

Let's get started!

9. Thomas S. Monson, "Guideposts for Life's Journey" (Brigham Young University devotional, Nov. 13, 2007), 5–6, speeches.byu.edu.

2

Exploring Your Goals

The purpose of wealth is to bless your life, your family, and those around you (see Jacob 2:17–19). Money is neither good nor evil. It's a neutral resource that enhances who we already are. The more you have, though, the greater the responsibility. After all, it's been said many times, "For of him unto whom much is given much is required" (Doctrine and Covenants 82:3).

For now, you need to understand that creating a plan is essential to reaching any type of goal, be it spiritual or financial. If you don't plan a direction for your life, you may end up somewhere you don't want to be. The same can be said about your money. I have firsthand experience with this. My late father is an excellent example of "failing to plan." He lived paycheck to paycheck and was often unemployed. In the end, he lived a needlessly difficult financial life. Forethought and planning could have changed his circumstances and brought peace to our family.

Think about it this way: would you haphazardly pick a destination, leave with no advance planning, and call it your next vacation? Of course you wouldn't. And yet, more often than not, that's how we live our financial lives.

I admit that no laid plan is perfect, but it doesn't need to be—it just needs to be managed and able to be adapted. Life will always have unexpected bends in the road. Any plan you create must be malleable and flexible enough to account for new directions, opportunities, and experiences. If you're single, what will happen to your plan should you marry? If you're married, what will happen to your plan should you find yourself single? Some of these questions may be difficult to ask yourself, but you can't be afraid to delve deep in pursuit of your best future.

Having the right plan, as simple or as complex as you need it to be, will make all the difference.

There are plenty of books, guides, and articles on building wealth over a lifetime. Many of them serve as a one-way path where you either follow the author's way or you fail. There seems to be no middle ground, no in-between, no measure of progress to build on. Money management isn't a "do it this way or the sky will fall" endeavor. Like everything in life, there are degrees of good, better, best, and in some cases awful. Consider this guide a hybrid approach. And even "awful" choices can still help you in the long run. Mistakes and follies, be they our ancestors' or our own, teach us valuable lessons. If we understand and apply what is to be learned from them, we can avoid repeating them.

John Toland, a Pulitzer Prize–winning author, summed up his monumental work *The Rising Sun* by declaring, "I have done my utmost to let the events speak for themselves, and if any conclusion was reached, it was that there are no simple lessons in history, that it is human nature that repeats itself, not history."[10]

Starting Your Plan

Effective financial plans always start with specific goals in mind. These goals vary, but some of the most common are things like retiring at a certain age, paying off the mortgage on your home, helping the kids or grandkids seek their higher education, leaving a legacy to your university, traveling, purchasing that special car or recreational vehicle, saving for children's weddings, helping pay for missions, or going on a senior mission yourself. We all have different goals and

10. John Toland, *The Rising Sun: The Decline and Fall of the Japanese Empire, 1936–1945* (New York: Random House, 1970), foreword.

priorities. What's important for you may not be important to someone else.

For example, over my lifetime I have written several lists of my ever refined life goals in the journals I have kept. Currently I have them condensed into four life goals: Financially Free, Good Health, Large Property, and Christian Family. For years these goals were engraved on my brass key fob. A few years ago I graduated from the key fob and had those very goals engraved on a ring I wear each day on my right hand. Always a reminder.

No two retirements are the same, but when it comes to your finances, there are objectives every retiree must prepare for. How do you transition from saving for a retirement to living off that savings? How do you replace your paycheck with an income stream and continue to manage risk? What goals do you have in mind? What are your priorities? What happens if health problems arise?

Again, these may be difficult questions to ask yourself, but that's the only way you'll be prepared to face the answers.

When starting your initial financial plan, the first thing you're going to need is a journal. I recommend the most expensive blank book you can afford. I'm serious—the most expensive you can afford. Why? Because you'll take care of it and cherish it. If you start with a cheap pad of paper, you may discover it discarded under the front seat of your car one day. But if you go for the higher-priced, leather-bound book that has a place for a pen, you'll find that value translates to how you treat the journal. In cases like this, spending more will pay off.

Next, you need a place to start. You can't know where you're going unless you know where you are and where you want to be.

Let's begin with a goal of retiring in thirty years with one million dollars in your retirement accounts. Sound good? Now, assuming you can earn an annual investment return of 7 percent (never guaranteed, but it gives us some numbers to play with), you will need to save about $882 each month to accomplish this goal. If that amount sounds too great, don't be discouraged. Start with what you *can* save, and as you develop discipline, you will make up for lost opportunity over your lifetime.

This is where my good, better, best, and awful come in. I will suggest what might be considered good, and perhaps you will see that you are better or maybe even best. Learn from the best and then avoid awful circumstances if you can. We all can learn from those who went before us and ended up in a very bad way. So if $882 a month (the best situation) is unreachable now, perhaps $200 a month is a good place to start. A better place would be $400 a month if possible. And of course, $0 a month is awful. Now you know what is good, better, best, and awful.

Knowing where you want to be and what it will take to get there will make all the difference in your financial life. Most people simply work paycheck to paycheck, and what they have left in their account when they retire is what they live on. This approach is the proverbial tail-wags-the-dog method. It's backward planning. Although this approach is very popular, we know that what is popular isn't always right. In my opinion, more people succeed with a plan. You can make one yourself or have a financial advisor help you, but either way, without a strategic plan in place, life will naturally put up roadblocks and very little will happen.

Let's briefly look at three case studies that help illustrate this point. Each example is about someone at a different place in their lives, with different financial resources and goals. By making plans now, they are best prepared for their futures.

Case Study #1

Jacob and Avery are fifty-two and forty-eight years old, respectively. They have four children ages eighteen, twenty, twenty-two, and twenty-four. Jacob works in the accounting field, and Avery chose to stay home to raise the children. She will enter the workforce after the last child leaves home.

Here are their financials:

- Jacob's annual salary is $140,000, and Avery will plan for a $48,000 salary in her preferred field beginning in two years. She plans to be employed for about ten years once she enters the workforce.
- Their home has a mortgage of $230,000 and is valued at about $485,000. They will continue to pay off their loan over the next thirteen years.

- Jacob and Avery own both the family cars. They plan to replace one of them in two years and budgeted about $40,000 for it. They intend to pay cash from their savings and investments.
- Jacob maximizes the company-sponsored 401k plan, and the company has matched $8,000 each year. The balance is roughly $500,000.
- Avery has a Roth IRA (individual retirement account). They contribute $5,000 each year and have a balance of roughly $47,000.
- Separately, their joint investment account contains stocks, bonds, and cash valued at $89,000.
- Although they have two credit cards, both are paid off each month.
- According to the social security statement Avery recently received, Jacob is entitled to $3,100 each month at full retirement age (FRA). Avery will likely choose one-half of her husband's benefit at her FRA, but she can make that choice later in life.
- During retirement, they want to maintain their standard of living, which will require about $80,000 each year. Their wants include serving a twelve-month mission, the purchase of a new car priced at roughly $40,000, and yearly travels around the world that would require about $13,000 each year for eight years.

Without getting in the weeds, the chances of this plan working are about 86%. Very good odds of success! Having this knowledge will help Jacob and Avery understand what they need to do in order to see their retirement plans to completion.

Case Study #2

Jamee is twenty-eight years old and has two children, ages five and nine. Jamee works in the medical field.

Here are her financials:

- Jamee's salary is $80,000.
- She rents her home for $2,000 a month and desires to purchase a home later in life.

- Jamee owns the family car but plans to replace it within the next five years through financing or outright purchase.
- Jamee maximizes the company-sponsored 401k plan, and the company has matched $6,000 each year. The balance is roughly $110,000.
- Her savings account has a balance of nearly $13,000.
- Each of her children have 529 education plans, which are tax-advantaged savings accounts designed to be used for the beneficiary's education expenses. She contributes $1,000 a year.
- She has two credit cards. Both are paid off each month.
- According to her most recent social security statement, Jamee is entitled to $2,300 each month at full retirement age (FRA).
- Retirement seems so far away, but she is a planner and settles on 80% of her current income, which calculates to $64,000 in today's dollars. Her "wants" include serving a twelve-month mission, the purchase of a new car, and seeing her kids get their higher education. She also would like to explore the world and would need approximately $10,000 each year for ten years to accomplish that.

The chances of this plan working for Jamee are about 92%.[11] Because she's starting young, the odds of success are far greater for her. The earlier you start your plan and understand what the numbers mean, the easier the process becomes.

Case Study #3

Jack and Roselyn are sixty-two and fifty-two years old, respectively. They have two grown children and five grandchildren. Jack works in the construction field, and Roselyn is a school administrator.

Here are the financials:

- Jack's annual salary is $85,000 and Roselyn's is $97,000.

11. The projections or other information generated by financial planning software regarding the likelihood of various investment outcomes are hypothetical in nature, do not reflect actual investment results, and are not guarantees of future results. Financial planning software results may vary with each use over time.

- Their home was purchased years ago and has a mortgage of $105,000 and a Home Equity Line of Credit (HELOC) of $43,000. The home is valued at about $325,000. They have about eight years left on the mortgage and about five years on the HELOC.
- Jack and Roselyn own two of their three family cars. The third is more of a recreational vehicle, and they owe about $11,000 on the loan. They plan to replace one of the vehicles in three years and spend about $50,000. They intend to finance that purchase.
- Jack maximizes his company-sponsored 401k plan, and the company has matched $4,500 each year. The balance is roughly $225,000. Roselyn also maximizes her 403b, and the school matches about $8,000. Roselyn's balance is roughly $435,000.
- They also inherited some stocks, bonds, and cash valued at $19,000.
- They have two credit cards. Both have balances of $3,500 and $2,300.
- According to their most recent social security statement, Jack is entitled to $2,900 each month at full retirement age (FRA). Roselyn is entitled to $3,250 each month at full retirement age (FRA).
- To maintain their standard of living in retirement, they'll need approximately $100,000 annually. Their wants include purchasing a recreational vehicle valued at $120,000 and a new car or boat equal to their lifestyle, likely at $40,000. Yearly travels around the country and world would require another $13,000 each year for ten years.

The chances of this plan working are about 74%. Even though their odds are lower than the other examples, knowing where they're at today will help Jack and Roselyn make better financial decisions going forward. Perhaps there are other ways they can adapt and save more to improve their chances. If they didn't know their current standing, they wouldn't know what appropriate changes to make.

The popular financial planning tool known as Monte Carlo will simulate a thousand scenarios at the high speed of a computer.[12] Simply put, your trusted financial advisor inputs some personal information to include your financial goals, income, debts, and all savings and investments. The Monte Carlo will quickly look back in history for market returns and run a thousand possible future outcomes based on your known information. Your output is a statistical probability of meeting all financial goals through retirement. (More on this later when we tackle planning.) Want a glimpse into your financial future? Sit down with a trusted financial advisor. Ask for your plan to be created.

Expenses and Saving

Making financial course corrections today can have a dramatic impact on your life going forward. President Dieter F. Uchtdorf has spoken many times about his experiences as an airline pilot and how constant course corrections are necessary for a safe flight.[13] If you're off by a few degrees early on in your journey, without a course correction, disastrous results can often follow.

The same holds true for your financial well-being. A few important critical changes to poor financial habits today have the potential for positively wonderful results to your future.

If you are like most people, saving for retirement is not your only responsibility. You likely have a mortgage or rent, other bills, obligations, and contributions each month. Add in vacations and entertainment to enhance your lifestyle, and before you know it, you have little or nothing to put aside for your retirement years.

If this is the situation you find yourself in, don't despair! There is good news. With proper planning and discipline, you can still achieve a comfortable retirement without sacrificing too much in terms of your lifestyle. One key component is keeping your expenses in check.

12. Will Kenton, "Monte Carlo Simulation: History, How it Works, and 4 Key Steps," Investopedia, last modified Mar. 26, 2023, https://www.investopedia.com/terms/m/montecarlosimulation.asp.

13. See Dieter F Uchtdorf, "A Matter of a Few Degrees," *Ensign* or *Liahona*, May 2008, 57–60.

Like everything in life, watching your expenses and saving money is a balancing act. If you save to the point that life is not enjoyable, you risk being miserable. Pain is the first clue. Sacrificing modestly now for something of great worth later is a worthy goal. Use measured discipline when saving. A wise lady shared with me that when she got a raise, half of the raise went into the company-sponsored retirement plan, and half improved her lifestyle. Seems reasonable to me.

Also, do not binge and fast when it comes to saving for retirement. Slow and steady wins the retirement planning race. I have dealt with people saving a bunch of money in the company retirement plan in the first few months only to realize they can't live on what is left over. They withdraw money early at great expense and under tax penalty.

These are the sorts of decisions that can derail your retirement train. Employ measured steps.

At the same time, there are incentives for employers that can pad your retirement account and help get you further ahead than you would by saving on your own. Some companies match their employee's retirement contributions to a degree. Some businesses also offer Health Savings Accounts (HSA), which let you set aside money on a pre-tax basis to pay for qualified medical and health expenses. These accounts can be saved now and used for retirement purposes later. This is another tool that can add money to your overall retirement goal. Basically, the employer match is free money. Your contribution coupled with your employer's match can add up quickly.

That's the saving portion. Now let's look closer at your expenditures and how they can affect your future.

Let's say you plan on retiring at a certain age with a certain after-tax income stream, and that plan is moving forward nicely. Prior to retirement, you feel comfortable and willing to splurge on a few things by pulling from your savings. A dream sports car catches your eye along with a vacation cabin in the mountains. These seem like important priorities right now, but purchasing them today can endanger your retirement plan. As another example, my cousin received company stocks each year from his employer, and each year he sold the stocks and spent the proceeds on entertainment. He reported to me in his retirement that his actions had been unwise, and he wished he had acted differently. That Ferrari you buy at age fifty will not bring you comfort at age seventy if you have little in the way of savings.

The same goes for college tuition and the like. When you are faced with the choice of saving for a child or grandchild's higher education or investing enough to meet your retirement needs, you should consider your retirement needs first. Students can get grants, obtain loans, or take on a part-time job to help pay for school. But senior citizens cannot get financial aid to retire!

Likewise, taking on unnecessary and expensive debt can derail your retirement. So can a withdrawal from your savings to help a family member. One time, a client called to ask my opinion about financially helping an irresponsible brother-in-law with his drunk driving litigation. The amount asked for was about $50,000. I was asked to help with their decision. I play the impartial role of financially counseling my clients, so I simply ran the withdrawal through their financial plan. The result showed that my clients would likely not realize a few of their retirement goals if they were to withdraw that money. I provided the mathematical answer they needed to say no to their reckless brother-in-law. It was their money to give, but now they knew the long-term impact on their future goals.

Except for emergencies, you should avoid premature distributions or borrowing from your company-sponsored retirement plan. Premature withdrawals are taxed as ordinary income, and a 10 percent tax penalty is added for those under 59½ years old. If you need to borrow, consider other sources. The term will hurt enough for you to pay it back quickly. Borrowing from your company plan is too easy and too comfortable, and you'll lose out on market participation with that money. There may be other financial consequences too. Check with your employer.

Planning to Succeed

Hopefully all of this helps you realize the importance of having a plan. Remember, the key to any successful strategy is that your plan needs to be malleable. Life is anything but predictable. You'll need to adapt, and so will your financial plan.

You can start by looking at your net worth and building your approach from there. I advise engaging the services of a qualified and trusted financial advisor (FA). Interview as many as you need to find a good fit. Ask your family and friends for referrals. Look for someone with experience in creating and maintaining financial plans and someone who will invest in a way that makes you comfortable. Above all, work with a financial advisor who listens to you and who you trust.

Your FA will create a financial plan by helping you prioritize and refine your goals, then monitor your progress. The FA will keep in touch with you as your working career or retirement life changes. Use that advisor as a sounding board for all things financial. If your FA is not willing to listen or take the time to answer your questions, get a new advisor. It's that simple.

Your financial future is too important to leave to chance . . . or to bad consultants who don't have your best interests at heart.

One Last Look

Good: Although you could be a better investor, you're saving a little and spending a lot. After all, life is short, and you want to enjoy the moment.

Better: You grasp the need to save for the future and are automatically contributing to your company-sponsored retirement plan. You have a handful of financial priorities, but they are dreams because they are not written down and measured. Die with experiences, not dreams.

Best: You're working with a financial advisor who creates a plan for you and monitors it regularly. Every year, you review your financial life and make necessary adjustments. You participate in adding funds to your portfolio and paying down debt.

Awful: A friend shared this true story about her uncle, Ron. Ron had a stable job that he really enjoyed, but the pay was never quite enough for his growing family. His paycheck never stretched to the next payday. His wife found things to do on the side to make ends meet. Ron had a lot of opportunities for advancements at work, but they required additional certificates or classes. He did not possess the ambition to move up and was content to stay at the bottom of the company ladder. They had no family goals to work toward. Everything they did financially was reactive. Each additional expense put them back and never forward. After their fifth child was born, Ron's wife felt she needed to enter the workforce. The financial stress was enormous. As a couple, they saw less and less of each other. They grew apart and eventually their marriage dissolved. Money is a huge part of every relationship.

Something for the Kids

Encourage your children to make a twelve-month plan with a documented financial goal in mind, like buying a computer or bicycle. Have them monitor it monthly on graph paper or a computer spreadsheet and summarize what took place each month—how much they spent versus how much they earned. Set a small reward when they reach four months, then eight months, and then the twelve-month goal. Ask, "How did the outcome change from what you thought when you started?" The lesson is learned from the journey, so make sure they stick with their plan for twelve months. Ask them to record what they learn in a journal.

At times I've agreed to match money saved by my children if they have a worthy financial goal in mind. This works very well.

3

Overcoming Money Fears

The Lord has said that if you are prepared, you shall not fear (see Doctrine and Covenants 38:30).

So how do we prepare financially? Before we can save or invest or do anything with our money, we need to learn to understand money. Starting with an understanding of how financial markets work will go a long way toward pulling back the mystery and dispelling the fear.

Remember Christ's parable of the talents (see Matthew 25:14–17)? He gave those talents to the servants so they would invest them and return more. We use this parable to talk about our personal talents and abilities, but the real-life principle works for money exactly as it's stated in the parable. The servant who had one talent gave into fear and buried it in the earth when he could have doubled it and used it to further the Lord's purposes.

We are asked to do the same thing. That's why we can't be afraid to invest, use our money wisely, and spend it to help ourselves and others.

I've heard it said many times over the course of my career that the stock markets are rigged. Let me say this very plainly: the stock markets are *not* rigged. Every company in existence (including the one you work for) is trying to gain some edge over their competitors so they can be more efficient in order to be more profitable. That is capitalism at its best, and until Christ comes, for disciples, this is our best business model. Even so, no one entity has the markets-at-large rigged to their advantage. Fear not and participate.

Now, that doesn't mean there aren't nefarious people out there trying to separate you from your money using phishing schemes and targeted attacks. They exist. It's part of the landscape. But if you pay attention—and realize that what seems "too good to be true" probably is—you'll avoid most pitfalls.

When false claims and impossible investment returns are presented, we must be wary. One of my clients fell into this trap after an investment firm in France guaranteed 17 percent interest on his investment. If anyone ever guarantees you a huge return like that and it seems too good to be true . . . it is. I tried to persuade my client from withdrawing $50,000 and investing in the French firm, but he was adamant. I could not change his mind. And unfortunately, he lost all his investment to the French firm and had no recourse to recover it. Remember, the US government is not going after crooks in overseas markets for you. All was lost. Gone.

Here's another example that hits closer to home. I recently saw an ongoing internet ad that read something like this: "The man that predicted the 2008 market crash has now predicted the mother of all crashes." Scary, right? We've all seen ads like this on social media or websites we've frequented. Well, this ad is "click-bait," trying to lure unsuspecting people down a rabbit hole with the intent of separating them from their money.

First off, no one can predict market fluctuations. No one. It's a complicated system based on thousands of companies and millions of investments all crashing into each other every moment. Think about the March Madness basketball brackets for a moment. Sixty-four teams are matched. Games begin and eliminations happen quickly. Soon there are only eight teams left, then four, then two, until finally a winner is crowned. That's a data set of only sixty-four points, and yet the chances of guessing all the possibilities and final outcome correctly are 1 in 120 billion.

When it comes to financial markets, you have thousands of people making thousands of predictions, half of them contradicting each other. Should one person get it right, odds are that it was a lucky guess. Do not fall for the "click-bait"—it's most likely a scam. Better yet, contact your financial advisor before acting. They have additional resources to help you.

Keep this in mind as you're looking to invest, and a lot of your fear will melt away.

And here's another bit of advice that you might not expect: don't take yourself too seriously, but just seriously enough. Investing is a long game. Losses will happen. Accept that they happen, remain calm, learn from them, and over time your market experience will improve. Remember, what matters is not market timing but time in the market. Best to learn with small amounts rather than big money. Successful investors are right more times than they are wrong, but they are wrong sometimes. Think of your investments like your mortal life; if your entire existence from birth to death was a single knot on a spool of thread, you wouldn't even be able to see the knot once you pulled all the thread off the spool and laid it out straight. The entire spool represents eternal life. Your mortal life is important, yes, but small.

This is a long game—life *and* our finances. Don't get caught in the weeds. Smile and allow for bumps. Believe in yourself and trust in the Lord.

Now, that doesn't mean we stand there and do nothing when things go awry. You may face a situation that has you paralyzed and needing some sort of corrective action. Write down the situation. Write down the worst outcome, listing as many details as possible. Write down the most acceptable outcome, and list as many positive details as possible. Your situation will most likely fall somewhere in the middle.

Now the question becomes: how can you make the "middle" better?

In the banking crisis that struck in 2008–2010, many banks failed. This was a volatile time with a lot of uncertainty and fear. A neighbor of mine sold her stocks and went completely to cash. In 2015 she admitted to me that she was still in cash . . . too frightened to re-enter the stock market. Unfortunately for my neighbor, between 2011 and 2015, the market improved significantly. Because of her fear, she missed out on the biggest recovery in years.

Expansion, Peak, Contraction, and Troughs in Our Life. Repeat.

Market expansion is prosperity for most of society. Market peak has exhausted the prosperity. Market contraction requires a realignment, and market troughs are hard times for society. Stated is the typical and often repeatable four-part market cycle. Life follows this same pattern closely.

I reflect on a lecture Jim Rohn provided me. He said something to the effect that the winters of life can be long and hard, but when does spring come? Right after winter. If you had to place spring among the seasons, where would you place it? Right after winter. God is a genius.

After all bad experiences, good still survives . . . always. If this were not true, then Satan would win and there would be no God. Let us look at some common and uncommon examples of good coming from bad.

Wars have littered the course of world history from the very beginning. Why does God allow such atrocities? The very first gift God gave His children was agency. We sometimes refer to it as "free agency," but in my opinion, there is no such thing as "free agency." All choices have consequences, both good and bad. You can't choose your consequences—they are the payment for your choices. If we choose to make war, war will likely be the consequence.

When I was young, I often wondered why a loving God would not intervene when wars claimed so many innocent victims. As I read the Book of Mormon for about the twentieth time, I began to get into the weeds. In the book of Alma, I read about Alma and Amulek watching as the wicked people of Ammonihah cast innocent people into the fiery pit and burned them to death. I thought very long and hard on Alma 14:11: "For behold the Lord receiveth them up unto himself, in glory, and he doth suffer that they may do this thing, or that the people may do this thing unto them, according to the hardness of their hearts, that the judgments which he shall exercise upon them in his wrath may be just."

God was there to accept His children home. The experience witnessed by Alma and Amulek was horrific, but even so, those innocent victims were welcomed home into the loving arms of Him who sent them to our world. Their cry for vengeance will bring the judgments of God upon the perpetrators of such gross wickedness. Later we read that the Lamanites did come upon those in Ammonihah and destroyed them (see Alma 16:7–10). Justice was served.

Obviously, we don't live in the Garden of Eden. We are subject to upsetting experiences. Fear is very real. We must seek help through tough times. Hardships I've personally gone through have been bitter. Afterward, though, my life improved because I held on to the gospel (the iron rod), worked to endure, and made it through each trial.

Bad experiences eventually lead to good ones. Being afraid of those bad experiences doesn't serve us in the slightest. Some bad experiences we bring upon ourselves, and some are brought on by others. Come to recognize the difference, especially if you brought on the bad experience. Take responsibility and corrective action.

What fear stops you from achieving your financial goals? Is it the idea that the world will end soon and thus you have no need to prepare for retirement? I used that excuse when I was about thirty. I had read from President Joseph F. Smith's address at a general conference in 1945 where he said that it was highly likely that some of those in attendance would see the Second Coming of the Lord.

If true, a young baby that happened to be in its mother's arms that day would be a great-grandparent today. It could still happen, but does that mean we're absolved from preparing for our future? I would say the answer is no. Live like the Second Coming is tomorrow, but prepare as if it's a hundred years away.

I Like Money, but I Don't Love Money

Ah, the love of money.

We have plenty of hang-ups and fears when it comes to this above statement. Many people have asked, "If I had lots of money, would I be wicked?" Then some say, "People with lots of money are jerks! It's more spiritual to be poor."

Lots of hang-ups. Lots of fear.

The thing about money, though, is that it is neither good nor bad. It is a neutral entity. How we use money and how we let it affect us is where the issue arises. If we love money more than our fellow men, more than our God, then we get ourselves into serious spiritual trouble.

First, here are a few scriptural passages that support the problem with loving money and riches.

The Apostle Paul writes in 1 Timothy 6:10, "For the love of money is the root of all evil: which while some coveted after, they have erred from the faith, and pierced themselves through with many sorrows." Also, Matthew 6:24 says, "No man can serve two masters: for either he will hate the one and love the other; or else he will hold to the one and despise the other. Ye cannot serve God and mammon." And Mormon 8:37 says, "For behold, ye do love money, and your substance, and your fine apparel, and the adorning of your churches, more than ye love the poor and the needy, the sick and the afflicted."

I could go on and on.

And yet money is an earthy tool used to satisfy commerce, taxes, and trade. Consider the interaction of Jesus and Peter in the Gospel of Matthew. Peter had just been asked by the tax collectors about Christ paying the temple tax. Even though Jesus was the Lord of the temple, He agreed to pay the tax, saying to Peter, "Notwithstanding, lest we should offend them, go thou to the sea, and cast an hook, and take up the fish that first cometh up; and when thou hast opened his mouth, thou shalt find a piece of money: that take, and give unto them for me and thee" (Matthew 17:27).

Jesus paid the tax.

Money is a tool. Christ used money for things during His ministry. Joseph Smith needed money as he worked to translate the plates. You and I need money to buy food and clothing, to experience the world around us, and to generally help others. Don't be afraid of money. Enrich your life, your family's life, your friends' lives, and all those around you with the proper perspective and use of money.

Oliver Cowdery was given a beautiful revelation through the Prophet Joseph Smith touching on this very subject. In Doctrine and Covenants 6:7, Oliver is instructed, "Seek not for riches but for wisdom, and behold, the mysteries of God shall be unfolded unto you, and then shall you be made rich. Behold, he that hath eternal life is rich." This instruction to Oliver to not seek only for riches can be good advice for all the Saints. Do not mismanage your priorities. Seek first for a hope in Christ. Keep His commandments, and then if you seek riches, you will receive them for the intent to do good. You are good, your family is good, and assisting others around you is good.

We can see examples of riches being used for the good of others almost everywhere we look—and many of the best examples are kept secret. Keep in mind that Matthew 6:1–4 records the Savior teaching that when you perform service, don't let your left hand know what your right hand is doing.

While attending BYU–Hawaii and waiting for my mission call, my religion teacher shared with me the story of his conversion. He had been a teenager, and after his baptism he felt a strong desire to serve a full-time mission. However, that was a difficult proposition for a young man who was the only Church member in his family and whose parents were unwilling to help pay for his service. He told me that while sitting in the celestial room of the temple one evening, a stranger approached him and a conversation started about his future plans. He explained that he was wanting to leave for a mission but that it seemed like a long shot given his circumstances. The stranger then offered to financially support the young convert on his two-year mission. My religion teacher's desire to serve was realized because someone chose to become successful enough to offer financial support to a total stranger.

This story drives me.

We can't be afraid of money. If we're always pushing money away because we're afraid of what it might do to us, we must remember that the Lord blesses the obedient with prosperity. He entrusts us with wealth when we show Him we will use it wisely. "Inasmuch as ye shall keep my commandments ye shall prosper in the land" (2 Nephi 4:4). In searching through the Book of Mormon, I found over forty-two instances where that phrase is used and some others with slight variations of the same meaning. God wants to bless His children on earth. If you are a parent, you understand the desire to bless the lives of your own children. After being grateful for what we have, we are encouraged to ask for blessings. Further, we are encouraged to be worthy of His blessings. When those blessings come, we can pass them on to others if we choose.

Please remember that Heavenly Father's plan is a plan of happiness, not a plan of prosperity. Having said that, God still wants us to work, to produce, and to share.

As a young father, I saw a bumper sticker that said "Commit Random Acts of Kindness." I decided to start doing just that. It didn't start out as big things—just simple things based on what monetary resources I had at the time. I was able to bring a little joy to others through random acts of kindness, even if by small means. Want to have some fun with your children next time you're in the drive-thru of your favorite fast-food restaurant? Tell the kids that you're going to pay for the food order of the car behind you. I have been doing this for years. The kids go crazy waving through the back window at the unsuspecting benefactors. It is amazing fun! The restaurant cashier at the window has always been happy to oblige our request. I pay for two orders and drive away. My children snicker with joy as they wave goodbye to those in the car behind ours. Out of little things, great things can be accomplished.

I've also chosen to use my resources on a bigger scale too. My family has owned several reliable cars over the years. When one vehicle gets old, we've replaced it. Instead of going through the process of selling the older car, we seek the advice of local Church leaders for a family who might benefit from receiving a vehicle without cost to them. We do apply one stipulation upfront, and this was our prerogative—that the receiving family use the car to attend church meetings and be willing to drive others to church should the opportunity arise. It is such a wonderful experience we've done more than once.

Now, I'm not telling these stories to brag but rather to show how the blessing of money and resources can be used to positively affect the lives of others. Since we had the resources, we were better able to serve.

This is the point I'm trying to get at. Money is a resource. If we have a lot, we can give a lot. If we love money and think only of ourselves, the money will do nothing for us other than amplify our worst qualities. If you drink and have more money, you'll turn into an alcoholic.

I want to believe the saying, "What goes around, comes around." I live a blessed life for many reasons. First, God blesses me in ways I can't enumerate. Second, He blesses me when I'm obedient and doing what He asks. And third, He blesses me when I apply myself to live the best life possible, using the talents He's given me. I can then in turn use those blessings to improve the lives of those around me. The Spirit will often dictate how and when to use those resources. Listen to those promptings and you'll never go wrong.

When I was young, I was taught never to give money to homeless people begging for money. I was told they would only buy drugs and alcohol with it. Once I became a teenager, however, I reversed course. I was reading King Benjamin's address in the Book of Mosiah:

> And also, ye yourselves will succor those that stand in need of your succor; ye will administer of your substance unto him that standeth in need; and ye will not suffer that the beggar putteth up his petition to you in vain, and turn him out to perish. . . .
>
> And if ye judge the man who putteth up his petition to you for your substance that he perish not, and condemn him, how much more just will be your condemnation for withholding your substance, which doth not belong to you but to God, to whom also your life belongeth; and yet ye put up no petition, nor repent of the thing which thou hast done (Mosiah 4:16, 22).

What a powerful scripture!

I keep a stack of dollar bills in my glove box for those that petition me for money. I always ask their name. I feel this shows kindness and respect for them as a human being. I suppose I could throw the money at the person and drive away, but I force myself to take a moment with that individual. Will they buy drugs and alcohol with the money I give them? Maybe, maybe not. At the end of the day, that isn't my concern. I don't judge them or their intentions with the money. I judge that they are in need. God is the ultimate judge, not me. I only help where I can. If I am wrong for giving away my cash, so be it. It is my hard-earned money, it is my prerogative, and I am trying to be a good steward over it.

Again, these are all personal decisions. I've had times where I didn't feel right or safe giving money to someone on the street, and I followed that prompting and continued on my way. How one person gives doesn't dictate how you should give. The important thing to remember is that money by itself isn't evil. Money is the grease that makes things happen on earth. We exchange time for money. Time is actually the most abundant resource you have. Money is replaceable—time is not. Trade your time for something of value.

Produce all you can while striving to maintain a balanced life. Once you produce enough for you and your family, you are encouraged to overproduce to trade in the marketplace and create wealth. Wealth can then grow through investments of different kinds.

Don't be afraid of money. Don't be afraid to invest. Don't be afraid to share.

A Story of Faith and Finances

Before we end the chapter, let's take a look at how the Lord can use your affluence to help His causes. President Monson once shared the following story:

> The glass [for the windows of the St. George Tabernacle] was manufactured in the East. The windows were placed on a ship in New York, then transported for the long and at times perilous journey around Cape Horn and up to the West Coast of America. The precious glass was then transported to San Bernardino, California, to await the overland trek to St. George.
>
> David Cannon and the brethren in St. George had the duty to go to San Bernardino with their teams and wagons to retrieve the glass, so that the tabernacle of the Lord could be completed. One problem: They needed the then-astronomical sum of $800 to pay for the glass. They had no money. David Cannon turned to his wife and his son and asked, "Do you think that we can raise the money, that we might obtain the glass for the tabernacle?"
>
> His tiny boy, David, Jr., said, "Daddy, I know we can!" He then produced two cents of his own money and gave it to his father. Wilhelmina Cannon, David's wife, went through the secret hiding places that all women had in their houses in those days. Her search produced $3.50 in silver coins. The community was scoured for money, and at length the sum of $200 was raised—$600 short of the required amount.
>
> David Cannon sighed in despair. He had tried his best but failed. The little family was too weary to sleep and too discouraged to eat, so they prayed. Morning dawned. There gathered the teamsters with their wagons and horses, prepared to undertake the long journey to San Bernardino. But they were $600 short.
>
> Then there came a knock at the door, and Peter Nielsen, from the nearby community of Washington, entered the house. He said to David Cannon, "Brother David, I have had a persistent dream

that I should bring the money that I had saved to expand my house—bring it to you that you would have a purpose for it."

All the men gathered around the table, including little David, Jr., as Peter Nielsen took out a red bandanna and produced gold pieces, one by one, upon the table. When David Cannon counted the gold pieces, they totaled $600—the exact amount needed to obtain the glass. Within an hour the men waved good-bye and, with their teams, set forth on their journey to San Bernardino to retrieve the glass for the tabernacle.

When that true story was told on a show "Death Valley Days," young David Cannon, Jr. was then eighty-seven years of age. He listened to the story with rapt attention. I feel that in his mind, he once again heard those gold pieces, one by one, produced as astonished men saw with their very eyes the answer to their prayers.[14]

One Last Look

Good: When asked, you provide time and money to a good cause.

Better: Setting up recurring contributions, you are able to financially support a good cause without any more participation. It's automatic, and you don't have to think about it again.

Best: You are actively engaged in good works because your faith and love of God moves you so. You follow promptings and go beyond the minimum requirement.

Awful: You see your wealth as evidence of your superiority. Those who have less deserve their poverty. You made good choices, and you've reaped the benefits. Other people made bad choices and now must suffer the consequences. It is not your responsibility to help them in any way. You are not your brother's keeper, after all.

Something for the Kids

The children of our day are the most fortunate of all previous generations. Children today enjoy incredible technological advances, medical advances, educational advances, and more. Sit down with your children and list all possible blessings. Ask them how their lives would be affected if they didn't have them. Then point out how others in the world, and even in our local communities, might not have

14. Thomas S. Monson, "Tears, Trials, Trust, Testimony, "*Ensign*, May 1987, 44.

access to these advances. I have used YouTube to present clips to my children on how other children in the world live.

Many blessings are realized through the generosity of good people. Teach your children how their blessings give them an opportunity to bless other people. Ask them to ponder how they might use their resources to make the world a better place. I recommend starting in your own community before reaching distant lands.

4

Why I Don't "Pay" Tithing, and Why You Shouldn't Either

God speaks to His children in the language of their understanding. For many years, the term "pay your tithing" meant just that: pay. I repeatedly hear leaders of His Church express in many ways the same message: "Pay your tithing." By definition, the Hebrew word *tithe* literally means "one-tenth." One-tenth of your interest (earnings) are freely donated to the Church to serve God's purposes.

The Bible indicates that God's people followed the law of tithing anciently. For example, it's recorded in Genesis 14:17–20 that Abraham gave Melchizedek tithes. The children of Israel were taught to bring their tithes to the Lord.

Through modern prophets, God restored this law not just once but several times. To fulfill this commandment, members of Christ's Church freely give one-tenth of their earnings to the Lord through His established Church. These funds are used to build up the Church's temporal resources, establish Zion, and further the work of the Lord throughout the world.

Tithing funds are used for the Lord's purposes—to build and maintain temples and meetinghouses, to sustain missionary work, to educate, and to spread the gospel to all the corners of the globe (see Doctrine and Covenants 119). Disciples and local leaders transmit tithing funds directly to the headquarters of the Church, where a council determines specific ways to use the sacred funds. This council comprises the First Presidency, the Quorum of the Twelve Apostles, and the Presiding Bishopric. Acting according to revelation, they make decisions as they are directed by the Lord.

With the widespread creation of credit cards, mortgages, and city utilities as an example—none of which was in wide use a hundred years ago—the Saints of today are often discouraged and weighed down by paying so many entities. Pay this, pay that. Tithing for too many has become just another bill—a hassle and often a painful experience.

But is that what the Lord intended with the law of tithing?

This law was given to the Saints in this dispensation so He could bless our lives through obedience and sacrifice. Let me be clear: my definition of spiritual sacrifice is the giving up of something for something better. Sacrifice does not always have to be thought of negatively or equated with losing.

Today, when it comes to the law of tithing, the idea of simply "paying" removes much of its meaning. Tithing is a law God gave His people so that He could bless His obedient disciples. The law also allows us to participate in building His kingdom here on earth.

So what if you decided to stop *paying* tithing and instead chose to *participate* in obeying the law of tithing?

Consider the paradigm switch for a moment. Contemplate changing a *demand* from leaders to pay into a personal *invitation* to freely participate and qualify for the promised blessings. This change in the way you participate is a liberating approach to how the law of tithing can improve your life and bless others.

Think about replacing the word *pay* with the word *participate.* Participate in the law of tithing. You're no longer merely paying tithing. There is a world of difference here that is truly liberating.

I've told many of my church-going friends that I don't pay tithing. You can imagine the eyebrows that furl, especially when leadership is nearby. Parents hurry to cover their children's ears!

Listen closely to what I'm saying. I pay my water bill, I pay my credit card bill, I pay my mortgage, but I refuse to pay tithing. Tithing is a commandment given to the Lord's disciples so He can bless us through obedience to that commandment.

Simple.

Elder Ronald E. Poelman of the Seventy took the old meaning a step further when he spoke in general conference, saying, "You and I are now among those generations given the privilege to know and to live the law of the tithe.[15] The blessings that flow from obedience to that law are both temporal and spiritual."

Privilege! When was the last time we thought about participating in tithing as a privilege? I believe Elder Poelman never simply *paid* his tithing.

This privilege is a double blessing. By participating in the law of tithing, Church members show their gratitude to God for their blessings and their resolve to trust in the Lord rather than in material objects. Members also help further the work of the Lord here on earth, blessing God's children with the opportunity to learn of Him, establish Zion, and grow in the gospel.

Remember, if God wanted money, He'd simply ask an apostle to go fishing! Funny line, but look at Matthew 17:24–27. They that received tribute (probably a tax collector) said to Peter that Christ doesn't pay tribute. Jesus then instructed Peter to go fishing, and from the mouth of the fish, Peter found the money needed to pay tribute. Did you know those verses were there? God does not need your money. He has plenty of resources He can draw upon.

I choose to *participate* in the law of tithing. I embrace the paradigm change. My attitude is completely different from those that are brow-beaten with guilt to pay tithing. Some Saints say the Church is rich. I don't know. I don't care to know. That's the Lord's business, not mine. My adherence is between Him and me. I have a cheerful heart when participating in the law of tithing.

There is a big difference here.

Tithing is irrevocably linked with gratitude and appreciation. God grants us the seasons, sunshine, rain, seed, and soil. Consider what is written in Doctrine and Covenants 38:17: "And I have made the earth rich, and behold it is my footstool, wherefore, again I will stand upon it." We can produce 100 percent from what He originally blessed us

15. Ronald E. Poelman, "Tithing: A Privilege," *Ensign*, May 1998, 78.

with. When I think about it that way, it becomes worthwhile to give back one-tenth of my gain. Doing so with a cheerful attitude allows for more blessings, and not all of them are financial.

Within this framework, "paying" tithing doesn't even count as a sacrifice. It's much more like a short-term investment. I cannot rightfully give the Lord ten cents and receive one dollar in return and then go around proclaiming my sacrifice.

This is beautifully illustrated in King Benjamin's address in Mosiah 2:23–24, which reads: "And now, in the first place, he hath created you, and granted unto you your lives, for which ye are indebted unto him. And secondly, he doth require that ye should do as he hath commanded you; for which if ye do, he doth immediately bless you; and therefore he hath paid you. And ye are still indebted unto him, and are, and will be, forever and ever; therefore, of what have ye to boast?"

Consider the biblical passage in Malachi 3:10 as well: "Bring ye all the tithes into the storehouse, that there may be meat in mine house, and prove me now herewith, saith the Lord of hosts, if I will not open you the windows of heaven, and pour you out a blessing, that there shall not be room enough to receive it."

First, take note that Malachi never said we should "pay tithing." Second, some pretty great promises are stated there.

In this discussion of tithing, we also need to consider some of the questions that act as distractions in all of this. There are ongoing debates on whether tithing comes from your gross earnings or your net earnings. The answer to this question is between you and the Lord. The scriptures are clear that you and I are not to be commanded in all things. That is why there is no clear answer. You have to seek instruction directly from the source.

Offerings are between you and the Lord. No one will check your accuracy.

Changing how we think about tithing goes beyond semantics as well. Have you ever obeyed a commandment out of resentment, personal benefit, or self-righteousness? If you fill out that tithing slip with bitterness in your heart, I can guarantee you're not going to see the same benefits as if you did so joyfully. And that's not the Lord saying, "You had a bad attitude when you paid tithing, so no blessings for you!" Instead, our attitude is keeping us from receiving blessings that are already there waiting for us. The angel Moroni spoke to Joseph Smith about his attitude and how it would need to change before he could receive the gold plates (see Joseph Smith—History 1:27–54). The plates themselves hadn't moved from their location in the Hill Cumorah for years—Joseph's attitude had just placed him in a spot where he couldn't receive them. Joseph's attitude about what to do with plates of gold had to change before he was permitted to receive them. Our attitude affects everything. How does your attitude toward tithing affect *your* participation?

I personally do not pay tithing, and I haven't for years. I do, however, fully *participate* in the law of tithing. Let me be clear: I freely give 10 percent to the Lord as I have been commanded—I just do so from a different state of mind. Yes, tithing still comes out of my bank account, it's still money, and it's still 10 percent. Nothing has changed about the process, just my way of understanding that process. Simply writing yet another check to pay God's bill does not resonate within my soul.

If you choose to participate in obeying His law, consider a paradigm change: your attitude. I recommend that you no longer pay tithing; choose instead to participate in the law of tithing. The Lord will take notice.

Today, participating in the law of tithing is mechanically easier than it's ever been. I simply calculate what I'm going to bring as tithes to the storehouse of the Lord and can do so through my online banking features. I can electronically transfer money to the Church effortlessly. Other offerings from my household are purposely accomplished the old-fashioned way, with the familiar gray envelope. That is a choice we've made as a family. My kids and I talk about the need to help those with less. We prepare the paper form and seal our combined contribution slips into the envelope. I invite one child to hand the envelope to our bishop on the appointed fast Sunday. This is critical for the children—so they can cheerfully interact with their bishop. It's important for their spiritual development to see their parents participate in obeying the Lord's commandments.

It doesn't matter how you choose to participate in the tithe. You can use cash, check, money order, highly appreciated stock, required minimum distribution (RMD), whatever. The key principle here is that you don't think of it as just another bill that you mark in your checkbook for tax purposes.

And there are innumerable promises given to us when we participate in the law of the tithe. You can't listen to general conference without a speaker detailing the temporal and spiritual blessings stemming from obedience to God's commandments. But this does not mean the blessings are exactly half spiritual and half temporal. The Lord knows our needs. As we obey, He will bless us accordingly.

Be leery of the speaker at church on Sunday who says that after paying tithing, they received more money soon afterward. There are plenty of stories out there of someone paying their tithing and then finding an unexplained source of cash. These sorts of tales make good apocryphal, faith-building anecdotes, but they don't promote real, lasting faith, and they shouldn't be our motivation for participating in tithing. Receiving more money may be a specific blessing to you (or a coincidence), but it isn't the real miracle we should be looking for.

The Lord also said that in the last days, He would not burn those willing to obey His commandment of tithing (see Doctrine and Covenants 64:23–25). That alone should be enough to provide your 10 percent as commanded.

And of course, in Doctrine and Covenants 82:10, Christ stated, "I, the Lord, am bound when ye do what I say; but when ye do not what I say, ye have no promise."

We have plenty of promised blessings. Today we can be faithful and understand why tithing is so wonderful for us individually. If we do that, it will become less of a painful experience and be transformed into the promised blessing it was intended to be.

Rich and Poor

The amount of tithing asked of us is the most perfect and equitable arrangement God ever gave His disciples. It is one-tenth of our increase. Today, increase is interpreted as income. Saints from the poorest to the richest are invited to participate in the law of tithing. Christ taught this principle in the story of the widow's mite:

> And Jesus sat over against the treasury and beheld how the people cast money into the treasury: and many that were rich cast in much. And there came a certain poor widow, and she threw in two mites,

> which make a farthing. And he called unto him his disciples, and saith unto them, Verily I say unto you, that this poor widow hath cast more in, than all they which have cast into the treasury: For all they did cast in of their abundance; but she of her want did cast in all that she had, even all her living (Mathew 12:41–44).

We don't know all the circumstances of the poor widow. We don't know the circumstances of the various members of our wards and stakes. Whether rich or poor, we are asked to give the same one from ten.

President Joseph F. Smith's mother was known as "Widow Smith." She was the widow of Hyrum Smith, who was martyred with his brother, the Prophet Joseph. She once rebuked the tithing clerk who stated that because of her poverty, she should not have to participate in the law of tithing. She said, "Would you deny me a blessing? If I did not pay my tithing, I should expect the Lord to withhold His blessings from me. I pay my tithing, not only because it is a law of God, but because I expect a blessing by doing it. By keeping this and other laws, I expect to prosper, and to be able to provide for my family."[16]

That was a strong woman right there—an example to us all on how we should look at tithing.

The Lord is not asking us to give Him all we have in the form of tithing or other material offerings. He wants us to give our hearts, our minds, and our talents. Today, we are asked to be stewards over our lands and possessions. Imagine the challenge: the Lord provides us with 100 percent of what we have and tries our faith by asking us to give back 10 percent.

I suspect that many good Saints participate in the law of tithing as I do. All are not blessed with material blessings equally. God knows what we need and want. President Spencer W. Kimball lived in a very modest home, but fit for a prophet? Sure—why not? Perhaps that is all he wished to acquire on his earthly mission. Blessings for obedience to God's commandments do not always translate into material blessings. Should you want more material blessings, then be sure you do your part to qualify yourself for them, which may include additional skills, licenses, certificates, or degrees. Meet the Lord halfway.

16. "Mary Fielding Smith," *Ensign*, July 2011, 73.

Can we do that much? Or maybe it would be better to ask, can we do that little?

Many people struggle parting with what is not originally theirs. Tithing is a trial of our faith in God. He has said that to tithe His people allows Him to bless them according to their obedience to this law.

In this dispensation, the Lord has established the law of tithing as the law of revenue for His Church. Without it, we could not carry out the eternal purposes of the Lord. It is also a law by which we show our loyalty to the Lord and prove ourselves worthy of privileges, ordinances, and blessings.

In 2022 the Church announced a paradigm shift away from tithing settlement to tithing declaration. It's a small word change but a big difference in meaning. *Settlement* meant to me that I was to settle my debt with the Lord. *Declaration* is closer to bringing your tithes and offerings to the Lord's storehouse (see Malachi 3:10).

To the many thousands of members joining the Church today, and to those who have been members all their life but still battle with their attitude over tithing each month, I encourage you to please exercise your faith. Participate in the law of tithing. This law may be different from what you were accustomed to prior to your conversion and subsequent baptism. But nothing you do as a new convert will more completely prepare you to enjoy the wonderful blessings that await you.

A peace that will surpass all understanding will come to you and your family as you participate with both heart and mind. You will find that all fears concerning finances and care of family will diminish—perhaps not disappear, but diminish. You will come to feel your Heavenly Father's love for you as you understand your place in His eternal plan.

God does not need your money. He made the heavens and the earth and all things therein. I think He likes fishing though.

To illustrate my point in a different way, consider the following insightful joke about a certain man who lived a good life. Because he was faithful, he received a personal revelation that he would be allowed to take with him one object from his mortal experience into heaven. At the appointed time, he passed peacefully through the veil into the eternities. True to the revelation, he brought one object with him: a solid gold brick. Upon reaching heaven, he was greeted by angelic hosts who said, "Look at this fellow. He was allowed to bring one object with him to heaven, and he chose to bring a paving brick!"

What "paving brick" are you holding on to?

It's hard to part with hard-earned money, especially when times are tough. But when you change your perspective, you'll find giving back to the Lord far easier than you ever expected.

Don't pay—participate!

One Last Look

Good: You donate, albeit sporadically, to various charities when solicited.

Better: You pay tithing to your church when it's convenient, in addition to donating to charity when solicited.

Best: You analyze the income God has blessed you with and gratefully give Him back a tenth, using the proper channels established to accept the donation.

Awful: You cannot stand the idea of parting with your hard-earned money. Your spouse insists, and you begrudgingly allow your spouse to pay tithing. You have no idea of the amount donated until tithing declaration with your bishop. Then you can only imagine the new car that money could have purchased instead.

Something for the Kids

It's very important to teach our children by example the importance of setting aside tithing each time they receive an allowance or earn money. Assist them in filling out the form. Encourage children to personally give the envelope discreetly to their bishop.

The earlier you start this, the better. Here's a fun rhyme I heard years ago that we taught our children in order to help them understand this principle:

> What is tithing?
> I will tell you every time.
> Ten cents from a dollar
> And a penny from a dime.[17]

17. Earl C. Tingey, "The Law of Tithing," *Ensign*, May 2002, 10.

It's easier to learn and develop good tithing habits when young. Kids start with ten cents from a dollar and move up from there. It is much harder for an adult to give up $8,000 from an $80,000 salary if they never developed a belief to obey God's law of tithing.

President Joseph F. Smith said, "Our children, as soon as they become old enough to earn means, should be taught to pay their tithing that their names may be written in the book of the law of the Lord."[18]

As we participate in the law of tithing, we set the example for our children. We lay the foundation of a family that is deeply rooted in making and keeping our covenants with God. Participating in tithing allows for so many blessings, such as entering the temple and being sealed for time and all eternity. To those who find themselves unable to enter the house of the Lord because of their difficulties with tithing, I suggest you exercise your faith, prove the Lord, and participate. Choose to be obedient and sacrifice. Qualify for the blessings that come. After all, He eternally keeps His promises to us (see Doctrine and Covenants 82:10).

18. Earl C. Tingey, "The Law of Tithing," 10.

5

Provident Living

Provident living is where balance, preparedness, and discipline come together to give you better peace of mind. It allows you to continue your dedication toward God, country, and family with limited financial disruptions.

Let's talk about a "balanced life" for a second. This term is something that is thrown around constantly in our modern world. Gurus tout the need for balance and sell courses on how to achieve it.

Balancing your life is as impossible as reaching perfection while in mortality.

Sound harsh? Let me get some backup from an Apostle of the Lord.

Elder David A. Bednar gave us all a pass when he said, "Quit worrying about it because there's no such thing as balance. It doesn't exist."[19] He then gave an object lesson that confirms how impossible it is to find perfect balance. He verbally painted a picture of a greatly skilled acrobat who spins a dish on one hand, then adds another to a foot, and another and another, all the while revisiting each dish to continue the arduous task of keeping them all balanced. It's truly an

19. Lindsey Williams, "'There's no such thing as balance': Elder Bednar shares an object lesson you may need right now," *LDS Living*, Mar. 3, 2022, https://www.ldsliving.com/theres-no-such-thing-as-balance-elder-bednar-shares-an-object-lesson-you-may-need-right-now/s/94216.

amazing trick. Now, if we only had four or five things to balance in our lives, we might be able to pull it off too. But unfortunately, that just isn't reality.

Elder Bednar continued, "Can you ever have all of the plates on all of the sticks rotating at exactly the same speed? The answer is no. You have to know which one will be the first to spin so slowly that it's going to fall, and you need to make sure that you're spinning that plate."[20]

We have dozens of plates spinning in our lives. Something has to give. Prioritize and do not be afraid to occasionally say no to some requests. This very much includes making other people's problems your own. Don't do it.

I learned a valuable lesson when I was in a leadership meeting one Sunday. The instructor said to us that as a church leader, you cannot take upon yourself other people's problems. You are in a position to help people find and apply solutions to their own problems. Some individuals want to unload their problems onto you and make you carry them. No! We all need to progress. Taking on someone else's problems does not help you, and it certainly does not help that person to grow.

Preparedness is the second aspect of provident living. The scriptures and our latter-day prophets continue to warn each generation to be prepared, and if we are, the faithful Saints need not fear.

What does preparedness look like? Well, we've been asked by prophets to have food storage for when lean times come. Personally, I have a year's food stored. It has a shelf life of thirty years, so I am covered there. I have tablets that purify water and several handy little devices that can also clean water. I have no idea how the food would taste if I were called upon to use it, but it's my starting place, not my ending place. The Lord doesn't ask us to all be at the same spot on our journey. He only asks that we be headed in the right direction. That goes for being prepared as well.

I learned a great lesson from Brother Gerry Buttle, my Scoutmaster, many years ago. He told us young Boy Scouts that when a favorite food product his family enjoyed would go on sale, he would purchase a case of it. It's pretty sound advice. This does not break the budget,

20. Williams, "'There's no such thing as balance,'"

and over time we can build and rotate a storage of food that we would actually enjoy if we had to eat it for any reason.

One purpose of that preparation is so we can avoid fear. There is no way we can prepare for every eventuality. But if we follow the admonition of our Church leaders, we will be blessed, and we can bless the lives of others. Imagine instead of needing your food storage to feed your family for an entire year, you are able to feed a hundred other people for a few weeks during a disaster until things go back to normal. That is what my wife experienced when the infamous Hurricane Katrina hit. Saints from nearby areas donated excess food they had stored. This also allowed the Saints to rotate their stock. We don't always know why we are called to prepare in specific ways, but you can be sure that preparation will allow us to bless the lives of others as well.

No discussion of provident living is complete without talking about discipline. Our understanding of the word *discipline* changes depending on context. For some, discipline means punishment for bad behavior. But the type of discipline we're talking about here has more to do with self-control, sacrifice, and determination.

Discipline is created over years and years as we are exposed to good examples. A baby has no discipline. A toddler has no discipline. Teenagers in general have very little discipline. As we age, however, we often discover how a bit of discipline can affect our future in disproportionately positive ways. We can learn this truth through observing the people around us, or through our own bad choices. When I was first married and had very little discipline, my immature choices seemed to compound every problem I faced. The older I got, the more discipline I developed. It seemed like it took forever . . . and I'm still honing those lessons sometimes even now.

Let us forgive ourselves if we have not yet mastered a disciplined life. However, a life best lived is a life that is disciplined.

Provident Living and Church Welfare

In 1986 President James E. Faust gave a wonderful talk in general conference about our personal obligations entitled "The Responsibility for Welfare Rests with Me and My Family."[21] In this address, he talks about his personal experience during the Great Depression, describing how if he didn't finish his oatmeal for breakfast, it would be fried up for lunch or dinner so the food wouldn't be wasted.

Few of us today have suffered through times as difficult as these. Even in those days, however, the responsibility for the welfare of individual families fell on those families first and foremost. In 1936 the First Presidency said in a great statement of purpose, "The aim of the Church is to help the people to help themselves."[22]

President Faust said in his talk:

> The purpose of the welfare program is to care for the poor and the needy and make the members of the Church, by their obedience to gospel principles, strong and self-reliant. At the center of caring for the poor and the needy in a worldwide church is a generous contribution to the fast offerings and personal and family preparedness. At the very heart of taking care of our own needs is our own energy and ability, with help to and from our own families.[23]

The Church's welfare program is an enormous blessing to the world. Even so, it is inadequate to take care of everyone. For those of us with physical, mental, and spiritual capacity, it falls to us to do everything in our power to support ourselves and our families. Each of us may at some point in our lives need a helping hand, but generally the vast majority of us will be able to meet our needs throughout mortality.

If and when financial hard times occur, before we go to the Church for help, we are admonished to first rely on our own families. This can be an embarrassing and humbling thought to seek financial aid from parents or siblings. Throughout my career, I've seen several innovative examples of how families have overcome this problem and benefited from working together to solve these issues.

One family's solution involved all the adult children banding together and creating a joint checking account. They all agreed to add a

21. James E. Faust, "The Responsibility for Welfare Rests with Me and My Family," *Ensign*, May 1986, 20–22.

22. Quoted in "Gospel Classics: The Road to Financial Security," *Ensign*, Mar. 2003.

23. James E. Faust, "The Responsibility for Welfare," 20.

designated amount of money to the account every month. The money was administered by two signers for the benefit of the greater family at large. Responsibility over the account rotated every few years. The signers then administered the funds to family members that found themselves requiring financial help. No one family member owned the funds in the account—the money belonged to everyone. The family member in need would petition the two siblings administering the account, and they would decide how to help financially. This way, the greater family was a second line of financial defense.

Every situation is different, and circumstances like the one discussed may not work in every family unit. Money often muddies the water when it comes to relationships. The point is, with a bit of creativity, prayer, and trust, conditions can be created where families can help each other weather the storms of life.

There are other things we can do individually that will buffer us from financial headwinds. Like all good general conference talks, President Faust's talk provides us a few prescriptions that will help. I would like to take a moment and focus on these five areas so we can better facilitate our own provident living.[24]

Thrift and frugality were both number one on his list. What does "thrift and frugality" look like? Thrift comes down to not wasting what you have, while frugality is all about paying attention to your personal economy and spending within your means. This is easily said but more difficult to accomplish in practice, especially in a world that is constantly enticing us to spend, spend, spend! Credit is easy to come by and difficult to pay off. Debt becomes a prison for everyone ensnared by its promises of "buy now, pay later." We've become so hypnotized by the regularity of monthly payments and the ease of credit card access that too many have been filed down to the river as if being led by the Pied Piper.

Part of living a provident life is avoiding debt whenever possible, particularly personal consumer debt. The best way to shake off debt is to focus on paying it off during times of financial plenty. There are

24. To read more about these points in detail, see James E. Faust, "The Responsibility for Welfare Rests with Me and My Family," *Ensign*, May 1986, 20–22.

numerous schools of thought on how to do this, but they all preach the same sound advice: escape debt as quickly as humanly possible.

Second on President Faust's list is to seek to be independent. He talks about being independent from drugs and alcohol, bad habits, and paying interest. Yes, he brings it back to debt and discusses how debt removes our independence.

I think this would be a good place to quote President J. Reuben Clark's classic statement on interest:

> Interest never sleeps nor sickens nor dies; it never goes to the hospital; it works on Sundays and holidays; it never takes a vacation; it never visits nor travels; it takes no pleasure; it is never laid off work nor discharged from employment; it never works on reduced hours; it never has short crops nor droughts; it never pays taxes; it buys no food; it wears no clothes; it is unhoused and without home and so has no repairs, no replacements, no shingling, plumbing, painting, or whitewashing; it has neither wife, children, father, mother, nor kinfolk to watch over and care for; it has no expense of living; it has neither weddings nor births nor deaths; it has no love, no sympathy; it is as hard and soulless as a granite cliff. Once in debt, interest is your companion every minute of the day and night; you cannot shun it or slip away from it; you cannot dismiss it; it yields neither to entreaties, demands, or orders; and whenever you get in its way or cross its course or fail to meet its demands, it crushes you.[25]

That is a mouthful, but I believe every word is true. If we want to be independent, we need to get out of debt.

Another surprising tip regarding independence actually takes us back to the law of tithing. Participating in the tithe will give you independence. I know that sounds counterintuitive since you are returning 10 percent of your increase to the Lord, but we're also promised huge blessings for doing so. If we want to be independent financially, we need to participate in the law of tithing.

Being industrious is third on the list. Industry is about more than just working. It's taking advantage of opportunities, being resourceful, and thinking about new ideas and applying solutions. We have to work and be creative, we must rest when needed (Sabbath Day observance), and we should ask our Father in Heaven for inspiration

25. J. Reuben Clark Jr., in Conference Report, Apr. 1938, 103.

and opportunities. Even when things look bleak, we still must act and do what we can, relying on the blessings of the Lord that we may not see at the moment.

The great poet Virgil said, "They conquer who believe they can."[26] If we believe that our own industry will pay off, then it will. The Lord will justify and consecrate (make sacred) our efforts. What's required of us is action.

Fourth on President Faust's list is becoming self-reliant. Self-reliance allows us to not only take care of ourselves but of others as well. This means we strive to gain the knowledge and financial support we need through our hard and smart work.

Self-reliance has been a huge focus of the Church since its early days, but over the last decade, greater steps than ever before have been taken to help members achieve this goal. Classes on self-reliance—ranging from getting one's finances in order to starting a business or continuing education—are offered at the stake level all around the world. These are inspired courses that will help anyone become more self-reliant.

Last on the list, and the most concrete of all President Faust's admonitions, is the counsel to have a year's supply of food and clothing. Even when President Faust reiterated this guidance in 1986, it was already a fifty-year-old plea. Again, following this counsel is easier today than it has ever been. Entire industries are built around food storage and preparation. Getting a year's supply can be fairly cost effective, and the meals are far more flavorful than they were even twenty-five years ago.

One of the most crucial sections of President Faust's talk touched on people's reluctance to get a year's supply of food since their parents and grandparents never needed such a safety net, even when they had the supply. He says pointedly, "Perhaps following this counsel could be the reason why they have not needed to use their reserve."[27] Aha—think about that blessing!

---

26. Quoted in John P. Bradley, Leo F. Daniels, Thomas C. Jones, *International Dictionary of Thoughts* (Chicago: J.C. Ferguson Publishing Co., 1969), 661.

27. James E. Faust, "The Responsibility for Welfare," 22.

Food Storage Basics

Now let's get into more detail regarding how exactly to accumulate the proper food storage for your family. We've already discussed a few options for gathering those supplies, but now we will focus on concrete numbers that can help you have the right amount of everything you'll likely need. With a proper plan, it becomes very easy to wrap your head around what you require and where to find it.

Gathering food storage and emergency supplies can be simplified by using twelve monthly emergency preparation lists. (See below for an example.) With different monthly goals, these lists can put you on autopilot and help you establish a habit of gathering year-round while you regularly shop.

Anyone with a desire to become self-reliant can use these same tools regardless of where they are in the country or world. The principles are the same no matter where you live. Each list suggests monthly goals for one adult, but you can multiply food and water amounts by family members, increase or decrease amounts, modify food choices, and create a list that's right for you.

These lists incorporate the four steps found in "All is Safely Gathered In: Home Storage," a pamphlet prepared by The Church of Jesus Christ of Latter-day Saints, along with additional home storage, emergency equipment, and preparedness goals you can work on as a family.[28]

The first thing you need to focus on is changing your mindset regarding food storage. Instead of burying food in your basement to use only during emergencies, learn to "store what you eat, and eat what you store." That way, when emergencies come, you have food that you and your family actually enjoy eating. If you don't like freeze-dried Brussels sprouts, you probably don't want them in your food storage. However, if you love pasta primavera, you should probably stock up when sales arrive.

Work on the following steps first. Remember the push for the 72-hour kits? There's a start! Next, gather a three-month supply of food, emergency drinking water, and a financial reserve. Then gather long-term foods, home storage supplies, and emergency equipment.

28. *All Is Safely Gathered In* (booklet, 2007).

Here are some good places to start right now:

1. Take an inventory of all the canned, bagged, boxed, and packaged foods your family regularly eats. (Sounds like a fun home evening activity.) You may already be further along than you think! If you tend to prefer fresh or frozen food, just remember: the shelves in your favorite store will be empty during a disaster. You need to buy in advance and be ready or have alternatives for those surprise calamities. During the recent COVID-19 pandemic in 2020, there was a run on the stores for food and necessities. Many of you have lived through an experience like this.
2. Take an inventory of your long-term foods with a twenty- to thirty-year shelf life, such as flour, rice, honey, beans, and toilet paper. These are great staples for families and last decades without spoiling. Some people store these under the beds.
3. Decide on a food storage budget that fits into your family economy. For example, $10 to $30 a month per person is a good start. If you live in a small apartment or are on a limited budget, begin with a one-month supply of food. Prepare as much as your circumstances allow.

Patience is key when it comes to gathering your food storage. Do not panic and rush to the store so you can have everything now. The purpose is to slowly cycle through your food storage without wasting money or allowing the food to spoil. Keep an inventory sheet on a cupboard door to track how much you want to store and what you use. Hang your grocery list next to it and write down what to buy next time you shop.

Anything you do to help yourself become self-reliant is a step in the right direction. I know this to be true because I live this way every day. We all have this same opportunity—a single can or a bag of food at a time.

Twelve-Month Emergency Prep List

Another way to build your food storage is through focusing on specific items each month of the year. Colorado State University[29] came up with a food storage preparation list that will help simplify the process of gathering.

- January: Water and Beverages
- February: Breakfast Foods and Communication
- March: Tomatoes, Pasta, and First Aid (including a basic first-aid book)
- April: Soup, Fish, Beans, and Sanitation
- May: Condiments, Spices, and Emergency Cooking
- June: Grains, Vitamins, and Bread Making
- July: Summer Foods, Emergency Drills, and Canning
- August: Fruits, Vegetables, Shelter, and Bedding
- September: Meat, Potatoes, and Earthquake Prep
- October: Oils, Fats, and Fire Safety
- November: Holiday Baking, Emergency Heat, and Clothing
- December: Baking Basics, Power and Light Sources, Personal Self-defense

Disaster Tips for Provident Living

Food storage is only one aspect of surviving a disaster. As long as we're focused on provident living, here are a few more tips that will help keep you safe and avoid fear in the face of uncertainty. Whatever the situation, knowledge of food safety and storage is important.

Yes, where you place your food storage is a big deal. You don't want to spend thousands of dollars on cans and bags of beans only to have it spoil because you put it in a place that wasn't conducive to food storage. Food should be kept in a dry, cool location that doesn't get below freezing or above about seventy degrees Fahrenheit. Remember that the cooler the storage area, the longer the retention of quality and nutrients. Also, try to keep your food storage off the ground if

29. Pat Kendall and Nancy Dimond, "Food Storage for Safety and Quality," Colorado State University, June 1991, https://nasdonline.org/static_content/documents/2082/d000066.pdf.

possible. This adds another layer of protection against moisture and rodents.

If you are storing perishables in a refrigerator or freezer, be sure to cycle through them, as they will expire more quickly than dried goods. And if you have any question about whether something has gone bad or not, never taste it—just throw it out. It's not worth getting sick over.

Other tips to remember include the following:

- Do not eat foods from damaged containers.
- Keep foods clean.
- Keep cold foods cold and hot foods hot.
- Boil all home-canned, low-acid vegetables and meats for ten minutes plus one minute per 1,000 feet in altitude before tasting.
- Do not leave cooked or opened cans of food at room temperature longer than two hours. Bacteria can travel through the air.
- Avoid storing too many foods high in salt, as this will increase thirst.
- Store single servings or one-meal sizes to avoid leftovers, as refrigeration may not be available.
- Canned foods keep almost indefinitely as long as cans are undamaged. The can also will work as the cooking and serving dish. Open the can and remove the label before heating.

Foods Recommended for Storage

Here are some common foods that are recommended for storage:

- Water—one gallon per person per day for drinking, cooking, and personal hygiene
- Ready-to-eat canned foods—vegetables, fruit, beans, meat, fish, poultry, meat-mixtures, pasta
- Soups—canned or "dried soups in a cup"
- Smoked or dried meats—commercial beef jerky
- Dried fruits and vegetables—raisins, fruit leather
- Juices (vegetable and fruit)—bottled, canned, powdered
- Milk—powdered, canned, evaporated

- Staples—sugar, salt, pepper, instant potatoes and rice, cocoa mix
- High-energy foods—peanut butter, jelly, nuts, trail mix, granola bars
- Ready-to-eat cereals, instant hot cereals, crackers, hard taco shells
- Cookies, hard candy, chocolate bars, soft drinks, and other snacks
- Store one or two manual can openers with your emergency food supply as well as waterproof matches

Remember my old Scoutmaster, Gerry Buttle? He also taught me that as food storage supplies approach their expiration, take them to the food bank so they don't go to waste. Both perishable and non-perishable items are cycled through very quickly and will be used before they expire. It's a great way to avoid waste and help members of your community at the same time. Brother Buttle would then replace those food storage products when he found an advertised sale and would stock back up. I learned a lot from that old Scouter!

Now that you have the basics, consider the challenge of producing extra garden vegetables, gathering additional chicken eggs, or canning homemade jam to barter with your friends, neighbors, and family members. The goal is to go through the motions and sharpen your personal skills on how to produce something others need.

All of these tips and lists will help you live a provident life, and more importantly, they will help you avoid fear. The Lord tells us to "fear not" (Isaiah 41:13), and this is one of the primary ways He helps us to do just that.

Follow His counsel and ye shall not fear! How does that work? He knows us from the beginning and believes in us and in our eternal futures. Mortality is a short amount of time when compared to the eternities. As President Russell M. Nelson recently taught, "Mortal lifetime is hardly a nanosecond compared with eternity. But, my dear brothers and sisters, what a crucial nanosecond it is!"[30]

30. Russell M. Nelson, "Choices for Eternity" (worldwide devotional for young adults, May 15, 2022), broadcasts.ChurchofJesusChrist.org.

One Last Look

Good: You have a complete 72-hour kit for everyone in your household.

Better: You've followed a plan and accumulated a three-month supply of food and water.

Best: You've followed a plan for not only food and water supplies but also seeds to plant, medicines and first aid, liquid cash reserves, and (where possible) fuel for your household for three months.

If you have the means, accumulate more than just a three-month supply. You may find that those who have stored gold and silver instead of food are willing to trade precious items for your excess cans of oats, flour, or beans.

Awful: I sat in a Christian congregation one Sunday at the invitation of friends. The clergyman referenced the most recent disaster that had darkened our region with the Nisqually earthquake on February 28, 2001. He noted the material shortages and the human suffering that followed. The clergyman specifically said to his audience, "When the next disaster strikes, seek out your Mormon neighbors, as they have stores of food for such occasions." He then added that these Mormons obviously do not live by faith because God will provide for His people.

To exercise faith means to follow the prophet of God. Our prophet asks us to be prepared.

That was definitely an interesting perspective. I took notice of how some people feel about faith and food storage during his sermon that day.

Two schools of thought here: prepare or not prepare. I am in the camp of being prepared. Joseph of the Old Testament interpreted Pharaoh's dream that warned the Egyptians to prepare during seven years of plenty before seven years of famine hit (see Genesis 41). He helped the Egyptians organize, and through his efforts, he saved that nation and more during the times of famine.

Above all else, we live by faith in Jesus Christ and are saved through His grace for us. Keep in mind that "faith without works is dead" (James 2:20).

Something for the Kids

We're all familiar with CTR rings. This, of course, stands for "Choose the Right." Always a good reminder. I suggest there is a dual meaning for the letters CTR—it can also mean "Clean Thy Room." There is an important lesson learned when cultivating the discipline to keep a room clean. As we grow with age and find ourselves taking on more and more responsibility, keeping our room clean can also mean that our life is clean and orderly. When our life is clean and orderly, we are capable of taking on more responsibility successfully, and we can become community and church leaders.

It is my observation that those who have grown up without the discipline of keeping their life clean and orderly are not very good leaders. Before you start to tell other people how to correct their life, keep your own room clean . . . both literally and metaphorically.

6

Time, Marriage, and Money

Time is the most abundant and important asset we have. Alma wrote, "For behold, this life is the time for men to prepare to meet God; yea, behold the day of this life is the day for men to perform their labors" (Alma 34:32).

No matter how much money you have, you will never be able to buy back a single second of time. This is important to realize as we trade our time for money.

For most people who work for a salary or an hourly wage, you do not get paid for the hour spent at the workplace but for the value your hour brings to the company to produce or service something. If you are paid $25 an hour, the company should be in a position to extract out of your hour at least $25 of value added to a product or service.

That's why the phrase "time is money" is so applicable in so many aspects of life. Time lost is money lost for both you and your employer.

Work for your employer and make a living. Work on yourself and make a life. Keeping this in mind, there are things each of us must recognize if we are going to enjoy our time and use it wisely. Many of these things have been taught by prophets and apostles in these latter days. They are things we should pay attention to. They will help us live fuller lives and enjoy our finances as singles, married couples, and families.

The first thing I would suggest is keeping a regular journal. Record your successes and failures, your dreams and needs, your truly exceptional life experiences, and your biggest heartaches. As you age, record these thoughts, impressions, and experiences as often as you can. This is a habit I have developed, and it has truly enriched my life. Coming back to a journal over the years helps me see how I have grown. I like who I have become, and you will too.

The second admonition would be to not wish your life away. Wasting your time today worrying or longing for some moment in the future that you perceive as being better than the present is the fastest way to miss out on your life right now. Too many times as I rode the elevator to my office on the thirty-fifth floor, I would overhear strangers commenting on Monday morning about how they wished for Friday to arrive. I always thought how sad life must be if the best part was some imagined moment that hasn't happened yet.

In the April 2022 general conference, President Nelson shared with us a favorite poem of his about the subject of time. It went like this:

> The shadow by my finger cast
> Divides the future from the past:
> Before it, sleeps the unborn hour,
> In darkness, and beyond thy power:
> Behind its unreturning line,
> The vanished hour, no longer thine:
> One hour alone is in thy hands,—
> The NOW on which the shadow stands.[31]

All we have is right now—the present. The past is gone, and the future doesn't exist. The present is a gift. If you do not like where you are at this very second, make a change now. Don't think about how things will be better in two weeks or two months or two years. Create something better at this very moment. You are not a tree. Move. You are not stagnant, unable to plot your own course. Take action and use every moment you have. These moments will never come back to you again.

31. Henry Van Dyke, quoted in Russell M. Nelson, "Now Is The Time," *Liahona*, May 2022, 126.

Explore Ways to Use Your Time—and Your Screens—Wisely

Cell phones, tablets, and electronic devices are ubiquitous in the twenty-first century. We have them in our pockets all the time, on our nightstands as we sleep, and in front of our faces when we should be living our lives. The average American adult spends more than three and a half hours a day on a mobile device, adding up to more than twenty-four hours each week, according to a 2019 survey from eMarketer.[32]

If time is money, then wasting time on devices is costing you more than just cash. It might be time for a little digital detox. The good news is that you do not have to dump the device entirely to benefit. Instead, focus on changing a few behaviors, and you'll find time open up to you like you can't imagine.

First of all, you'll want to actually measure your digital intake and look for patterns. You probably have a strong suspicion that you use your smartphone or tablet too much, but having the data stare you in the face can jolt you into taking action. Apps exist for pretty much every digital device that will tell you your usage each week. If you're embarrassed by the data at the end of seven days, you'll want to make some changes.

Another great way to avoid losing yourself in your screen is to make plans for your free time. There is power in being intentional about how you spend your day. Think about activities that can replace your phone time in your regular schedule, whether it's doing a quick workout, reading a print book, or completing a crossword puzzle. Planning will impact every aspect of your life, not just when it comes to your devices. You'll find that the more you plan for the future, the less fear you have.

One more tool to save time on phones and tablets is to use different devices for work and play. We tend to want to use our smartphones to multitask—answering work emails on a personal cell phone or using the work laptop for online shopping when it's more convenient. However, it is better for your privacy and your mental health to create

32. Yoram Wurmser, "US Time Spent with Mobile 2019," Insider Intelligence, May 30, 2019, https://www.insiderintelligence.com/content/us-time-spent-with-mobile-2019.

firm boundaries for device usage. This means that at the end of your workday, put your work devices away. This will also signal to those in your household that you are in "leisure/family mode" and will invite them to interact and encourage them to keep their own noses out of screens. Here's something to try: don't allow phones or tablets at the dinner table.

For Time and All Eternity

The gospel of Jesus Christ teaches us about time and all eternity. When we imagine "time and all eternity," we tend to think about the marriage relationship. A majority of adults will marry someone at some point in their lives. Currently, 48.2 percent of Americans age fifteen and up are currently married.[33] That percentage is even higher among members of The Church of Jesus Christ of Latter-day Saints.[34]

When we talk about marriage, we need to talk about finances. If you are married and sealed in the temple of God, your plan is to be with this person forever. You chose them for time and all eternity. That desire doesn't guarantee that any specific marriage will last; after all, there are a lot of decisions that can lead to the dissolution of a couple. But when a man and wife choose to be sealed for time and all eternity, the goal at that moment is for the marriage to last through the ages.

No one goes into an eternal marriage with the objective of letting their finances tear their relationship apart. And yet couples who argue over finances at least once a week are thirty times more likely to divorce than their peers.[35] Also, couples with no assets at the beginning of their marriage are 70 percent more likely to divorce by the end of

33. See Grant Suneson, "These states have the highest by and lowest by percentage of married people in the US," *USA Today*, Mar. 7, 2019, https://www.usatoday.com/story/money/2019/03/07/marriage-us-states-highest-percentage-married-people/39043233/.

34. See Micheal Lipka, "Mormons more likely to marry, have more children than other U.S. religious groups," Pew Research Center, May 22, 2015, https://www.pewresearch.org/short-reads/2015/05/22/mormons-more-likely-to-marry-have-more-children-than-other-u-s-religious-groups/.

35. See Jeffrey P. Dew, "Financial Issues as Predictors Of Divorce" (paper presented at the annual conference of the National Council on Family Relations, San Francisco, CA), Nov. 2009.

the first three years than couples with at least $10,000 in assets.[36] And once you have been divorced, you are 90 percent more likely to divorce again.[37]

Money affects your marriage. Anyone who tells you "love is all you need" never stared down the stress of an empty bank account and mounting bills.

This being the case, talking about money is incredibly important in every marriage, right from the start—even *before* the start. When deciding to marry, learn about your potential spouse's spending habits, their position on debt (and amount of debt), their expectations for money management, and their work ethic. Knowing these things before you jump into marriage can help in innumerable ways. For those of you who have been married for ten years and have never had this type of conversation with your spouse, do it now! There's no time like the present. Conduct a financial check-up. Discover where the assets and liabilities are.

If you're only now starting to evaluate your finances as a couple, that's okay. The first thing you're going to want to do is sync up your financial picture. Let's say the wife loves gardening, so she handles the yard work. The husband loves to cook, so he handles the grocery shopping. Splitting household tasks by preference and ability is a fine idea . . . except when it comes to financial matters.

You must be on the same page and know where you are monetarily.

Having one partner in charge of all financial decisions—a sort of household CFO—creates a financial risk for the "non-CFO" in the marriage. For example, nearly 74 percent of women who outsourced the money management to their male partners discovered an unpleasant financial surprise after divorce or widowhood, according

36. See Jeffrey P. Dew, "The gendered meanings of assets for divorce," *Journal of Family and Economic Issues* 30 (2009): 20–31. https://doi.org/10.1007/s10834-008-9138-3.

37. See "Divorce Statistics: Over 115 Studies, Facts and Rates For 2022," Wilkinson & Ginkbeiner, accessed May 27, 2023, https://www.wf-lawyers.com/divorce-statistics-and-facts/.

to a 2019 UBS survey of high-net-worth women.[38] Financial secrets are dangerous, and if open money communication does not exist in a marriage, you're inviting doubt, unwanted surprises, worry, and mismanagement.

It is important for both you and your partner to understand the basics of shared finances, even if you're the one who prefers to be hands-off or the one who prefers to take the lead. In the same survey, nine out of ten women who said they share responsibility with their spouse for long-term planning and investing reported more confidence in their financial future and their marriage as a whole. This proves how collaboration can enhance the quality of your relationship. According to TD Bank's 2018 Love and Money Survey, couples are happier when they talk about money matters regularly.[39] Nearly 90 percent of happy couples discuss finances at least once a month.

Here are four ways to ensure you are working as an equally empowered team on all things fiscal.

Financial Date Night

There's value in setting aside distraction-free time to discuss what's on your mind when it comes to money. Having a monthly budget check-in over a relaxed dinner with your partner can help you connect everyday spending with the big-picture goals you are planning for, whether it's a vacation home or your retirement. Personal finance author Farnoosh Torabi suggests the following script to get the ball rolling: "I know it is not the most exciting thing to talk about, but it would make me a lot more comfortable if we could go over our finances together. I just think it's helpful if we share the basics so that we're both on the same page and can work toward common goals."[40]

---

38. See "Women put financial security at risk by deferring long-term financial decisions to spouses, UBS research reveals," UBS, Mar. 6, 2019, https://www.ubs.com/global/en/media/display-page-ndp/en-20190306-financial-security.html.

39. See "2017 Love and Money Survey TD Bank," TD Bank, Nov. 22, 2017, https://stories.td.com/us/en/article/2017-love-and-money-survey-td-bank.

40. Farnoosh Torabi, interview with Todd R. Tresidder, "Money and Relationships with Farnoosh Torabi," Apr. 28, 2015, in *The Financial Mentor Podcast*, podcast, https://www.financialmentor.com/podcast/money-and-relationships/15717.

It's also a good idea to have your first "money summit" with your spouse at one of your favorite restaurants over a good meal. A fun and familiar setting will help ease any potential tension. Money discussions can be awkward for the best of couples, so put each other in a place that will bring quicker smiles and warmer feelings.

If you're in the habit of discussing spending and budgeting, take the conversation up a level when discussing big milestones in your shared future. Are you planning on having children (or more children)? Do you want a bigger home? Do you want to downsize? What is your retirement fund looking like? These questions, and any others that are pertinent to your situation, will allow you to speak honestly and share things that otherwise would be left unsaid. These types of dates can be incredibly powerful and empowering for any couple.

Here are four questions you might ask that will help get you started:

1. What three things do you most enjoy buying?
2. What are three things on your "bucket list"?
3. What does it mean to you to be "good with money"?
4. What is our biggest money failure as a couple?

There's an App for That

Financial spreadsheets are very popular, but sometimes they don't translate well for some couples. If you're going to be on the same page regarding your finances, you need to both be able to understand the program being used. Many different budgeting apps exist that put financial transparency at both of your fingertips. Choose one that is safe and secure and that allows you both to see your assets, debt, and spending trends through charts and graphs. Your bank may have features to track spending.

I call this a financial plan—a higher-level, big-picture view of where you are and where you are likely headed. Ask your financial advisor for one. There should be no cost.

Back to spreadsheets. Most of these kinds of apps have notifications that will prompt your significant other to check cash flow, as well as alerts that show when your shared spending has exceeded a preset budget. Using these tools together will allow both of you to know what is going on with your finances and hold each other accountable.

Keep It Simple

The simpler you can make your finances, the better. As you get into investing and such, things can get more complex, but when it comes to your day-to-day accounts, avoid complications whenever you can. If you are going through an intricate bill-paying process to earn cash back on a credit card, switch tactics and set up bill-pay through your bank for all-in-one convenience. If you have a sprawling number of accounts to keep track of, consolidate as much as you can so both of you know where your money is, where it's going, and where it's coming from. This is why living debt free is so liberating.

Avoid Even the Appearance of Secrets

As I said before, financial secrets in a marriage are disastrous. If one partner has multiple bank accounts and keeps the other partner in the dark regarding money matters, even if there has been no impropriety, it invites doubt and resentment. That mixture of doubt and resentment in a marriage is like acid. It corrodes the good will and love that are the bedrock of any eternal relationship.

The only cure for this is open communication and honesty. If you aren't currently keeping secrets from your spouse but your finances are opaque or unknown to them, open everything so they know where every dime is going. This will build trust and strengthen your relationship. If you are not the one caring for the family finances, do not be critical. Family finances are hard to manage.

If you currently are keeping financial secrets from your spouse, I advise you to confess them, no matter how embarrassing or damaging. Keeping these secrets will not strengthen your marriage. The longer they fester, the worse the consequences will be when they finally do come out. And they *will* come out, whether you want them to or not. They always do. Always.

Divorce

When talking about time, marriage, and money, we cannot avoid having a discussion about divorce. It isn't a pleasant subject, but like so many things regarding money, unpleasant subjects are just as important as the pleasant ones. Sometimes more so.

Divorce occurs more today than ever before. It happens for a variety of reasons: infidelity, dishonesty, lack of compassion, laziness, and many other reasons. Author John Grey suggests in his book *Men are from Mars, Women are from Venus* that the other side of the "coin" to the divorce story is that there exists a desire from one spouse to be in a loving relationship rather than stick with a marriage that is simply too painful.[41]

Divorce was not what I wanted. It happened to me. I speak from experience.

There is opposition in all things, the Lord tells us. Divorce has been with civilization for ages, even in biblical times. Although the good Lord exhorts a married couple to be one, the reality is that two people do not always accomplish this goal.

As I've already mentioned, finances play an outsized role in a great number of divorces. Once the difficult decision to end a marriage has been made and the process is set in motion, you are suddenly faced with making choices that will deeply affect you for the short- and long-term. With all the legal, financial, and emotional complexities that must be confronted, keeping track of all the information you will need can be difficult.

Take comfort in knowing that you are not alone. Rely on your support circles: siblings and other family members, close friends, the Relief Society or elders quorum, your doctor, a therapist, and priesthood leaders. There are people outside these circles who can help you a great deal as well, like your accountant, financial advisor, attorney, and mediator.

During a divorce, there is no time to waste in getting a grip on your economic standing. Before you consult a lawyer or a financial professional, gather documents they'll need to help you assess your situation. Consider these items in creating your personalized list and remember to keep everything in a secure location:

- Prenuptial agreements
- Birth certificates of any children
- Marriage certificate
- Estate plan documents

41. John Gray, *Men are from Mars, Women are from Venus* (New York: HarperCollins, 2004).

- Bank, brokerage, credit card, and retirement account statements
- Business ownership and financial/tax records
- Life, health, and disability insurance policies
- Auto, homeowners', and renters' insurance policies
- Tax returns for the past five years
- Mortgage or home equity loan documents
- Online bank account usernames and passwords
- Pay statements for you and your spouse
- Loan applications and related personal financial statements
- Personal property documentation for valuable assets
- Outstanding bills or obligations
- Real property deeds
- Motor vehicle titles
- Credit reports
- Current income and expenses
- Wills, living wills, powers of attorney, and trust documents
- Inventory of safes and safety deposit boxes and keys

Common Steps in a Divorce

If divorce becomes the only option for you and your spouse, it's important to know what you're in for. There are many necessary steps you'll want to go through to get things accomplished as quickly as possible without adding more pain to an already painful situation. While all divorces are different, here are commonalities you can typically expect along the way.

Filing the divorce petition comes first. One of the spouses files a petition (called a complaint in some states) with the court. This document typically will explain the grounds for divorce.

The "service of process" petition is then served on the other spouse along with a summons that requires a response. The spouse who receives the summons must respond indicating whether they agree with the petition. If no response is received, the court assumes that he or she agrees to the terms.

From there, you go into the investigation and discovery phase. The two parties share information on income and assets to determine how to divide them and how to proceed with things such as alimony and child support.

At this point, negotiations will begin. If couples can resolve their problems through mediation or settlement, the divorce process is significantly shorter. But if an agreement can't be reached, the case heads for pretrial conference, offering a last chance for settlement before preparing for a full trial.

If a divorce goes to trial, it will likely be a very difficult process for all parties. Emotions will run high, pain and faults will be put on display, and wounds will likely be deepened. During trial, lawyers will present evidence and arguments for each side, and a judge decides on contested issues and grants the divorce.

If you have children, all of this is compounded. States calculate child support in different ways. Factors that weigh in include the income of the parents, the number and ages of the children living at home, any special needs of the children, and basic living expenses and school fees.

From there, assets will be divided. Even short marriages accumulate quite a bit of joint assets. It's important to identify those that should be part of a fair and equitable distribution. Consider the following:

- Real estate
- Vehicles and boats
- Bank, retirement, and brokerage accounts
- Furniture, tools, and appliances
- Stake in a business
- Jewelry
- Insurance policies
- Pensions and annuities
- Collections (art or hobby)
- Pets

Even the best divorces can be agonizing processes, especially regarding children. When going through a divorce involving kids, parents need to go out of their way to be civil toward each other and make sure their children understand it is not their fault that their parents are splitting up. The parents need to understand the implications of the divorce on the family members and their relations outside the family unit as well. Neither party can afford to be selfish over material possessions. Parents must look for the best resolution for all parties involved and not just theirs. Tools like counseling should be considered for everyone involved. Divorce is a process that leaves everyone battered. Don't be afraid to ask for professional help.

Children will hurt emotionally during these proceedings. There will be collateral damage. That is a fact. But even if the marriage needs to end, you still have a choice regarding how you respond to the situation and how your kids are treated. Try to understand their pain, and never use them as leverage to harm your soon-to-be ex-husband or ex-wife. Contention is of the devil, says the scriptures (see 3 Nephi 11:29). That isn't the Lord's way.

Death of a Spouse

Time never slows down or stops. That being the case, death is another unpleasant subject we need to look at. Just because someone dies doesn't mean their financial impact or burden suddenly goes away too. We need to get our house in order before we, or our spouse, pass through the veil.

Many of us do not want to think about our own mortality, much less that of those we hold dear. But death is something we will all face eventually, and sadly, it can happen at any moment. While the topic may be unpleasant, wouldn't you rather be prepared as much as you can be? Or better yet, wouldn't you want to have the comfort of knowing that your loved ones will be taken care of after you pass through the veil?

Although it may be tough, start with an open and comprehensive discussion with your family about end-of-life matters and "afterward." There needs to be a dialogue about quality of care and quality of life in your later years. You need to have conversations about how you want your property and finances to be handled. It's never too soon to start talking. When you are married, there's usually one hands-on financial person, but both spouses need to know exactly what you own, why you own it, and how to access it.

Planning beforehand can help in the aftermath of a loss, lending a sense of order to a tumultuous time. Preparing in advance can also provide guidance to friends and family and is one of the greatest gifts we can give to those we leave behind.

Obviously, whatever plans you put in place will need to be carefully considered and thoroughly discussed by all relevant parties, and they must cover short- and longer-term considerations. There's a lot to think about, which can be overwhelming, so it may help to break up the planning and take it one step at a time.

Put It in Writing

Involve your family as you make important decisions that will affect them after you die. You and your spouse will want to make sure they clearly understand your wishes to help avoid conflicts down the road. Store anything you put in writing regarding your estate, along with your other important documents, and make sure your family knows how and where to find this information.

On non-qualified accounts at an investment company, consider a transfer on death (TOD) designation. Should an older family member die, the beneficiary listed as TOD will have immediate access to the account funds and records. Banks typically use a payable on death (POD) designation. Speak with your financial representative about which is best for you.

Create a Will

First and foremost, everyone—and I mean everyone—needs a will. We'll get into wills and trusts in more detail in a later chapter, but know now that this is a step you're going to need to take sooner rather than later. Use your will to clearly document your wishes for the transfer of your financial and tangible assets. The goal here is to transfer assets smoothly.

Work with the appropriate professionals to help ensure everything is thoroughly and accurately documented. Without a formal will, the state will decide how your property will be distributed after your death, and the state really doesn't want that burden.

On my will, I write the date next to my name each year, indicating the last time I read my will. This helps remind me to keep it up to date.

Set up a Trust

A will may be adequate to cover your estate, but there are benefits to also setting up a trust. You may want to dictate how your assets are distributed (maybe through a charitable trust or endowment fund) or keep your affairs private and confidential by avoiding probate. Work with your attorney and financial advisor to help determine what type of trust would work best for you. Be sure to review your will and trust documents at least once a year to ensure all information is updated and that your wishes reflect your current circumstances.

WRITE A LETTER OF INSTRUCTION

Everyone in your family will benefit from you writing a letter of instruction that covers any wishes you have that are not covered by your will or trust. Consider the physical objects left behind, like the keepsakes and furniture. You'll want to contact your loved ones and then friends and ask them if there is anything of value they might want from your estate. Include these in the letter to your family. You may want one of your children to have Grandma's old piano, only to find out they detest the instrument and would much prefer Grandpa's arrowhead collection. Maybe you thought you would divide up the jewelry equally, then you find out that only one person in the family was interested in the jewelry at all. Some want the photo albums, others don't. Many future squabbles can be removed if you act now while you can still make things happen.

My grandpa used to bounce me on his knee when young, and he'd show me his Buck pocket knife that he cherished. Time after time, he told me that the pocket knife would someday go to me after he passed. While I was on my mission, my grandpa passed away. Where did that pocket knife go? No one knows. Grandpa's bequest was never written anywhere, and back then you didn't call family but twice a year while serving a mission, so I went without.

NAME SOMEONE YOU TRUST AS DURABLE POWER OF ATTORNEY

A power of attorney will manage your financial business on your behalf should you become incapacitated. Carefully select who you trust to do so, and make sure the paperwork is in place while you're still in your right mind.

Create a list of people to contact after you pass away. Beyond family and friends, include contact information for those who would need to be informed about your death.

Provide Document Security Codes, Passwords, and Keys

In the event of your death, your survivors will need to access or shut down a variety of business and online accounts. Make sure to record the necessary security codes and passwords and provide anything else they may need.

Write Your Own Obituary

This one can actually be a lot of fun if you let it be. Take the time now to decide how you want to be remembered in print and which photo you want to include. You may want to go a step further and write love letters to your family and friends or record your thoughts on video for future generations.

Plan Your Own Funeral

It may sound morbid, but planning your own funeral will make things easier for your family once you or your spouse passes away. Each person is different. You may want a celebratory affair, while others may prefer a more solemn occasion. Whatever your wishes, research the costs now and make arrangements in advance so your loved ones won't have to worry about all the details during an emotionally draining time. You may want to also consider prepaying for the services to relieve your family of the financial burden and to lock in today's pricing.

My sister is single and has some health issues. That got me thinking, and so I acted. I purchased for her a grave site near our mom and dad. I did not tell her for years, but it is all paid for.

Personally, I want to leave enough money for all my family to take a trip to an amusement park for a big party. That is the way I want to be remembered. I have always had wonderful experiences with my family at theme parks. Silly perhaps, but you know what? After I pass, they will get a chance to party, and that makes me feel good!

Obtain Adequate Insurance

Research life insurance and long-term care policies while you're still in good health. This is especially crucial if you are the primary breadwinner and your spouse or children will need covered financial support. Life insurance death benefits can help your beneficiaries pay off large debts, pay for higher education, and provide cash flow immediately after the loss to help cover daily expenses or the costs of a funeral (if not prepaid). And long-term care insurance can help alleviate financial stress if you face a debilitating illness or incapacity.

We'll go into life insurance more deeply later in the book, but for now, understand this is an important aspect of end-of-life planning and should be at the top of your list now, as long as you have enough wealth to cover all your financial needs currently.

Update Your Beneficiaries

Review all assets, accounts, and properties to make sure your listed beneficiaries reflect your current wishes. Be sure to look at your retirement accounts and insurance policies as well. We've all heard stories of old documents causing problems for families when a parent dies, so be sure to pay attention and get things updated regularly instead of assuming anything.

After Death

Losing a spouse is overwhelming and emotionally draining. And in the wake of that loss, money may be the last thing on your mind. It is wise to put off major money decisions while you are grieving. Conventional wisdom recommends taking a year to heal. That may not be possible, but even so, avoid jumping into any large purchases for as long as you can.

During the initial weeks after the loss, your main concern should be your own well-being. While many other decisions can be postponed, there are practical matters that may need your attention. Never be afraid to ask for help when these issues come up. Call family, friends, ward members, and even professional counselors when you need emotional support.

Life will continue to go on, even if you think you don't want it to. Make sure mortgage and insurance payments continue to be made so you don't find yourself in a worse financial position than necessary. Review all your accounts and remove your spouse's name from any joint accounts and transfer them to your name. (You will need a death certificate and other documents to do this.) Any automatic payments or debits should be reassigned before closing any accounts. You'll also want to notify creditors and close any credit cards as necessary.

A Promise of Peace

Our finances touch every aspect of our lives: our time, our marriages, our families, and our friendships. We must understand that we are to avoid mistakes that will harm those relationships and our own well-being.

Christ said, "These things I have spoken unto you, that in me ye might have peace. In the world ye shall have tribulation: but be of good cheer; I have overcome the world" (John 16:33).

He promised us peace. Pretending like our financial problems will just go away, or that the love of our life is never going to die, puts us in a place of denial. But denial will not bring us peace.

Communicate and be honest and prayerful. Fear is not our ally in any part of our lives or finances. Right now you have the time to make the changes you need to make.

Use your time wisely.

One Last Look

Good: You and your spouse have a relative understanding of your finances. One of you handles the books and shares where your accounts stand with the other. You keep no financial secrets from each other.

Better: Each half year or so, you and your spouse go on a financial date night and discuss current expenses and future plans. You work together to make sure spending is controlled and that you are saving at appropriate levels.

Best: In addition to your financial date nights, you and your spouse have living wills for each of you, life insurance policies, and all the proper documents should one of you pass away or become incapacitated. You've discussed funeral and estate plans with your family so everyone is on the same page. You've even taken time to write your obituaries together and turned it into a fun and memorable experience. This is kept in a binder and in a safe, secure location.

Awful: Once a client called to take a large distribution from her Roth IRA. Though she didn't need to explain her reasons to me, she shared that she felt she needed to make the withdrawal because her massive amount of debt had grown too large to keep from her husband. About 80 percent of the Roth IRA was distributed when she was only forty-five years old.

More Awful: In one case I heard about, after a divorce, the first wife remained on the 401k plan as the beneficiary. The man remarried and died twenty-one years later. Guess who received the balance of the 401k? The first wife . . . not the second one. (Yes, this really happened.)

Even More Awful: A man was named the executor of his deceased brother's estate. His brother's handsome company retirement plan had his ex-wife of twenty-five years ago as the beneficiary. Worse, the ex-wife had passed away seven years earlier. Now the question became, who gets the handsome retirement account? What a mess for the surviving brother to sort out.

Something for the Kids

Have your children write an obituary for themselves, pretending they lived to be a hundred years old. Encourage them think about what they would want the obituary to say. Ask things like "What type of person were you during this fictional life?" and "What did you accomplish?"

Now that they have an idea of what they would like their obituary to say about them, ask them to start planning how to make that imaginary life a reality. Ask what choices they will need to start making now, and encourage them to start living that best life!

7

The Prison of Debt

Debt is a bigger part of most people's lives than other dollar-denominated areas. We always have plenty of reasons for accumulating debt, but doing so for simple comforts and luxuries is the incorrect way to go about it.

Time is money. Time is what makes debt work. Over time you pay on your debt. All debt is not bad. Debt incurred for business, a home, education, and transportation can be justifiable. Your goal—over time and with prudent discipline—is to tip the scales where you have more assets than debts. Life is best lived debt free. This creates freedom from financial worry, and I'm a huge advocate. Worry less, be free. But remember, debt is not evil. Debt is a tool to be used wisely. Educate yourself on how to use debt to your advantage. This is something I concentrate on with my clients. I educate them on the use of debt and the eventual retirement of all financial obligations. Although investment, credit card, and other debt varieties are out there, learn to be cautious when stepping into waters that will require you to pay interest over time for something you buy now.

Debt can be considered a necessary evil. Church leaders regularly caution members about the use and accumulation of debt. There is a good reason for this, outside of helping members live more providently.

It is widely understood that Joseph Smith was a kind and compassionate man but not a great businessman. Business was not his calling. Historical records show that Joseph was often in financial debt to others, and not by small amounts. In Nauvoo, Joseph operated a store known as the Red Brick Store. When someone came to him needing supplies but unable to pay for them, he would often give supplies away to help that family. (I guess he was part capitalist and part bishop's storehouse.) Unfortunately, the store failed because he gave so much away, and his investors were pretty unhappy. Some of them even left the Church over it.

With this historic example of indebtedness, it's clear to see why Church leaders warn us about debt. The ramifications can be massive in our own lives and the lives of those around us.

Before we get into too much detail on the effects of debt and how to avoid it, I want to make a few things clear. If you are in heavy debt right now, do not get a second or third job and sacrifice your family to get out of it. Everyone can tighten their belts, so to speak. Family time is still the most important time. This is not a misprint: family time is still most important. Live a little, and understand that your children need you too. Your spouse needs you. Yes, debt is a heavy burden, but it won't be lightened by trading relationships away for momentary respites. Today there are no debtor prisons. Seek professional help if necessary.

Prophets have said repeatedly that we ought not place matters of mortal importance in front of matters of eternal importance. Read to your children and take a long walk with your spouse, if that applies. Neither of these activities cost money, yet there are eternal rewards in building those bonds. This is not a race; it is a slow jog. There is no praise or reward for sacrificing your family over your finances. Children grow so quickly, and if you are not there, they will turn to others.

Living in debt makes for a hard, unsettled life. In a previous chapter, we quoted from President J. Reuben Clark as he talked about interest on a loan taking no vacation days, no sick days, and always working on weekends and holidays.[42] It's 100 percent true and sort of scary. The effects debt can have may reach deep into our relationships and can shake our very foundations.

I once encountered a young couple engaged in what looked like a loving courtship, and they had plans to marry. Their relationship fell

42. See J. Reuben Clark Jr., in Conference Report, Apr. 1938, 103.

apart, however, when one of them discovered the enormous debt accrued by the other. That debt created too much of a financial burden to accept just starting out. I do not blame in the slightest that person who broke off the engagement, as this was an indicator of a much bigger problem that would only have grown worse in a young marriage.

Many of you may know of seasoned, decades-old marriages destroyed by excessive indebtedness. Learn from them.

A Need for Discipline

If we're going to talk about debt, we need to also discuss discipline. I know we've hit on this before when going into how to live more providently and amass food storage, but when it comes to debt, discipline is key. If you can't stop yourself from buying things on credit, you'll never be financially free.

My brother gave me a book when I was a teenager called *The Richest Man in Babylon*, authored by George Samuel Clason. That book contains the story of a young man being taught the following disciplinary principle: each time he crossed the city bridge, he was to pick up a pebble and throw it into the river below.[43] Filling up the river with pebbles was not the long-term goal. The repeated cognitive action of doing something consistently was the goal.

Creating a simple habit will allow you to create more habits on top of it. If you want to be able to develop a habit of only buying things with the cash available in your accounts, you need to start somewhere.

What action can you do each day without fail to develop the discipline to succeed in life? Think about it. You could read your scriptures daily, walk around the block, stack toothpicks in a pile, write in a journal, or yes, even toss a pebble into a nearby creek as you walk over a bridge. Choose a simple task you know you can accomplish and stick with it. I am told it takes thirty consecutive days to develop a new habit. And by the way, if you miss a day, you cannot make it up by doing it twice the next day. You must start over. By tackling small and simple tasks, you will eventually be able to conquer life's biggest challenges.

43. George S. Clason, *The Richest Man in Babylon* (New York: Penguin Books, 1988), 18.

And getting free from debt *will* be a challenge. I'm not going to sugarcoat it. Getting out of debt is really hard.

Credit card companies are like cigarette and alcohol peddlers that market their addictive products by using fashion models, perks, and opulent surroundings to make you think you belong with them. We were taught that in these last days, evil designs will be created to get you addicted to products for immediate satisfaction. Revolving credit card debt is one of those products promising immediate satisfaction, and some offer a rewards program too!

While there are those few who have the discipline to outmaneuver their marketing traps and master their benefits, the vast majority remain under the influence of credit cards for a very long time. That's one of the reasons the poor stay poor.

Consumer debt in 2008 was reported to be $12.68 trillion.[44] In 2020 that number rose to $14.5 trillion. More than 191 million Americans have credit cards, averaging 2.7 cards each.

If you know you have a problem with overspending and using credit cards, now is the time to admit it to yourself and start taking steps toward creating habits that will help break those patterns. It is an addiction every bit as powerful as drugs, pornography, and alcohol. Seek the Lord, seek help from professionals if needed, but don't wallow and believe you're a lost cause. You're not! You can't change yesterday, but tomorrow will be a lot brighter if you start making changes today.

Figuring Out Your Debt Load

Let's look at consumer credit cards for a moment, also known as "revolving credit." Revolving credit refers to a situation where defined credit limits replenish monthly up to the agreed upon threshold. As the customer pays off debt each month, they are allowed to access up to the established credit limit. So if you have a $10,000 limit, and you purchase $1,000 of products then pay off the $1,000, you can go right on and spend to the limit again the next month. This balance can fluctuate monthly depending on the customer's usage.

44. See Bill Fay, "Key Figures Behind America's Consumer Debt," Debt.org, last modified Apr. 3, 2023, https://www.debt.org/faqs/americans-in-debt/.

Now is the time to introduce you to how compounding interest works. I will teach you the Rule of 72. The Rule of 72 is a simple way to determine how long an investment or debt will take to double given a fixed annual rate of compounding interest. Of course, in the case of a credit card, it can be used to determine how fast the amount you owe doubles. If you invested $100,000 into a venture that you expect to have a return of 8 percent, you would then expect your $100,000 to become $200,000 in approximately nine years (72/8% = 9 years). Conversely, if you want to estimate what annual rate of return you might need to make a given investment double in five years, the rate would be about 14.4 percent (72/5 years = 14.4%).

Now let's apply that same simple math to your credit card situation. If you are being charged an interest rate of 27 percent on your credit card and your balance is $5,000, from the above example of the Rule of 72, you can begin to understand why the credit card company wants you to keep spending to your limit and paying the minimum payment owed. When you include annual card fees, late fees, cash advance fees, and so forth, they are making a killing off of you. This is because 72 divided by 27 equals 2.7 years—a little more than two and a half years is all it will take for the amount you owe to double!

There are plenty of books and different schools of thought on escaping debt, but since we're here together, I will share my thoughts and what my experience has taught me on this subject.

Getting Out of Debt

Follow step one: destroy your credit cards and forego future point programs. (Note that this doesn't mean you can't have a credit card again sometime in the future—it's just better to establish the skills and discipline to correctly use them to your advantage first before you dive back in.)

One of the ways credit card companies grab people is with their reward points. These programs offer between 1 to 5 percent cash back on purchases. Sounds great, right? Credit card issuers are able to offer rewards to cardholders because of the high interest rates and fees they collect from you, other customers, and merchants. So the key to making the most of your rewards is to avoid paying any interest on the balance. That requires paying the balance off every month. Even a small balance left on the card will accrue enough interest to almost certainly outweigh any rewards. Remember, the average interest rate on a credit card is almost 19 percent. For most retail store cards, you're looking at interest rates upwards of 25 percent and higher. If you're paying even a fraction of that interest, your "rewards" are meaningless by comparison.

Here's a personal example I'm sure most of us have experienced. I recently received an unsolicited credit card offer from one of the largest US banks. It came with a dazzlingly famous Mickey Mouse logo across the front. The marketing department at the bank teamed up with the company that brings us all the fun family movies we love to watch. It's an incredibly smart move since we have grown to trust certain companies above others. That's the power of a strong brand.

Here's the teaser: "Receive a $200 statement credit after you spend $500 on purchases in the first 3 months after opening the account." This is the hook, and it sounds easy to do. Then the points program is lauded. Earn 1 percent in rewards on all card purchases, then be eligible to receive 10 percent off select purchases at their overpriced exclusive retail stores. Lastly, the teaser indicates you can shop with ease because the 0 percent promotional APR (annual percentage rate) will last for 6 months. After that, the variable APR starts at 15.99 percent.

Notice the word "variable" in this circumstance. The rate can go up without them having to notify you.

Just imagine! All this can be yours with no annual fee.

Although it sounds good so far, they are laying the trap to ensnare you. In the accompanying disclosure form, which looks like it was written specifically to people with law degrees, I see the pricing information. Under "Fees," I read about a proprietary bank plan that allows eligible purchases to be placed in a 0 percent interest program. But get this: the monthly fee for the program is 1.72 percent on every purchase. Trickery.

Nothing is free. These programs are intended to confuse the consumer. Remember that when using credit cards, it is you against a mighty and highly funded marketing team. You are alone against an army of brilliant people. They study the habits of how the millions of customers out there think. They know the tricks and have created many of them. They will win and win big over most people.

What angered me most about reading the fine print on this particular card offer was the section directed at our brave soldiers in the military. It said that members of the military and their families were protected because interest rates for them could never, quote, "exceed an annual percentage rate of 36 percent."

Look at that—36 percent!

Really? Who is protected with this interest rate cap? Thirty-six percent will bankrupt you so fast your head will spin! If you're choosing to play this kind of consumer credit game, you better have a rock-hard, disciplined plan because the bank has a track record of financially destroying people like you. Game on? Not for me. I'll pass.

My definition of sacrifice is the giving up of something now for something better later. Cutting up your credit cards may feel like a sacrifice, but in truth, you are freeing yourself and removing temptation. Go ahead and redeem the points you can, or transfer them to charity, then close out the credit card accounts.

Step two: list every single debt you have—from mortgage to car payment, revolving credit cards to student loans, and everything in between. Next to each of them, in column form, write down (1) the interest rate, (2) the minimum payment required, (3) the balance owed, and (4) the date the minimum payment is due. Reorder the list with the smallest balance owed at the top (which was item #3) down to the largest balance listed last. So if you owe $5,000 on a truck, $3,500 on a credit card, and $120,000 on your house, the credit card would be listed first, truck second, and mortgage last.

Step three: immediately focus all your resources on paying off the debt with the lowest balance—the one at the top of your list. Put all your extra money toward that one debt, while paying the minimum payments on time on all the other debts. If you need to bring in some extra cash to help facilitate this first push, hold a yard sale, donate plasma, or sell something you own that holds value and you won't miss. Think: sacrifice for a better life. Skis, a trading card collection, an old coin collection, guns, the extra car, or whatever. These early sacrifices will go a long way to helping eradicate your debt load.

I recommend paying off debt in this order (small balance first) because people need a success sooner rather than later. This is wisdom. Accept it for now, debate it later. Pay off the smallest balance owed first.

Once the obligation at the top of your list is paid off, apply the same cash payments from the first debt (now retired) to the second debt, along with what you were already paying on the second debt (minimum payment). You can see how this starts to build on itself and can eliminate what you owe in short order. More money is now going to pay off the second debt than with the first debt. You are learning discipline here and compounding what you pay for each obligation. By the end, imagine how much you will be paying toward your most substantial debt!

Throughout this process, you'll need to reward yourself. Getting out of debt is not easy, so I recommend that you celebrate those little victories to help keep yourself on the path of success. Once the second debt is eliminated, reward yourself with something that does not cost money. Be creative and figure that one out yourself. Have it be something you will enjoy and will continue to give you motivation.

Continue on to the third debt listed. Brag a little to trusted family and friends. Now you are adding the last two debt payments with the minimum of the third. Continue this new discipline and congratulate yourself once you reach the end of your list. Celebrate and be proud of what you've accomplished. Once you're out of debt, feel free to buy something you need or want using the cash now at your disposal every month. If you keep this momentum, you will never need to go into consumer debt again.

Another way—an old-fashioned, tried and true way—is the envelope method. Before all the electronic ways to move money, some people placed carefully budgeted money in labeled envelopes. When the money in any envelope was depleted, then no more money was spent on that item or service. Done for the month. All debts and living expenses were paid personally with cash. Since we do not live a hundred years ago, some businesses today may not accept a cash payment; in that case, exchange your cash for a money order or something similar and pay the obligation. The envelope method takes discipline and a safe and secure location. Repeat this process monthly until your debts are relieved.

Avoid New Debt

An easy way to save money for your future is to avoid taking on new debt. It's hard to save when you're paying extra money in interest. Like we discussed earlier, though, there will likely be debts you'll be paying off for years at a time, and that's okay. Three types of debt are considered acceptable by most financial and religious experts: home, education, and reliable transportation.

Outside of those specific things, you should not accrue more debt once you've escaped its hold. And even when buying a house or paying for education, you need to be smart about how you do it. Just like with credit cards, these industries have powerful marketing machines in place to get you to overspend. Have you ever heard about a great deal offered at a car lot, only to discover that hidden fees coupled with high financing rates completely eliminate the savings you had in mind? This is what I'm talking about.

Let's take a closer look at each of these three potential debt sources and see how we can be smart about taking on their debt load.

What Kind of Home Do You Really Need?

Bigger is better, right? At least that's what the housing market tells us. The size and prices of homes have grown exponentially during my lifetime. Let's look at some numbers provided by the California Association of Realtors.[45] These are averages for the entire nation, so depending on where a family lived, their price would of course vary:

> 1950s: The average new home in America sold for $82,098. It had 983 square feet of floor space and a household size of 3.37 people, or 292 square feet per person. Homes had more bathroom space than sleep space: 1.5 bedrooms and 2.35 bathrooms. The most popular colors for kitchen appliances were canary yellow and petal pink.
>
> 1960s: The average new-home size grew to 1,200 square feet and cost $118,857 on average. This gave its 3.33 residents a spacious 360 square feet of room apiece. The bedroom/bathroom ratio flipped from the previous decade, with 2.5 bedrooms and 1.5 bathrooms. Turquoise and coppertone were the appliance colors of choice.
>
> 1970s: Homes continued to get bigger by an average of 1,500 square feet. As houses grew, the household size actually shrunk to 3.14. Each person enjoyed more space than before, with 478 square feet each. The average price was $160,338. Kitchen appliances

45. See "Have American Homes Changed Much Over the Years? Take a Look," Compass, Apr. 15, 2016, https://compasscaliforniablog.com/have-american-homes-changed-much-over-the-years-take-a-look/.

achieved an iconic color balance: avocado and harvest gold. Television sets per household totaled 1.57.

1980s: By the mid-1980s the average price of a home had more than doubled since the 50s, climbing to $216,338. Square footage per household resident more than doubled as well, to 630 square feet (a total of 1,740 square feet for a household of 2.76 people). Kitchen appliances eased back on the color schemes to almond and beige.

1990s: The average new home sold for $268,055. It had 2,080 square feet of floor space and a household size of 2.63 people, or 791 square feet per person. In the kitchen, black was the favorite color for appliances. The number of bedrooms and bathrooms were little changed from the 1960s: three and two, respectively.

2000s: Square footage per person continued to climb, now at 865 per person. That equaled 2,266 total square feet for a household of 2.62 people. The price at this time came out to $281,141. The number of television sets per household reached two for the first time since they hit the market. Black appliances gave way to stainless steel.

2010s: The average new home during this decade reached $292,700 and offered 924 square feet per person. The average household consisted of only 2.59 people at this point, allowing 2,392 total square feet, or three times the space afforded in the 1950s. Television sets per household jumped to 2.93, while kitchen appliances held steady with stainless-steel finishes.

2020s: The average levels off to about 2,333 total square feet for 2.53 people. That comes to 926 square feet for each person. A whopping $336,900 is the median new construction cost. Stainless-steel remains the favorite.[46]

The trend is obvious—bigger and more expensive across the board. With natural inflation, you would expect the price of homes to rise over the span of sixty years, but these housing gains easily outstrip the rate of inflation.

The cost of a larger home also comes with larger costs on furniture, heating and cooling, flooring and lighting, insurance, and maintaining the property. When you buy bigger than necessary, you may

46. Peter Andrew, "Is Your House the 'Typical American Home'?," HSH, Apr. 20, 2022, https://www.hsh.com/homeowner/average-american-home.html.

be paying far more than you planned since so much more must be maintained.

So you need to ask yourself, how much house do you really need? Obviously, the more children you have (and members of the Church are notorious for large families), the more space you are likely to require, but that doesn't mean you need to keep up with the Joneses, as it were. Look closely at your finances and what you can afford. Keep yourself within that budget. If a 2,000-square-foot home is sufficient for your needs, don't go chasing one that is 4,000-square-feet just so you can prove to the neighbors how great you are.

Be humble, prayerful, and smart when choosing which home to finance. It's a big decision. Bring the Lord into it, and you will end up in a much better position than if your only criteria is "How much home can I buy?"

I have one last word of advice about wanting to keep a mortgage balance because you like having the tax deduction it brings you when paying tax-deductible mortgage interest.

If you have a $100,000 mortgage balance at 5 percent interest, and you have over $100,000 in your investable assets, *and* this is what you honestly believe will be the last home you will occupy, then by all means pay off the mortgage loan. Live debt free. The myth of keeping the mortgage purely for the tax deduction is the myth I will now dispel. Simple math. With a $100,000 mortgage at 5 percent over a 30-year term, the monthly payment is $536.82. After one year, $1,475.37 is applied to the principal and $4,966.49 is applied to interest to service the debt. The next year, you receive the 1099 form that shows the interest you paid the bank for the mortgage. From last year's tax filing, you are in the 25 percent tax bracket, and nothing material has changed for this year's filing. The $4,966.49 when applied to your tax liability will provide you with a 25 percent deduction, so that means 25 percent of the $4,966.49 is $1,241.62, which is a credit toward your taxes. However, if you were in the position to pay off the mortgage, then you would be able to keep the *entire* interest money of $4,966.49, which is by far a better financial move than getting a tax deduction which equalled a small 25 percent, or $1,241.62.

I know of only one person who competently showed that he had a portfolio of corporate bonds at a sufficiently higher fixed interest rate above the mortgage rate he was obligated to. But he is not most people, and mortgage rates are increasing today. That window may be closed for a season.

Higher Education

There is more and more pressure on families to pay for their children's post–high school education. This may be a benevolent and highly important priority on your list of life goals. I applaud you for that. It is a worthy objective. Higher education can separate you and your children from the millions of others competing for the best careers and jobs.

But that doesn't mean you are obligated to pay tuition for your children. Do not feel guilty if you are thinking along these lines. Higher education costs have grown at an alarming rate, even a higher inflation rate than home costs over the past sixty years.

Personally, my parents paid for one semester of my undergraduate costs and nothing for my master's degree. I truly appreciate the part my mom and dad played both in helping me at the beginning and allowing me to figure the rest out for myself. Like many students, I worked a part-time job, applied for government grants, and took out a couple small student loans. I graduated and received a job offer. I eventually paid back the loans and became a tax-paying citizen for the next thirty-plus years. I turned out just fine after being almost exclusively responsible for my own education. You may find reasons to be different—your money, your choice.

That begs the question: if our kids choose to go to college, how do we (or they) pay for it?

There are numerous ways youth get through college or trade school without parents fitting the bill for sometimes hundreds of thousands of dollars. I worked through college. My-son-in-law went the military route to pay for dental school. A friend made her way through college with grants and scholarships. The point is that you qualify yourself (or your children qualify themselves) for a better life through training or schooling, and you need to find ways to pay for it.

Of course, for many students and families, the easiest way to pay for schooling (though easiest isn't always the best route) is through student loans.

Currently this country's higher education system has been raising tuition rates disproportionately higher than inflation. Universities know that the federal government will guarantee loans that students take out for their schooling. This guarantee means that even if a student files for bankruptcy, their loan is still owed and must be repaid eventually. Too many students saddle themselves with excessive student loan debts, and the universities are the ones that benefit. We all know stories of people (or perhaps ourselves) still paying off student loans a decade or more after graduation.

In my opinion, if the education these universities are providing is so valuable, the universities should be the ones guaranteeing the student loans. Students could then dislodge themselves through bankruptcy courts should the education prove worthless. You can imagine how different the tuition and loan situation would be for students if the university were on the hook.

A viable alternative to attending a university is to attend a local junior college or trade school. Classes are usually smaller and resources tend to be more available compared to the large universities.

Like everything else regarding credit and loans, think hard before you go into debt for education.

Luckily for those of you wanting to avoid student loans for your kids, there is an alternative: saving! That's right—you can start right now to save in a college savings program and take away the sting of university debt before entering higher education.

Today there are 529 educational plans available to save for post–high school education. We'll get into more details in our next chapter, but rest assured—there are ways to save for college that are pretty amazing. My remaining children all have 529 plans.

Or, as an alternative, you could just make your kids pay for their own schooling. That is a legitimate route. It's your money, so it's your call.

On Transportation

Cars are a wonderful tool. They're also the one major purchase you make that depreciates in value the moment you buy it.

I have a very simple rule when buying a car: pay cash for it. I know that's easier said than done, but if at all possible, try to make this a reality.

Now obviously, that doesn't work for most people, which is why an automobile is seen as an acceptable purchase using credit. If you can't pay cash for your vehicle and must finance, set a purchase limit right from the beginning. Be disciplined (there's that word again!) and don't spend over your limit. From there, I say thirty-six months of financing is all you can afford—no more than that ever. Surely the salespeople will show you that over a longer-term loan, you can get that car with all the extra features including the stereo and custom wheels. Of course they'll say that! They make more money off a higher-priced sale with a longer-term loan. Don't fall for it! Stick to your purchase limit, pay what you can afford, and don't finance for more than you need. Thirty-six months is the finance time limit.

Get preapproved by your preferred lender prior to shopping so you know the terms and shop around for the best terms before buying. You will likely be pressured to finance more than your budget allows.

Another tip is to not mention your down payment (if you have one) until after the price of the car has been finalized in writing. Most automobiles are financed for the same amount whether a down payment is provided for or not. This way, you'll know that your down payment is going toward the price of the car. You would be amazed how your down payment can disappear in fees and extras. You want your down payment to go toward the actual price of the car you're buying.

And finally, no discussion of a vehicle purchase is complete without talking about vehicle insurance. I know insurance is not always an interesting subject, but we need to cover it if you want to keep within your budget.

Before you buy, call your automobile insurance company and share with them your two or three finalists. Your agent will tell you what the costs will be to insure each car you are looking at. A simple phone call can save you thousands of dollars and may even help you decide on the right vehicle.

I was at a point in life where I wanted a nice new-to-me car (something most people call a "used car"). I could pay cash. I was looking at the Nissan 350Z and the convertible Lexus 430SC. The auto insurance company told me the semi-annual cost of insurance for each. To my surprise, because the convertible Lexus 430SC had a rear seat, it was considered a sedan and therefore was much cheaper to insure. The Nissan 350Z was classified as a sports car, and the insurance on that car was considerably higher. I chose the Lexus. Calling the insurance company before my final decision saved me thousands on future car insurance payments. Since I wanted each car equally, the cost of insurance became the deciding factor.

Becoming Aware of Excessive Spending Habits

Do you overspend?

I know your defensive gut reaction is to say no.

But let me phrase it a different way: do you keep track of your finances and what you're spending your money on?

If the answer to that question is no, then I can guarantee the answer to the first one is yes.

Overspending is incredibly easy if you're not paying attention to where the money goes. I've known clients who chose to look closely at their spending and discovered that almost 25 percent of their disposable income was used at restaurants and fast-food places every week. They didn't realize they were eating out so much and didn't like the habit they formed. With a few changes, they were able to start saving substantially more, all because they started paying closer attention to their habits.

Money spent on non-essential expenses should be reallocated toward your new savings goals. What are "non-essential expenses"? The answer to that question is different for everyone. It's a question we all need to ask ourselves and figure out. Here's a clue: What can we do without? What has become a crutch because it's convenient?

Perhaps you collect model airplane kits and it brings joy to your life, but you discover you're spending hundreds more on your hobby each month than you realized. Will cutting back on that spending be detrimental to your happiness? Probably not. You don't need to cut off the things that bring you joy, but you should learn to control them.

Here's an example from my own life. I like chocolate candies. Cherry cordials are one of my favorites. My local grocery store sold a large box of cherry cordials for a relatively low price, so I bought one box. After eating two pieces, I decided that the chocolate quality was not to my liking. I thought, "Why am I putting this poorly produced product in my body? These ingredients cannot be good for me." Even so, did I stop buying cherry cordials? No. I decided to spend more money on higher quality cherry cordials and buy fewer of them. Are cherry cordials non-essential expenses? Probably. But for me, they make life a little more enjoyable, and that is an important luxury I occasionally seek. I choose this indulgence and live life a little outside the lines, so to speak.

Do not constrain yourself or others in the family to the point that life is no longer enjoyable. Strike the elusive balance as best you can. Rather than waste money on a lesser value product, I purchase a smaller quantity of a higher quality cherry cordial and eat fewer . . . but the taste is out of this world! Employ discipline and enjoy life—but in smaller portions. Americans are mostly overweight anyway, myself included, but I am working on it while I enjoy life.

The point is, we all have essential things in our lives that may not be essential to someone else. What is essential to you? And is it truly essential? Will sacrificing some of these things now help you have something better in your future? These are hard questions, but unless we're willing to dig deep and answer them honestly, we will never develop the discipline necessary to change our financial lives.

Consumers of all ages are confronted with about a million products to purchase every day. You can buy nearly anything you want in the world through online retailers. You do not need all that stuff, and you do not need to buy someone else in your life stuff they don't need.

Save your money. My mom told me that everything you buy requires a little more time in your life—to use it, store it, fix it, dust it, and so on. Your precious time and money is being sapped away.

Stop it. Stop filling your life, and in some cases your children's lives, with material possessions that merely take up space and require time and energy to maintain. You will find yourself far happier and at greater peace without them.

And making these small changes can have huge compounding results.

Something as simple as skipping the daily $5 hot chocolate or energy drink can help you save about $1,825 a year! If you invested those savings every year for twenty years at a 7 percent annual compounded return, you would have around $75,000 saved for your future. Live life, but just understand where your money is going and how it all adds up.

And trust me, getting out of debt and staying out of debt is the most wonderful, freeing feeling in the world. When you know you are in control of your financial future, it's like the horizon opens up, and possibilities you never imagined are right there at your fingertips.

It's amazing to live debt free, and I highly recommend it.

One Last Look

Good: You have some debt, but it's manageable. You keep a low balance on your credit cards. Your home equity line of credit (HELOC) is being paid down.

Better: You have a few credit cards but pay off the balances immediately each month. Whether they're low or high interest rates doesn't bother you since you pay the balance off each month. Once in a great while you miss the payment deadline, but who doesn't? Life is busy. Some of the cards have a reasonable annual fee for the reward programs they offer.

Best: You are debt free. The cash flow from what would otherwise be used to service debt provides an exhilarating feeling of freedom. You save each month so you can purchase a new automobile, family vacation, or unplanned expenses. Your plan is to pay cash for your larger purchases if at all possible.

Awful: You sign up for nearly every credit card that comes your way. (Incidentally, applying for credit cards lowers your FICO credit score, which qualifies you for higher interest rates, not lower ones.) You are enticed by the many freebies offered. You ignore the fine print regarding the interest rate escalation, and after the teaser interest rate period expires (usually after six months), your interest rate soars. You feel it is a game worth playing, so you look to transfer the debt to yet another low-interest rate credit card, but then many have fees associated with that too. You have freebies and points, but now you are over your head in debt. You're making the minimum payments and occasionally falling behind. Late payments are ratcheting up the balances. You realize you need help.

This is exactly how the poor stay poor. Credit card companies fought the legislative laws requiring credit card companies to report year-to-date fees, interest paid, and current interest rates. Review your statement to see the costs you pay to service debt.

Don't end up in this spot. If you're already in deep, now is the time to pull yourself out. It's not too late. Look for credit counseling in your area.

One Last Awful: In our previous church ward, a family boasted about the many credit card programs they finagle constantly. That may be fine for them, but because they brag about it to others, other families close to them are tempted to jump in and do the same with credit cards. This family is exporting the very dangerous desire to play the credit card switcheroo finance game. I do not think this will end well for many families there. Others may not be up for the time and determination required to finagle the switcheroo debt game.

Do not encourage others to get into debt. You never know which family is not prepared, and you may end up destroying their financial lives.

Something for the Kids

One day your kids will benefit from establishing a history of good credit usage. Review these four considerations with them.

First, consider obtaining a secure card from a financial institution that is known to report credit behavior to the large credit bureaus. The financial institution will accept your deposit upfront. As you use the card, the charge comes from your own deposited funds. You regularly replenish the account on a consistent basis. This will create a credit history.

Second, consider becoming an authorized signer on an established credit card account. My sister-in-law began this way when she went off to college. Her parents felt good that she had a credit card for emergency purposes. Mostly she used the credit card to purchase airline tickets home for the holidays.

Third, establish a checking account and credit card. When you use the credit card, enter the payment information into your check register as if it were drawn from your checking balance. Deduct the credit card purchase from the available balance. At the end of the billing cycle, you have the funds in the checking account to pay your credit card balance.

Fourth, consider obtaining a cosigner for a small loan. There is risk to the co-signer who is equally responsible for the loan amount. Your attention to this will create a credit history.

8

The Importance of Saving

Jim Rohn taught me the following life lesson that has served me well: save some of your "Pepsi money" for something really big. I did just that recently. I bought tickets for the "Get Back" concert on May 31, 2022—row 1, seats 11 and 12, with Sir Paul McCartney. Totally worth the Pepsi sacrifice.

During our youth, saving for retirement is usually low on our list of priorities. After all, it's decades and decades away. Just because something is currently beyond the horizon doesn't mean we won't eventually collide with it.

Whether you accept it or not, eventually you're going to want to retire peacefully. While pursuing that retirement goal, you may apply for a mortgage, and having a sizable retirement account bodes well with the lenders.

In the last chapter, we focused on avoiding debt, and once you've accomplished that, saving money should be your next major goal. Retirement is obviously the big thing you'll want to be looking at, but saving money goes beyond just putting cash away for when we reach a certain age. It means having the ability to enjoy a lot of freedom you just don't have when you're paying off credit cards and car loans.

So where do we start? How much should we save? Where do we save it all? Stocks? Banks? A mattress?

All good questions. (Except the mattress one—don't do that!) Let's dive in and start demystifying how to maximize your savings.

Without thinking too much on retirement specifically, start by saving 10 percent of your gross income in an employer-sponsored retirement plan or similar vehicle. Done. Once you've got that taken care of, permission granted to think more about a home purchase, education, and reliable transportation needs.

Obviously, for members of The Church of Jesus Christ of Latter-day Saints, one-tenth is a religious number. There is power behind a tenth, or 10 percent. If I asked you what 10 percent of $1,389 is, you would quickly calculate in your head $138.90. You were taught to move the decimal point to the left one place. If I asked you what 20 percent of $1,389 is, you probably wouldn't be able to calculate $277.80 in your head. You may quickly double the approximate tenth ($140) to come up with a close $280, but still, 10 percent is an easy calculation we don't need to put much thought into.

The Lord's number of one-tenth has helped me figure prices and savings on products pretty easily over my life. There is something special about a tenth. So start now by saving 10 percent of your gross income. There is power in that number.

When we get to the chapter about creating a financial plan, we'll dial this number in. For now, 10 percent.

A Changing Employment Landscape

Gone are the days when most Americans could rely on their companies to provide lifetime employment, including a guaranteed monthly pension upon retirement.[47] Employers are transitioning away from offering pensions and toward defined contribution plans. The accumulation phase refers to those who work from about their mid-twenties to mid-sixties. People are working to afford a place to live, transportation, vacations, and stuff—lots of stuff. Retirement should be a part of what we are working toward. People in this retirement-accumulation phase are forced to be more personally responsible for saving and investing enough to provide themselves ample income during their retirement years. These defined contribution plans allow

47. See Barbara A. Butrica et al., "The Disappearing Defined Benefit Pension and Its Potential Impact on the Retirement Incomes of Baby Boomers," *Social Security Bulletin* 69, no. 3 (2009). https://www.ssa.gov/policy/docs/ssb/v69n3/v69n3p1.pdf.

the employer to make contributions for the benefit of the employee without the heavy costs related to older-style pension plans.

Ironically, shifting the burden of saving and investing away from the employer to the employee coincides with a decreasing rate of personal savings in the United States. Following World War II, the savings rate in this country rose. It peaked in 1982 at over 10 percent. Only during the pandemic of 2020 and 2021 did levels rise again to those heights, but they quickly dropped back down afterward.

The decreased savings rate and the disappearance of pensions, coupled with uncertainties in the stability of Social Security, creates a compelling argument for why you need to start taking responsibility for your own retirement savings right now.

When we talk about saving, we're not implying that your money simply sits in an account for decades and that's it. You can do that, but it isn't the smartest way to use your time and hard-earned cash. What we're talking about is the need to invest your money. Some people choose real estate and others choose the stock market. I choose the stock market for its liquidity. Personal preference.

If you've never invested before, it can feel incredibly daunting. It doesn't have to be scary though. We're going to get into more details about investing in the next chapter, but for right now I'm going to provide a few simple reasons why it's a good idea and how relatively easy and reliable it can be (emphasis on "relatively").

One of the easiest ways to start saving inside or outside of a retirement plan is to use the method called Dollar Cost Averaging, or DCA.[48] You may be participating already.

Many investors struggle to find the optimal time to invest. (Hint: the optimal time doesn't exist.) Question for you: when is the best time to plant a tree? Answer: twenty years ago. But we can't do that, so start today. Trying to find the optimal time can lead people to avoid investments altogether. They may feel the market is "too high" right now or fearful because it's "too low," thinking that if they invest now, they will lose money when the market goes even lower. Conversely, an

48. See Adam Hayes, "Dollar-Cost Averaging (DCA) Explained With Examples and Considerations," Investopedia, last modified Apr. 26, 2023, https://www.investopedia.com/terms/d/dollarcostaveraging.asp.

irrational investor can be overly anxious about investing even when the economy is doing well.

A common refrain from people who stopped investing sounds like this: "One time, I invested in the stock market and lost big-time. I'm not going back in until it's safe to do so." The problem is, there is no "safe" time to invest. There is always volatility, but like I've stated before, over time the market goes up and therefore your investments follow. Even if you invest at the height of the market, another downward trend will likely follow at some time in your future. The market will eventually hit a new market high. That's how markets have worked. My compliance department would want me to say here that past results do not guarantee future results. You get it. Life has risks. This is true of any investment.

Enter Dollar Cost Averaging (DCA) to calm the nerves. The DCA approach helps eliminate all these issues by systematically establishing regular investing in all market cycles—good, better, best, and awful. Over time an investor will achieve an average investment price on all purchases. If you're investing when the market is high, those eventual market losses will be offset by purchases when the market prices are lower. The added benefit is that when the market is too high, few shares or units are purchased. When the market is lower, many shares or units are purchased. When the markets smooth out, the profits on the lower-price investments can outweigh the few purchased at higher prices.

In a perfect world, we would purchase all our investments at their lowest possible price and, like magic, the market would skyrocket and we'd be able to retire immediately with millions in the bank. It's a wonderful fantasy, but unfortunately, the world does not work that way. DCA is the best proven alternative. The market will always fluctuate, much like the tide waters every day. But let me tell you a little secret that has been true for longer than I've been alive on God's good earth: markets grow higher over time, always, 100 percent of the time. The key is *over time.* Remember it is not *market timing* that works—it's *time in the market.* That should give you some courage when you're dipping your toe into investing!

The most common example of DCA is through payroll deductions in a company-sponsored 401k or similar plan. Consider an employee earning a salary of $100,000 a year and contributing 10 percent of her gross salary into the company 401k. The employee is purchasing some stocks at higher prices and some at lower prices throughout the entire year. As long as the contributions are reoccurring, she too is using Dollar Cost Averaging.

As you can see, investing really isn't that difficult. Just be sure to make it a priority and stick to it. This is discipline. Time will pass and your accounts will grow. You will be astonished to see how effortless it was to accumulate your first $100,000. Then the $500,000 mark comes into view. It's incredibly exciting! You have a sizable asset. Once I hit my first million in my IRA, I truly witnessed the magic of large numbers. A ten-percent market growth on my million-dollar portfolio meant $100,000 added to my retirement's market value. Consider that this $100,000 market gain may be more than what some people make in a year. That's the power of large numbers. To be clear, these are market gains and not cash in hand, and markets change daily.

I'll tell you right now—the first million is the hardest to make, but the second million comes far more quickly with far less effort.

How's that for motivation?

To understand this growth principle, consider that each year I put away about $40,000, but the compounding on my first million continues to propel me toward the second million, say $50,000, giving me a total of about $90,000 each year. It grows and grows without me having to worry too much about it—just a little.

Of course, there will be down times, but we're not looking at the next year or even two—we're looking at the next decade and beyond. With that type of time on your side, growth will occur, and you will reap the benefits of your discipline.

Pay Yourself First

One of the oldest and wisest axioms of financial health and saving is this: pay yourself first. What this means is that you put money into your savings before you do anything else with it. Obviously, as members of the Church of Jesus Christ, we would switch that slightly and give to the Lord first as we participate in His law of tithing. Once that's done, however, we put money in our savings right off the bat.

This may not feel like "paying yourself first" since the money is being put into the investment, but think about it another way: the rest of your earnings are going to pay other people for food, your housing, automobiles, movie theater tickets, and so on. That money will never stay with you. It is spent each month. Your savings belong to you and no one else. When you're saving, paying yourself first is key to lasting growth and a future where fear isn't constantly on your doorstep.

This mental accounting concept segregates your paycheck automatically before you have the opportunity to spend it. I pay myself first by having a ten-percent payroll deduction go straight to my 401k. A payroll deduction takes a certain percentage of each paycheck and places it directly into your retirement plan. The money is immediately invested and grows tax-deferred. Contribute at least what your employer is matching. If they're willing to put in anything, like $500 a month alongside your $1,000 a month, then put in $1,000 a month! Do not pass up free money from your employer in the form of a company match.

If you already contribute, experiment by increasing your contribution a little each quarter or when you get a bonus, raise, or promotion. Some plans offer an automatic increase feature. This allows your contribution to adjust over time and increase so slightly you likely won't even miss the money going into your retirement plan. In the end, you may even hit the maximum allowable by IRS rules and be completely surprised at how much you saved over the course of a year.

In the event you don't have a company retirement plan, you can take the "pay yourself first" approach to saving money in an Individual Retirement Account (IRA) or a brokerage investment account. In the case of a brokerage account, you can use those investment funds whenever and however you like, but they may be taxed like any capital investment.

If your employer allows you to deposit funds from your paycheck to multiple direct deposit accounts, consider having 10 percent go to the IRA then another percentage to a brokerage account. If you're able to continue with additional direct deposit locations, consider a portion going into yet another account earmarked for a life goal, like the down payment for a house, a 529 educational account, or an important family vacation.

Higher Education Savings

Higher education is a noble pursuit. Whether it's a trade school, military experience, college, or the school of hard knocks, one of the best earthly gifts to pursue or bequeath is a learning opportunity for yourself and others. The Lord encourages us to seek learning (see Doctrine and Covenants 88:118). Today there are terrific vehicles to help better prepare you for your higher education goals for yourself or those you love.

President Gordon B. Hinckley, then a member of the First Presidency, shared his thoughts on education:

> First, educate your hands and your minds. You belong to a church which espouses education. To you young women may I suggest that you get all the education you can. Train yourselves to make a contribution to the society in which you will live. There is an essence of the divine in the improvement of the mind. "The glory of God is intelligence, or, in other words, light and truth." "Whatever principle of intelligence we attain unto in this life, it will rise with us in the resurrection."[49]

College was important to me and my parents. I didn't qualify for any scholarships, and my parents were only able to help pay for one semester of tuition. I graduated with my degree and a small amount of student loan debt. Over the next couple years, I developed a strategy for paying off my loans. I consolidated my student debt into a mortgage refinance. After a couple more years, we sold the property, and the mortgage that I once refinanced (and thereby the student loan) was eliminated. I believed in myself and this strategy at the time. Mortgage interest was tax-deductible (student loan interest was not), and I believed that I could increase the real estate value quicker than I could repay the student loan, which I did.

Like with any debt, there are strategies that will allow you to maximize your ability to pay them off . . . if you're disciplined and forward-thinking. The same goes for student loans. But if you can avoid them all together, you're going to find yourself in a much better situation, whether you're planning to attend college yourself or help pay for one of your children or grandchildren to attend.

Speaking for myself, I do not plan to leave much cash to my living children when I pass through the veil. That's a decision I have prayerfully made, and my reasons are many. If something were to happen to

49. Gordon B. Hinckley, "Rise to the Stature of the Divine within You," *Ensign*, Nov. 1989, 96.

me before my younger children reach college age, however, I do plan to leave enough money in their 529 savings plans to pay for at least four years of higher education. Today's 529 education savings plans have so many positives, with only a couple restrictions.

Let's take a look at these plans and how they may work for your family.

This is how my 529 savings plans function. My wife is the owner. Our child is the beneficiary. These are the two most important facts to understand right from the beginning. I am the successor owner, which means I only take over the account if my wife dies before me.

As the owner, my wife can contribute money into the 529 savings account, up to the allowable IRS limits. As a father, I can also contribute the same amount of money each year up to the annual amount allowed by the IRS. Any other family members can contribute money to the account as well, up to the same allowable limits. As the account owner, my wife holds all the power of distributing the money when the right time comes—in this case, when the beneficiary child goes to college or trade school. Additionally, should my child receive a full scholarship and not need the money, my wife, as the owner, can change the beneficiary to another child. If that child is not in need of the money, the beneficiary can again be changed to any family member, even to my wife or me. This is a powerful tool. I advise you to reread this paragraph. It is that important. So hypothetically, if money is left over, another family member could go to college and enroll in a tennis, foreign language, or pottery class.

The contributions are invested across multiple securities, which are similar to mutual funds that grow without taxation until the money is needed for all college expenses excluding transportation. This should not be a deterrent since no college student needs to purchase a Tesla with 529 plan money to get to school. Also, 529s don't cover airline tickets. Those two examples fall under transportation. College students do not need to fly first-class to and from school using 529 tax-favored funds. Outside of transportation needs, however, all lodging, tuition, books, stationary, computers, lab fees, food, and utilities qualify. My wife has the flexibility to send the funds directly to the school for the benefit of the student, or she can write a personal check and have the money reimbursed to her checking account.

This is a program seriously worth looking at. Now consider, how many birthdays, graduations, and holidays come into a child's life? How many adults blow money on plastic toys made overseas during these celebrations? Consider spending half of what you were planning for plastic toys and contribute the other half to a 529 plan. Then pass this same message on to the relatives. They may choose the contribution over the plastic toys too. Over time it all adds up, and in my case, my wife is the owner of the funds. The child is the beneficiary and cannot legally demand money from the 529 plan.

Individual retirement account (IRA) monies can be used for college fees as well. When you take money out of an IRA for valid college expenses, the distribution is not penalized by 10 percent like it would be for other early withdrawals. Taxes are due on the money when it is taken out, however, so pay attention to that.

Not Saving for College

Any discussion of saving money for a child's college fund also must include the discussion of *not* saving for a child's college fund. This is a decision every family must make on their own. I paid for the vast majority of my schooling, and I am happy with how I turned out. I know many successful individuals who chose not to go to college at all. Just because something is common doesn't mean it's right for your family and individual children.

There are plenty of alternatives to the common college experience and the high costs associated with it. Don't discount trade schools or the route of the bold entrepreneur. Even starting out in fast food can lead to lucrative careers for the enterprising individual. Success comes from all angles if you're willing to put in the work, gain the experience, and use the brain God gave you. If you live in America, you have every advantage to succeed.

Now ask yourself how many fast-food restaurants serve millions of people every day around the world. How many people are employed in those fine facilities, from the fry cook on up to the store manager? Are these the highest-paying careers? Can a person support a family on those wages? Ask yourself how many orthopedic surgeons are serving millions of people every day around the world. These represent some of the highest-paying careers. Can a person support a family on those wages?

Now consider what you want out of life. Do you desire God to open the windows of heaven and have Him pour out a blessing of prosperity, so much that you don't have room to receive it? Then you best qualify yourself to receive those blessings. Keeping the commandments is a great first step, then turn yourself into the most skilled person you can be. I believe that a person of honesty, integrity, and perseverance can excel at any vocation and live the best life possible . . . if that person is willing to qualify for it at all levels.

Follow the acronym ASK: Always Seeking Knowledge.

Some readers will say, "I am only a local mechanic and cannot achieve financial success because I am just barely making it as is." Feel free to remove the word "mechanic" and insert your career if you feel discouraged. If you're feeling that way, allow me introduce Bridget and Garrett. (Those aren't their real names, but it's a real couple I have known and admired for years. They work smart.)

Garrett was a high school teacher when I met him. His wife, Bridget, worked for a collection agency. They lived modestly. They appeared to be frugal, smart, working people. They owned a home (mortgage) and managed to rent the home Bridget had when they first met (another mortgage). They started a family. Garrett eventually qualified for a teaching position at the local community college. Bridget worked and received her college degree. They have three children now, and Bridget manages the family and the rental, among other things. They have multiple newer cars, all paid with cash. Their credit score is in the 800s. They have two credit cards that carry no balance. They recently purchased a modest mountain cabin for the family. In a nutshell, I bet their taxable income is modest, and yet they remain money smart and have just as much stuff as the Joneses down the street. They qualify themselves for a nice lifestyle while raising their family, and mostly on a teacher's salary! You can too. Don't fool yourself thinking that success is accomplished by others, and without excuses or inheritance!

Would you be interested in becoming a millionaire collecting other people's garbage for a career? Consider Harry Wayne Huizenga.[50]

50. See Howard Cohen, Adam Beasley, and Barry Jackson, "H. Wayne Huizenga, billionaire entrepreneur and Miami sports icon, dies at 80," *Miami Herald*, Mar. 23, 2018, https://www.miamiherald.com/news/local/obituaries/article206530794.html.

Huizenga started his garbage hauling business near Fort Lauderdale, Florida. He borrowed $5,000 from his father and then sweet-talked a competitor into selling him used trucks. Starting with his first garbage truck in 1968, Harry eventually grew his business into a Fortune 500 company. By the time he took his company public in 1972, Huizenga had completed the acquisition of nearly 133 smaller garbage haulers. In the early 1980s, Harry had grown Waste Management into one of the largest waste-hauling companies in the United States.

Harry Huizenga didn't stop there. He eventually invested in and later purchased Blockbuster Video. The visionary man then sold that business at its peak. Huizenga went on to create AutoNation as well. At the time of his death from cancer in 2018, Harry Huizenga owned professional football, baseball, and hockey teams, became known for his philanthropy, and won the "Distinguished American" award for his massive funding of scholarships throughout the state of Florida.

Here's a man who never graduated from college but used his fortune to pay for complete strangers to do what he didn't do. This is a perfect example of how resources can be used for the greater good. No government mandated his philosophy. He was free to bless the lives of those around him.

And Harry did it all without a college degree.

Some capital, drive, good advice, and grit can elevate a person to unimaginable heights. No one knows what your children can achieve. Be prepared to give them the best start you can, and then let them run on their own.

The Balance of Saving

Like everything in life, saving can be taken to the extreme. In this case, the saved money doesn't help to alleviate fear but becomes a source of fear in and of itself. "I'm never saving enough!" "I won't have enough money saved if something bad happens!"

Saving money is part of the ever elusive balance we try to strike in our lives. If it becomes too much of a focus, hindrance, or burden, then it loses its purpose in helping us find peace.

One mistake a friend of mine ran into was being so eager to save money for his future that he began saving too much money for too many goals. Before the year was up, he lost interest in saving anymore because he had deprived himself and his family of the common comforts of life. He wasn't happy, his wife wasn't happy, and his kids weren't happy. My friend went too far, got frustrated, and gave up.

You must use discipline to master the ability to save while also living in the moment at the same time. Give that first 10 percent to the Lord, and place the second 10 percent right into your savings. I discourage investing more than 10 percent when (and only when) that higher amount impacts the ability to provide basic needs and comforts for your family. The Lord counsels us to walk before we run. Find a good fit and apply discipline. Automatic deduction to your employer-sponsored retirement plan is a great way to start saving for your future.

Saving doesn't have to be complicated, scary, or overwhelming. You'll be amazed at what you can accomplish if you start simply (like with a 401k), follow sound principles (like with DCA), and listen to the counsel of the Lord (much of which flows directly from the prophets and apostles at any general conference).

One Last Look

Good: You have a savings account, and you deposit a defined amount from each paycheck.

Better: Your employer has a matching program for contributions to your company-sponsored retirement plan. You contribute just enough to get the full match.

Best: You maximize your company-sponsored retirement plan to the IRS allowable limit, and you are collecting the matching amount your employer puts in also. Your spouse does likewise. Saving is comfortable against family needs, and you live life to the fullest without fear of spending for your needs and wants.

Awful: A recession hits and your balance drops in the stock market. You pull all your investments out until you feel safe that the market has stabilized. As the economy improves, you remain skeptical and are too nervous to reinvest and end up losing the opportunity to maximize your savings as the markets go higher. After another five years, you discover you could have earned tens of thousands of dollars in market value had you only cast your fear aside.

Something for the Kids

Cameron started mowing lawns at age fourteen. He saved about one third of each payment he received in a bank account. Eventually he put himself through college using the same discipline of working and saving. Cameron plans to retire in 2022 at the age of sixty-four. He is a multi-millionaire because he paid himself one-third of his paychecks for fifty years. Cameron is a special case. What is your case?

Now that's a success story! Discipline learned early. I only ask that you start with 10 percent.

If your children can save even one-tenth of the money they receive in a bank account during their youth, and continue that discipline through their working career, they too could retire relatively wealthy and do so on their own terms and at their own time.

Most adults absolutely hate their job. It's true—ask the next ten people you meet. If your kids were able to build a respectable account balance while young, should their career become cumbersome, they would have the resources to do something positive about it. If your savings is large enough while you're young and you didn't like your career or job, you'd have the money to alter your path. Most adults cannot do that.

9

Investing Your Talents

Before I go any further and start delving into investments, my attorneys want me to state the following:

> As stipulated by law, I cannot and do not make any guarantees about your ability to get results or earn any money from the ideas, information, tools, or strategies presented. The risk of loss in trading securities and options can be substantial. Please consider all relevant risk factors, including your own personal financial situation. Before investing or trading any investment, understand that stocks and options do involve risk and are not suitable for all investors. Use caution and always consult your attorney, accountant, financial advisor, and tax advisor before acting on this or any information related to a lifestyle change or your finances. Past results of any individual or trader or trading system published by the author are not indicative of future returns by that trader or system and are not indicative of future returns that may be realized by you. All strategies and examples are provided for informational and educational purposes only and should not be construed as investment advice under any circumstances. Such set-ups are not solicitations of any order to buy or sell a financial security. Any financial numbers referenced here should not be considered average earnings, exact earnings, or promises for actual or future performance.

In the Gospel of Matthew, Jesus Christ shares a parable about servants and talents (see Matthew 25:14–30). We all know this parable backward and forward. Three servants are entrusted with the property of their master in the form of talents. The first two invest them, growing the master's wealth, while the third buries the talent in the ground because he's afraid of losing it. The first two are then rewarded and the last is cast out of service.

We often interpret this as an invitation for all of us to share our talents and gifts with the people in the world. This is a beautiful interpretation. But have you ever thought about this parable in terms of investing your own money? The parable is surprisingly straightforward. It talks about investments and interest and all of that.

The key takeaway for me is that the third, or "slothful," servant was lazy or afraid to act, fearing he'd lose the talent (or, in this case, the money entrusted to him), and thus he did nothing productive with it.

Investing is all about expending your extra money with the expectation of achieving a profit or material result by putting it to work in the financial markets, buying shares, owning property, or using it to develop a commercial venture as an example. Always keep in mind that there is always the risk of loss in any investment.

Is it scary? It can be if you've never done it before.

Should you do it? Absolutely! Grow yourself and grow your money as well.

Investments can include a primary residence, rental property, stocks, options, bonds, mutual funds, unit investment trusts, structured investments, precious metals, collectibles, and more.

The beautiful thing about investing is the power of compounding returns. Albert Einstein called compounding interest "the eighth wonder of the world."[51] Compounding interest is simply receiving interest and then reinvesting that interest to earn even more interest. Essentially you're earning interest on your interest. Think of it like one of those cartoons where a very small snowball starts rolling down a mountain and by the end it's gigantic. Imagine your interest like that—growing and growing over time. Time is money.

51. "The 8th Wonder of the World," Guardian Savings, Sept. 1, 2019, https://www.guardiansavings.org/blog/2019/9/1/the-8th-wonder-of-the-world.

Time is the key element of compound interest. The more time you have, the bigger your snowball can grow, so to speak.

I presented the Rule of 72 when we discussed credit card debt, but it really shines when applied to compound interest and investing. You'll remember the Rule of 72 as a simple way to determine how long an investment will take to double given a fixed annual rate of compounding interest. By dividing 72 by the annual rate of return, investors obtain a rough estimate of how many years it will take for the initial investment to double. If you invested $100,000 into an investment that you expect to have a return of 9 percent, you can expect your $100,000 to become $200,000 in eight years (72 / 9% = 8 years). On the other hand, if you want to estimate what annual rate of return you might need to make an investment double in five years, the rate would be 14.4 percent (72 / 5 years = 14.4%).

Let's say you had $100 to invest. If you could invest that money for ten years at an annual rate of 10 percent interest that was *not* compounding, you would have simple interest of $200 after ten years, or $10 per year. On the other hand, if you invested the $100 for ten years at an annual rate of 10 percent *compounded* daily interest, you would have $271.79. The longer you allow the money to compound, the more dramatic the difference will be.[52]

Now think bigger.

Consider $10,000 at a 12 percent rate per year for twenty years, and your money compounded would be $110,188.29! If that same scenario was experienced without compounding, then with simple interest your money would only grow to $34,000 over the same period.

A more practical example is Christopher, who starts with $10,000 and adds $200 each month for twenty years. Miraculously he has been getting 7 percent daily compounding interest. His value after the twenty years will be $145,277.61.

This principle is applied in the stock market and for millions of investors every year. The results are always astounding when you project them into the future. I believe it was Warren Buffet who was asked if the stock market could ever reach one million. Is that even possible?

52. See "Compound Interest Calculator," Investor.gov, accessed May 27, 2023, https://www.investor.gov/financial-tools-calculators/calculators/compound-interest-calculator.

Well, let's do a little math using the Rule of 72 and see what we get. We'll look at the Dow Jones Industrial Average, or DJIA, which is a price-weighted measurement stock market index of thirty prominent companies listed on the stock exchange in the United States.

At the end of 2022, the Dow Jones Industrial Average (DJIA) was at 33,147.

In seven years it could be at 66,294.

In another seven years it could be at 132,588.

In another seven years it could be at 265,176.

In another seven years it could be at 530,352.

In another seven years it could be at 1,060,704, over one million!

I will be in my mid-90s by then. I could live to see it happen. Where will you be? Will you participate?

How Stocks Work

Entire libraries have been written about stocks—how to buy, sell, diversify, avoid risk, embrace risk, lower risk, and every other aspect of the investment trade. Stocks have been romanticized, vilified, embraced, and feared, but at the end of the day they come down to one thing: using money to make more money over time.

Now, you may ask yourself, "Where did all this stock market madness start?"

I am so glad you asked!

Somewhere around the year 1792, some folks gathered around a Buttonwood tree and, although simplistic, began buying and selling existing companies using paper certificates as the vehicle to represent ownership.[53] The intent of the stock market, as it became known, was an investment tool that allowed anyone with a beneficial business idea to bring that idea to market and get investors to financially support the idea. This would help an entrepreneur who did not personally have the money needed to bring the idea to fruition. In the purest form of goodwill for all, the stock market represented the place to obtain the money to financially support these ideas. It was believed that all

53. See Olivia B Waxman, "How a Financial Panic Helped Launch the New York Stock Exchange," *Time*, May 17, 2017, https://time.com/4777959/buttonwood-agreement-stock-exchange/.

parties would benefit: investors, entrepreneurs, and the general population. This is what the stock market was originally for.

Today, greed often overshadows the stock market's humble beginnings. There are wildly diverse opinions about the nature of today's stock markets. Some see it as the purest form of business, while others look at it as legalized gambling.

Here's how it really works. Today, publicly traded stock shares are issued by companies and represent an ownership portion of the company itself. Basically, when you buy a stock, you are buying a tiny percent of the overall business. You are becoming an owner in that company because you now own a share of its overall market value. That's why when someone owns 51 percent of the stock in a company, they now have a controlling interest. They make the business decisions going forward. They own a majority of the shares in the business itself. For this reason, stocks are also referred to as equity because you have an equity position in the company.

In the case of common stock, the most popular and widely available kind, this ownership interest may give you the right to vote for the leadership of the company and other proposed measures as well as participate in any dividends. In the case of common stock, these dividend payments may fluctuate depending upon the profitability of the company and whether the company board of directors allow dividends to continue. Some companies retain all the money for future expansions. Dividends are not guaranteed.

Stocks are traded through an exchange where market price fluctuates throughout the business day. You can buy stocks representing any publicly traded company with the hope that the market value—determined by those who want to purchase shares and those who want to sell shares—will rise or fall over time. You may be able to sell shares at some future time for more money than you bought them for originally.

Investing in stocks can offer one of the best opportunities for higher returns, but there are risks. One risk is that the market value of the stock may be lower when you want to sell it. By doing so, you may realize a loss. Alternative to a stock is a bond. A bond functions much more like a loan you give to a company, and thus businesses have the obligation to pay them off under the agreed-upon terms. If a company were to declare bankruptcy, owners of common stock would not have the same priority in recovering their investment as a bondholder. But if a company is hugely successful, a bondholder won't reap the benefits like a stockholder will. It's a balancing act between risk and reward.

Stocks are often classified as "growth" or "value." Growth companies are typically in an expansion phase where they are reinvesting their cash flows into growing the company to take on greater market share. Value companies, on the other hand, are classified as such because the company may have reached a major market share peak and experience little growth as they strive to maintain their products or services from competitors. Value stocks tend to be mature and well-established companies. Sometimes these companies fall out of favor and lose their way in the business world. Look at Kodak and General Electric for example—once darlings of the stock market.

Stocks are also classified according to the size of a company. This is referred to as market capitalization, or "market cap" for short. This market cap implies the total value of all stock shares a company has outstanding. It is calculated by multiplying the price of a stock by its total number of outstanding shares. For example, a company with twenty million shares selling at $50 a share would have a market cap of $1 billion.

Companies worth over $10 billion are classified as "large-capitalized" companies. They have access to huge amounts of money to keep operations going. Companies in the $2 billion to $10 billion range are classified as "mid-cap." If a company is smaller than $2 billion, it is called "small-cap." Generally speaking, smaller companies historically provided a higher investment market return with, of course, a higher level of risk for the investor.

In today's complicated legal world, stocks remain a reasonably convenient way to buy and sell ownership in various companies. The internet has enabled common citizens to access the stock markets on their own, whereas years ago it was difficult and expensive through established brokerage houses.

And just like originally envisioned, people with a good business idea can search for investors willing to trade cash for partial ownership in their company. The new business then issues stock, and the cash received from the investors is used to buy materials or tools, purchase a factory, hire employees, and so on—whatever that specific company needs to grow. Of course, there is a risk of failure in any new business.

The perceived value of the stock will fluctuate based on the business's performance. This performance is measured in many ways, and the stock price will fluctuate based on that perceived value.

As an example, consider a fictitious company, ABC, that receives $1 million for the initial sale of 100,000 shares of stock. That makes each share worth $10. As time passes and the products begin to sell, company ABC is perceived by the investing public to be worth $2 million. As news of their success reaches investors, the shares may reach a value of about $20 each. Initial investors have doubled their market value in this investment!

It doesn't end there though. More fluctuations enter the equation when an investor believes the company's value is greater than a mere $20 per share. He offers $22 per share. For a time, the company is perceived to be worth $2.2 million. Investors are pleased because their stock value is higher. The shareholders that purchased each share at $10 have an unrealized gain of $12 for each share.

Unrealized gains are a prince, but never forget that cash is always king. Those *perceived* gains are just that: perceptions. Prices may drop for any number of reasons, and suddenly the stock gains evaporate. Imagine that same investor who bought shares at $22 now thinks the company is in trouble and dumps them for $6 a share. The company is now perceived to be of less worth than when it started.

You can see how this whole thing can seem like a roller coaster. The important thing to remember is that in my lifetime, history shows that the stock market as a whole has risen over time. I've said it before, and I'll say it again: the stock market is a long-term market for individual investors. It is not market timing that makes a difference but time in the market. If you choose to play it for the short-term, you may get disappointed. Stick with it over a few decades and you will get the returns you deserve. Jump in and out with every market correction and you'll be crying over your losses and yelling about how the market is rigged against you.

I advise people to invest and stick with it the best they can.

My first priority as an investor and advisor, with few exceptions, is that the investment must pay the investor cash on a periodic basis, usually in the form of a dividend. Dividends are payments a company makes to its stockholders as that company is profitable. Profits are shared with the investors. Dividends are paid on a regular basis and are one of the ways investors earn a realized return from their stocks.

My second priority is in unrealized gains. (Like I mentioned earlier, I call the unrealized gain a "prince," but cash remains "king.") This unrealized gain is the second priority because you can't spend unrealized gains. Unrealized gains are black ink on white paper. After it's printed on your statement, the next business day will show that all values have changed. Whenever the stock market drops, you'll hear from the media about how billions of dollars of wealth vanished overnight. It wasn't cold hard cash suddenly disappearing—it was market value. Over time your stock may double in price on paper, but until you've sold it and have the cash in your account, it's all unrealized wealth and susceptible to further market fluctuations each business day.

My third priority is diversification. There are many strong companies producing products or services in different areas of industry. If you only invest in one sector of the market—say oil, for example—then when the prices drop, you could lose your investment and be left with less. An excellent strategy to follow is to spread out your ownership throughout the market so negative fluctuations don't impact your portfolio of stocks so harshly. (Though please note that diversification does not ensure a profit nor protect against loss in a declining market.)

Investing in Stocks

We're advised to do what we love in life, right? Well, that truth doesn't just translate to our jobs and hobbies. It is equally true in our financial lives as well.

I want to tell you what I love to do with my investing.

I love to buy and own individual stocks, then sell call options.

I love to investigate their story, discover the reasons they're successful, and understand their financials, dividends, products, and services. I only purchase stock I have grown to like very much. I nearly always sell a call option on the stock I own, especially if no dividend is present. There will be more on this "call option" topic later and in more detail, but bear with me for right now. The call option that I sell will bring me cash that will be in my account the next business trading day. The stock that pays a dividend is also in cash and is usually paid to shareholders quarterly.

To summarize: I own a stock I like. I believe it will appreciate in value over time (the prince). Super important point I want to drive home: time is money. I may get a cash dividend quarterly, and I will receive cash (the king) for selling the call option on the stock I own.

It may sound complicated, but trust me, it is so interesting and rewarding!

I love this whole process—researching the stock, buying, selling, and everything in between. That's why I do it. If I disliked the process, I would avoid it at all together. On the financial journey you're beginning, you will find aspects you enjoy and aspects you despise. By focusing on the parts you love, you'll find the parts you don't love becoming less burdensome.

I want to start with the aspect of finances that I absolutely adore, which, as you now know, is buying individual stocks. I'm going to try to help you understand why this is so rewarding and why you shouldn't be afraid of investing in the stock market. It isn't as terrifying as you may think. And heck, you may be like me and enjoy every aspect of it.

Let's start with a real-life example and go through some of the details so you can get an idea of how stock buying works. Let's look at company ABC again. Stock ABC trades on the major stock exchange and can be purchased by any investor (which includes you). On a given day, the volume of shares trading back and forth are about 3 million individual shares. I buy 100 shares of ABC stock for $14,198 (that is, $141.98 for each share).

ABC has a history of paying cash dividends of $6.56 for each share to the owners of record for the following 12-month period, or $1.64 each quarter. That means if the board of directors continues to allow dividends, I will receive $656 on that stock investment for the year through the dividend.

Now, I mentioned call options a bit earlier, so let me give you a bit more information on those. Call options are financial contracts that give an investor the legal right (but not the obligation) to buy a stock, bond, commodity, or other asset at a specified price within a specific time period. One equity call option contract controls 100 shares of stock.

Options on stocks are bought and sold on a public stock exchange (known as exchange-traded options) or over the counter. If you own a call option, you can use it to buy a defined number of shares at a guaranteed price and have a determined amount of time, whether the stock goes up in price or not. A call option buyer profits when the underlying stock increases in price during the specified time. As a call option seller, I receive the cash premium the following business day in my account. The details of the call option sold will state the date of expiration and the price I am willing to sell each share of my stock for. I profit when the stock price does not reach the price indicated in the call option contract. This is called the strike price. In this case, I retain the stock, dividends paid by the company, and the cash premium the buyer gave me for the call option. I could also profit should the underlying stock price exceed the price on the call option by the expiration date. I am then entitled to all of the following: cash for each share I sell, any cash dividend from the company, and the cash premium.

Simply put, if you purchased a call option on Microsoft stock for $1 per share for the following month, for example, you would exercise your contractual right to buy the stock at a given price—say 100 shares at $120 a share—and you would own that option for the following month. If Microsoft stock rose to $130 a share in that time, you would buy the stock at $120 a share as agreed. You would have earned $1,000 ($10 of profit x 100 shares) minus the $100 to buy the call option, giving you a net gain of $900. However, if at the end of the next month the price hasn't risen past $120, the option expires and you don't buy the stock, and you lose your $100 to the seller.

Still with me? Good!

When someone buys a call option on a stock, they pay a fee to the stock owner. This is known as the premium. In the above example, it was $100. If they don't end up buying the stock, the original holder always keeps that fee and retains their stock.

I sell the stock option, collect the cash fee called a premium, and move on. I personally do not buy call options. I sell call options, but that's just me.

I sell a call option on the stock I own. Owning the stock makes the type of option I am describing a covered call. Covered only means that I own the underlying stock. By owning the stock, I am capable of delivering the stock should the buyer exercise the right to buy the stock at the agreed price, which is called the strike price. I am entitled to the cash premium paid and receive it in my account the next trading business day. That cash premium is mine—deal done. I don't have to wait until the expiration date to get the cash premium.

I sell the call into the future, say one to three months. I choose the strike price I am willing to sell my shares for, preferably higher than I purchased it for. The market chooses the cash premium price, and it's published for all to see. This is the market. There is a complicated algorithm too lengthy to describe in this guide that determines how the cash premium is priced. Suffice it to say that time and volatility are two large influencers. By entering the call option order, I am agreeing to the terms of the strike price and future date.

Let's look a little deeper into the ABC stock example from earlier. If I were selling a call option on that stock, I could choose the expiration date of three months into the future and a strike price of $160 for each share. An investor interested in that stock would accept those terms and pay a cash premium fee of $1.22 for each share on my 100 shares to guarantee the shares will be held at that price no matter how high the stock market value might soar during the next three months.

If the three months pass and the stock price is under $160 on expiration day, then the contract is expired, worthless to the buyer. I continue to keep the stock, any dividend owed me by the company, and of course the cash premium the investor paid at the start. You can calculate the result: $1.22 x 100 = $122.

Not a bad return on a stock I didn't even have to sell!

If, on the other hand, the three months pass and the stock price is at or above $160, then the buyer will exercise their right to purchase all 100 shares for $160 each. Is this bad for me? Not at all. I made a short-term profit minus what I paid for the stock originally. I also keep the quarterly dividend paid by the company, and I keep the cash premium too. From the original investment of $141.98 for each share, I keep the profit ($160 - $141.98 = $18.02), the quarterly dividend of $1.64, and the cash premium of $1.22. That's a $20.88 gain per share, or $2,088 for the whole 100 shares.

Not a bad return on a stock I sold!

From the above example, if I replicated the trade without selling the stock, I may have received $11.44 on each of my 100 shares of ABC over a year's time. I could spend this money on products or services, or I could buy more stocks that I think will increase in value.

Here is a list of the stocks I will hypothetically purchase today, and how things will likely evolve over time:

- ABC $141.98 per share
    - Annual Dividend $6.56 / Quarterly Call Cash $1.22
- DEF $229.65 per share
    - Annual Dividend $5.16 / Quarterly Call Cash $1.75
- GHI $188.20 per share
    - Annual Dividend $3.72 / Quarterly Call Cash $1.45
- JKL $188.44 per share
    - Annual Dividend $2.64 / Quarterly Call Cash $3.10
- MNO $88.13 per share
    - Annual Dividend $2.00 / Quarterly Call Cash $0.92
- PQR $32.83 per share
    - Annual Dividend $1.12 / Quarterly Call Cash $0.80
- STU $114.63 per share
    - Annual Dividend $5.20 / Quarterly Call Cash $0.93
- VWX $23.72 per share
    - Annual Dividend $1.80 / Quarterly Call Cash $0.24
- Y&Z $59.60 per share
    - Annual Dividend $2.32 / Quarterly Call Cash $1.31

You can see from this list how these types of call option transactions can add up over time. If it's something you have an interest in, they can turn your investment work into something a bit more like a serious hobby.

That's how it is for me—a professional interest.

I very much enjoy selling covered call options. I own individual stocks and am engaged in selling the call option contracts. I collect the dividends (if any) and the cash premiums. A few times I've ended up selling the stock because the price rose beyond what I had anticipated, but most of the time the call option expires, completely worthless to the entity that paid me cash to potentially buy my shares at a higher price than I paid for them.

I've heard it said before that this strategy leaves you selling the best stocks and keeping the losers. I disagree. I have actively been engaged with this strategy for over twenty years. Sometimes a stock needs to be sold if it becomes too overvalued. Sometimes a stock drops in value too. If the stock drops, the worst-case scenario for me is that the cash premium may become very low later. Should the stock price rise over time, then cash premiums may rise also.

This strategy can be performed in an Individual Retirement Account (IRA) or taxable account too, but only when the account is approved for selling covered calls by the firm. There is no tax reporting for the IRA account. The taxable account will be taxed on the profits. A detailed report will show in a 1099 form distributed yearly.

In my opinion, this strategy helps reduce overall risk. Take our earlier example of ABC stock at $141.98. Every time I get a cash premium paid to me, in essence my original cost declines proportionally. The best case is that I live long enough to keep collecting $1.42 each quarter of a year for many years. As I reduce my original investment by selling covered call options, I reduce the risk I made in my original investment.

And always keep in mind, you don't have to do all of this yourself. That's what some financial advisors can do for you. If you want to try investing but don't want to deal with the details, there are skilled financial advisors who can help. You don't need to do it alone.

A professional financial advisor can oversee a covered call writing strategy for you with the goal of generating additional income on your stock positions. These programs have position minimums and other requirements that must be met. Your financial advisor can help you determine whether or not this is the proper direction for you. Consider your time horizon, life goals, objectives, and risks you are willing to take.

To summarize, I find individual stocks that I believe have the potential to appreciate over time. I try to select stocks that pay a dividend. I will likely sell a covered call option on the stock I own for a higher strike price than the price I originally paid. If the stock is purchased away from me, I still realize a profit and keep the cash from two sources: option cash premiums and dividends (if any are declared). If the option expires, I still make a realized cash gain that I can use to buy groceries, travel, or purchase more stocks I like.

These yields excite me. If this could be replicated as I get older, then my goal is to receive all the money I spent on my principal investment back in my account. Remember, time is money. The more time I can give to this process, the greater my rewards will be over time. Whether I replicate this exact trade for the next few years or not, the fact remains that I am growing older each day. Time is money.

So start investing now because time is like the grains of sand that pass through an hourglass. There is no stopping time. It is your most abundant resource, and it is always slipping away.

My Bad Example

Alright, I can't talk about call options without going into what are called "naked call options" and how, when I was a very young investor, I lost my original investment being a bit too naive.

When I was out of college, I dabbled with buying call options. I studied a little about them but discovered too late that I hadn't learned nearly enough. I opened an online no-help account. I followed a shoemaking company and heard that they would report earnings the following week. I purchased about $1,000 worth of short-term call options. In the week prior to the announcement, the stock price did appreciate a bit. I got excited! The big day arrived and the company earnings matched the analysts' expectations to perfection. The stock then began to plummet. I said, "Hey, hey—wait a minute! The stock should go up because the company did what everyone thought should happen. Why is the stock going down?"

I ended up losing the $1,000, but it at least bought me some valuable experience from the school of hard knocks. I invested in naked call options. A naked call option is when an investor purchases a call option but not the actual stock itself. These are very risky because most of the value tends to be in the amount of time available to exercise the option. If the stock declines, there is little time left to overcome the trend and reverse any losses.

Another vitally important lesson I learned is this: "Buy on rumor and sell on fact." Most investors had read the same public earnings announcement I did, and we all agreed that the shoe company probably would report earnings in line with expectations. Once the announcement was verified, the more speculative shareholders sold their shares on the confirmed fact and moved on to the next quick trade to be made elsewhere. I was left holding the bag, thinking that since the announcement was positive, magically every investor was going to pile into this stock, driving it even higher. Nope.

That lesson cost me a thousand dollars, but I at least learned several good lessons. You might say my tuition was expensive. Experience is important when you're investing, which is why it's wise to consult with trusted experts when you're first starting out. Don't follow my bad example and jump right in buying naked call options. You don't know what you don't know, and if you want to avoid some pain, trust those who walk in front of you.

Cryptocurrency and Alternative Investments

Cryptocurrency is a relatively new way to invest that has people excited and terrified all at the same time. A cryptocurrency is an encrypted data string that denotes a unit of currency.[54] It is monitored and organized by a peer-to-peer network called a blockchain, which also serves as a secure ledger of transactions (e.g., buying, selling, and transferring).

Put in simple terms, it's digital currency not backed by the United States Treasury. Cryptocurrency (crypto) is independent. Crypto has no backing in the form of a nation, major bank, or precious resource, and there is no guarantee of its base value. Bitcoin, Dogecoin, Unobtainium—all these cryptocurrencies are only worth what the market says they're worth, and the market is made up of people around the world. The only way for the crypto to increase in value is to convince someone else into buying yours at a higher price, as there is no real value, unlike gold. Gold has value because it has industrial purposes like jewelry, electronics, and medicine. Ever since men and women have been on God's good earth, gold has held value. That is a longstanding record.

Cryptocurrency has some similarities to many traded commodities like soybeans, corn, lumber, copper, coffee, and sugar. They all have fluctuating values that are impacted by demand and availability.

54. See Jake Frankenfield, "Cryptocurrency Explained With Pros and Cons for Investment," Investopedia, last modified Apr. 21, 2023, https://www.investopedia.com/terms/c/cryptocurrency.asp.

Cryptocurrency vendors control their own supply but can't prevent new vendors offering yet another cryptocurrency from entering the market. There is actually no limit to how much cryptocurrency can be created. Anyone can enter this industry. According to CoinMarketCap, a crypto tracker, in 2019 there were over 2,100 cryptocurrencies created, and today my last count was nearly 5,520 cryptocurrencies available.[55] This is what makes calculating cryptocurrency prices based on usage quite challenging.

As a rule of thumb, institutional investors allocate less than 1 percent of their overall assets into alternative investments like those of cryptocurrencies. It's just too much of a risk. Individual investors buying crypto may want to consider their risk tolerance. Unfortunately, this can be difficult to do with cryptocurrency since things in this field are still evolving.

It's kind of like the Wild West, and nobody knows who the sheriff is with cryptocurrency. Watch the FTX debacle unfold.

It is only my closely held opinion that crypto will become a story where future generations will study its demise. I do not buy or sell crypto. Crypto actually devours a tremendous amount of electricity to create a digital Bitcoin you cannot hold.

In 2020 and 2021, expectations that many national currencies would lose value in the wake of COVID-19 (among other factors) led to a surge in the price of crypto. Some people thought cryptocurrency would even supplant national currencies and become the primary unit for purchases worldwide. El Salvador actually adopted Bitcoin as a legal currency in September 2021.[56] That experiment is continuing, with very mixed results, while other nations have done what they can to push back against crypto.

55. See "Global Cryptocurrency Charts," CoinMarketCap, accessed May 27, 2023, https://coinmarketcap.com/charts/.

56. See MacKenzie Sigalos and Arjun Kharpal, "El Salvador's bitcoin experiment: $60 million lost, $375 million spent, little to show so far," CNBC, Oct. 13, 2022, https://www.cnbc.com/2022/10/13/el-salvadors-bitcoin-holdings-down-60percent-to-60-million-one-year-later.html. See also Christopher Brito, Bitcoin is now legal currency in El Salvador — but its rollout hits major snags," CBS News, Sept. 8, 2021, https://www.cbsnews.com/news/bitcoin-el-salvador-legal-currency/.

Governments simply have a lot to lose and not much to gain by allowing the cryptocurrency revolution to supplant their own fiat money.

Cryptocurrency is a new commodity, and that very novelty contributes to its volatility. Cryptocurrencies do not have a long track record over which experts can collate massive amounts of data about its inherent trends, risks, and rewards. Investors thus lack the knowledge to make truly informed choices.

Some things appear to have a value just because they are popular, but as their popularity falters, so does their value. Some people have become overnight millionaires trading cryptocurrencies, and these stories have driven the demand for investors to get in on the action. But the big question remains: can cryptocurrency continue to grow in value, and is it a good or bad investment?

It remains to be seen whether or not those overnight millionaires will be able to hold on to their wealth. Unfolding before our very eyes is the FTX cryptocurrency bankruptcy.[57]

You may not want to choose crypto or some other alternative investment strategy, but I urge you to invest in businesses you believe in. The stock market isn't rigged or set up to take your money like a casino is. It's time to cast aside any fear you might have in sound investments, trust in the Lord, and prudently send your talents out into the market to grow and maybe even do some good!

One Last Look

Good: You purchase a few stocks and hold them for years. Sometimes the stocks appreciate, sometimes the stocks depreciate. Over time the unmanaged stocks record an unrealized gain.

Better: You are diversified and own over a dozen stocks in different sectors. The dividends are meaningful, and the stocks reflect the companies that align with your values and the products your family uses on a regular basis.

57. MacKenzie Sigalos and Rohan Goswami, "Crypto firm BlockFi files for bankruptcy as FTX fallout spreads," CNBC, Nov. 28, 2022, https://www.cnbc.com/2022/11/28/blockfi-files-for-bankruptcy-as-ftx-fallout-spreads.html.

Best: You own over a dozen or more individual stocks, researching individual companies with the help of a financial advisor. Your advisor sells call options to add cash premiums to the accounts on a regular basis and this inflow of cash, together with investment and market advice, more than pays for the professional services you receive. You have a financial plan. You know where you are and where you are heading.

Awful: You invest in a handful of hot stocks you heard about in chat rooms and on social media. These stock tips are all the rage. There are also trading platforms that charge next to nothing to trade stocks, so you can frequently turn over your account as much or as little as you want. This feels like "Vegas baby" without the travel. In this environment, you tend to buy a stock on the hottest tips but soon find that the stock value tends to decline after purchase. Impatience gets to you. Why do you always feel like you are the last to buy on the latest hot stock before the value tanks? You form an opinion that the stock market is a racket that rich people use to lure in suckers like you. You conclude that people like you buy high and sell low. Investing in stocks is risky and you always seem to lose money. You quit, grow bitter, and complain about how you never have enough for retirement.

More Awful: When I say "do what you love" when talking about buying stocks, I don't mean something illegal, unethical, or unwise. There's a movie I think everyone over age sixteen should watch entitled *Blow*, featuring actor Johnny Depp.[58] It's an excellent story about how George Jung (played by Depp) interacted with the Medellin Cartel, headed by Pablo Escobar, and how they established the American cocaine market in the 1970s in the United States. Here you see how George Jung uses his talents for all that is wrong in the world.

Halfway through the movie, George is on the run from the law, and he reconnects with his loving father in his dimly-lit living room late one night. Quietly his father essentially asks his son why he participates in these illegal acts. George looks at his father and quietly says, "Because I'm good at it."

58. *Blow*, directed by Ted Demme (New Line Cinema, 2001), https://www.amazon.com/gp/video/detail/B0BX1XM8X6/. Note that this movie is rated R for pervasive drug content and language, some violence, and sexuality.

Bingo! Stop the movie and think hard about that singular scene. That was a powerfully wrong answer that leads George to no good. You will see George Jung lose everything in the end. Everything!

We are commanded to be honest and show integrity. True lasting success doesn't come from cheating investors or cynically saying, "Everyone does it, so lying and stealing is no big deal." Follow the example of Christ and feel peace when you look at yourself in the mirror each morning.

Something for the Kids

Investing requires a few necessary ingredients: time, discipline, study, and experience. Help your kids learn a few things about investing now. Perhaps let them choose a company to invest in and buy a single share with their earned money. Have them track it over time. This will help them feel comfortable putting their money in the stock market and teach them early how to remain calm when stocks go up and down.

Back in the day, I purchased one single share of Disney stock for each of my seminary students. They received the actual certificate. I helped them start investing young by owning a piece of the Disney Corporation. I hope that spark led to greater success for those teenagers, who are now adults.

10

A Practical Guide to Gifting

As you follow the commandments and precepts God has provided, you will reach a point of "overproduction" where you bring in more resources than you personally need. I feel this is a promise fulfilled from our Father in Heaven. He will open the windows of heaven and pour you out abundant blessings. God wants to bless you. Be obedient so He can. One of the many reasons for blessings of prosperity is so we can use our agency and choose to provide help to other people.

According to a study conducted by Indiana University's Center on Philanthropy, 62 percent of high-net-worth donors cited giving back to the community as their chief motivation.[59] There are more practical factors at work as well, like setting an example for younger generations, establishing a charitable legacy, and maximizing tax benefits. Even so, altruistic motives are cited as the most important. Winston Churchill phrased it best when he said, "We make a living by what we get, but we make a life by what we give."[60]

59. See Una Osili, Chelsea Clark, and Jon Bergdoll, "The 2021 Bank of America Study of Philanthropy Charitable Giving by Affluent Households," IUPUI, Sept. 9, 2021, https://hdl.handle.net/1805/26654.

60. Winston Churchill, "We make a living by what we get," Goodreads, accessed May 29, 2023, https://www.goodreads.com/quotes/857718-we-make-a-living-by-what-we-get-but-we.

On a similar note, Bessie Anderson Stanley said, "To know that even one life has breathed easier because you have lived—this is to have succeeded."[61] Giving draws us closer to the people around us, promotes happiness, and strengthens empathy. A study conducted by researchers at the University of British Columbia and Harvard Business School found that "spending money on others promotes happiness more than spending money on oneself."[62]

We've been taught that we love whom we serve, right? (See Matthew 6:3–4.) Charitable giving is a service and will help us love our neighbors. Donating time, money, and resources are vital components of a wealthy and healthy life.

There are many good reasons for giving. What are yours? Making a difference? Helping those in need? Fulfilling a moral calling?

One of life's greatest rewards is sharing your wealth with those less fortunate yet deserving, and it seems there are as many good reasons to give as there are ways to give. Perhaps you want to leave a legacy or establish a family tradition of giving that can instill these values for generations to come. Maybe even save a little (or a lot) on taxes. It's all possible.

And just like with saving and investing, having a good plan will maximize your ability to bless lives. There are well-known ways to gift away your surplus wealth for the highest good and personal satisfaction. Whether you call it philanthropy, charitable gifting, or donating, a plan will help you make the most of your generosity.

Where to Start

With so many options, each with its own benefits and considerations, you may wonder how to best start or continue a giving plan. When you come from a place of compassion, it's easy to be overwhelmed by all the possibilities of where your money can do the most good. A lot of need exists in the world, after all, and we can't

61. This quote is often misattributed to Ralph Waldo Emerson. See "What Is Success?," The Tale of Sir Bob, Mar. 26, 2010, http://thetaleofsirbob.blogspot.com/2010/03/what-is-success.html.

62. Elizabeth W. Dunn, Lara B. Aknin, Michael I. Norton, "Spending Money on Others Promotes Happiness," *Science* 319, no. 5870 (Apr. 2008): 1687–1688. https://doi.org/10.1126/science.1150952.

singlehandedly solve all of it. Narrowing your philanthropic focus is necessary in order to get the most penetration out of your generosity.

To do this effectively, you need to ask yourself some pertinent questions like the following:

- Which charitable causes do you care deeply about?
- Is there something in your personal or family history that makes one organization more interesting to you than another?
- Do you want full control over your philanthropic giving?
- Do you prefer long-term or short-term giving?
- Do you want to volunteer your time, money, or both?
- What are your funding sources?

Your answers can help bring your charitable giving goals into clearer focus and lead you on a path that fulfills your wishes for yourself, your family, and your community.

Now you need to match your giving style with the right giving strategy. For some, your Required Minimum Distribution (RMD) goes straight to charity. For others, their highly appreciated stock goes to charity.

If you don't already have a philanthropic philosophy baked into your financial plan, you've got a lot of options—from simple to sophisticated—to help you give back and pay it forward. The focus should be on matching your giving goals and preferences with a strategy that makes sense for what you'd like to accomplish.

Let's take a look at a few possibilities.

Flexibility/Simplicity Plan

Like many people around you, you may prefer the simplicity of directly donating cash or volunteering with an organization. Both give you a more direct relationship with a charity and more flexibility in responding to immediate needs within your community. Setting up a donor-advised fund, or DAF, is also relatively easy. A donor-advised fund allows you to control how your donations will be distributed, receive a deduction when it is most tax efficient for you, and give to a variety of charities when it makes sense to distribute.

Think of a donor-advised fund like a charitable investment account. Its sole purpose is to support your charitable giving. When you contribute cash or any other type of security, you are eligible for an immediate tax deduction. You can then invest the funds for tax-free growth and recommend grants for almost any public charity that is qualified by the IRS.

Sophistication/Control Plan

If you have ample means and seek a strategy to maximize your charitable impact, a private foundation may be the next step. While it requires legal setup, it offers more control, allowing you to fully immerse yourself in executing your giving strategies. Creating your own private foundation will allow you to create international grants, award scholarships (and choose the recipients), and give funds directly to individuals for disaster relief and hardship assistance.

Privacy/Anonymity Plan

Gifts given through a donor-advised fund can include the donor's fund name so that your family can receive recognition if it wants, but they also provide a way to give anonymously. Only money going into the fund is reported on a tax return, not gifts coming out of the fund. It can be a great way to do good and have no one ever be the wiser. Like it says in Matthew 6:3–4, "But when thou doest alms, let not thy left hand know what thy right hand doeth: That thine alms may be in secret: and thy Father which seeth in secret himself shall reward thee openly."

Versatility/Benefit Retention Plan

Setting up a trust is another way to donate money to good causes. Charitable remainder trusts enable you to fulfill your philanthropic intentions, provide income for you or your beneficiaries for an extended duration, and capitalize on immediate tax incentives. Charitable remainder trusts help with tax relief today while also having the potential to keep an asset to benefit your beneficiary after you pass away. We'll get into a little more detail on these trusts later in this chapter.

Collaboration/Family Involvement

Would you like to make giving a family affair? Setting up a private family foundation is one way to go, but it requires significant assets and responsibilities. A foundation isn't the only way you can partner with loved ones. Donor-advised funds also offer a flexible way to help achieve your family's philanthropic mission. Your family can name the DAF (The "Your-Last-Name-Here" Organization for example), and you can collaborate on creating a mission statement that will focus intent and help direct your generosity.

Why is a mission statement important in this circumstance? It can outline your giving goals, identify the causes you believe in, and clarify each family member's role to keep everyone engaged. Consider naming your children and nieces or nephews as the successor advisors on your DAF so that after you pass away, they may continue the tradition of giving in your family name for years to come.

Longevity/Legacy Plan

Do you want your philanthropy to live on? For how long? A few years? Forever? If so, a private foundation is the way to go. Now, as I stated previously, a private foundation requires major assets and runs like a corporation with a board of directors. But if you want your giving to continue long after you've left mortality, this is an excellent way to make it happen. A private foundation can exist in perpetuity, creating an enduring family legacy. The collaborative board structure actually encourages family engagement. However, a donor-advised fund can also have successor advisors or accommodate a legacy giving plan as well. You can name a percentage of your assets to be distributed annually in perpetuity once you've passed away.

Some other unique ways to plan your giving may include naming your favorite charity as the beneficiary of your insurance policy or IRA, or even naming a donor-advised fund or charitable remainder trust as the beneficiary of these accounts. As an example, as an alumnus I have been contacted by Brigham Young University to leave a portion of my estate to them once I pass. There are ways to accomplish this with other entities as well.

Donating Outside the Box

Giving cash is the most common charitable strategy. We rarely think twice about donating to the Girl Scouts outside the grocery store or the Santa-clad bell ringers each holiday season. You may even be in the habit of writing a yearly check to the local pet shelter each December. Donating money directly helps fund organizations that serve in our communities. It's a wonderful way to serve without needing to be too hands-on if your time doesn't permit a deeper dive into the charity.

But there are many other ways to fulfill your giving goals in a meaningful and impactful manner. It's just a matter of finding the best fit for your individual financial situation. Here are some robust strategies that can help you fulfill your philanthropic, financial, and personal goals.

Volunteering

Giving of your time can often be even more fulfilling than simply giving money. By volunteering, you get to experience firsthand the positive impact you are creating. You can meet new people, learn new skills, and feel more connected to your community.

The opportunities for volunteers are endless, so chances are you can find one that fits your interests. Do you like sports? Be a volunteer coach. Too much? Then consider an assistant coach! Do you have a green thumb? Volunteer at a community garden. Are you handy with tools? Build houses for the homeless. I believe former president Jimmy Carter lent a hand building homes with Habitat for Humanity. Have you tried your local Just Serve website? The point is that fueling your passion as a volunteer is easy, and the lives you impact and change are right before your eyes the entire time.

Donating Stock

Besides cash, you can also donate long-term appreciated stock. That's right—you can actually donate stock! Not only does your charity get to the full benefit from a valuable donation, but you can also claim the fair market value as an itemized tax deduction. This allows you to avoid paying the capital-gains tax that would result if you sold the stock and then donated the cash. This is how the rich do it. It's a simple yet effective strategy to maximize the amount of money you can give.

You may also donate complex and illiquid assets such as private company stock, restricted stock, real estate, automobiles, boats, collectibles, alternative investments, or other long-term appreciated property. This requires more time and effort than donating marketable securities or cash, but it has distinct advantages. These assets often have a relatively low-cost basis. In fact, for company founders, the cost basis of their private stock may effectively be zero.

You can even donate highly appreciated stocks to participate in the law of tithing instead of using cash. The Church is already set up to receive stock from your brokerage account. This is easy to do—just speak with a financial advisor.

Keeping your cash gives you control over your money, which is liquid. Cash is king. You can buy the same stock, another stock, or use your cash for whatever, but you retain control when you keep your cash, and the law of tithing is satisfied when gifting highly appreciated stock.

Let's say I purchased 100 shares of XYZ stock for $50 per share three years ago. It was the right choice and has grown to $100 per share. To keep within the commandment of participating in the law of tithing, I want to contribute $1,000, as this represents the tithing from my current salary. I could write a check for $1,000 and joyfully give, or I could contact the Church and arrange for ten shares of XYZ stock to be transferred to the Church at a current market value of $1,000. I paid $500 for those shares years ago. I currently contribute $1,000 in appreciated stock, and I keep my cash in the bank. I get the full tax deduction since I do not get taxed when giving the stock to the Church. It is a pretty clean accounting process too. Cash is king. The Church will sell the stock for the market value once they receive it, and since the Church does not pay taxes on contributions, the full market value is applied to the needs of the Church. Win-win.

That is a great strategy. Make no mistake about it, the Lord still loves a cheerful giver, whether they're giving cash or stock. What's important is to consecrate the gift. Remember that the bishop's storehouse originally received potatoes, eggs, and other such items.

Know Your Charity

When we talk about maximizing the amount of good you can do through your charitable donations, one of the biggest requirements is learning about your charity of choice.

Be sure to invest some time in knowing the expenses that a charity encounters when they solicit you for money. How much of your donation goes directly to help those in need? This might not matter to you if you're only giving ten or twenty bucks, but when looking to give large amounts of money, you should do some research.

Sadly, some charitable organizations pay incredibly high salaries to executives, much like they would at a Fortune 500 company. They also may have other expenses that will eat up a good portion of your donation long before it reaches the people you intend to help. Even worse, there is sometimes cases of outright fraud as well. One Texas couple ran three different charities that claimed to help cancer victims, but they were pocketing all the money. They were finally shut down for fraud but not before stealing millions from unsuspecting people just trying to help cancer victims.

A common first step is to read the 501c3 profile of the charity you're looking to support. You can find out about executive pay among other aspects of the nonprofit. If you feel your donation isn't going to end up where you would like it, that's probably not the charity to support. If fifty cents of every dollar goes to pay a number of executives, you may want to rethink your donation.

For example, search for Scripture Central from your computer (once known as Book of Mormon Central). When I do so, I see a wide blue bar with the word DONATE. I also see a yellow wide bar that says DONATE FAQ. All sorts of information is listed about how donations are used. There's also information about their leadership and if they receive salaries (which they state they do not). I also see they retain a firm to audit their financials. If this isn't enough information, a contact hot link is provided for inquiries via email. I contacted them and asked if they accept donations in the form of cash, credit card, stocks and bonds, real estate, cryptocurrency, and Qualified Charitable Distributions (QCD) from an IRA. They do.

Searching out your charities is a relatively easy thing to do. You probably have excess reserves in your bank or investment accounts. You are in a position to help promote something wonderful throughout the world. This is what I think the excess of money is for. You are a steward over that excess money you generate, so begin now.

DIY Charitable Giving

At the end of the day, you don't need to give to a specific charity at all. You can do it yourself without actually forming an organization or anything along those lines. A close friend told me about efforts done to offer grants to deserving BYU students based on academics and service rather than need. They have full control over every aspect of this endeavor, thus keeping it very straightforward and without creating any entities or tax shelters. This is something your family could do as well.

This is their program. If a student is enrolled at BYU, they can apply for the grant off-campus. A winner is chosen from among the applicants that year. Go over the applicants, notify the winner, and transfer money directly to the school on behalf of the student. Give to deserving students. It's that simple, and with the right attitude, it could bring some family fun to gifting.

Again, keep it simple. First, there is no need to set up the IRS 501c3 nonprofit. Your family could self-fund the grants and weigh the benefits. Doing it this way means you don't need to worry about additional tax shelters or be beholden to government audits and changes in their rules. Something to consider.

Now, if you want full control over your philanthropic decisions and desire to go even bigger than a single grant, setting up a private family foundation may be exactly what you are looking for.

Unlike a public charity, a private foundation makes donations, called grants, to other charities—and the choices are up to you (with some IRS-imposed restrictions). This means a private foundation usually does not conduct its own charitable operations. The foundation supplies money to the charities of its choice, and they do all the work. It's important to note that the activities of a private foundation must benefit the public in order to maintain tax-exempt status.

Depending on your level of wealth, private foundations may be a good option. You would have more control, but realize that more control can also mean higher administrative costs. Family members can be hired to administer the foundation. You will need to have a board made up of people willing to help govern the foundation and keep records of the board's meetings and giving activities. Private foundations can use their assets to pay staff or fees related to running the foundation. You must make grants worth at least 5 percent of the foundation's investment assets each year, and grants should be made to other nonprofits. Under some circumstances and with proper documentation, it may be possible to make grants to individuals as well, but that is not the norm.

Another thing to note: there's a 1 to 2 percent excise tax on the organization's investment assets. Other IRS restrictions apply, so you must be sure you receive the guidance you need to comply.

But again, if you want to go big, this is the way to do it.

Charitable Gifting During Retirement

Just because you're retired doesn't mean it's time to stop gifting. Even if you find yourself on a fixed income, donating to charity should still be a part of your expenditures, even if it's a small amount. Remember, this is about the quality of our own lives as much as it is for those we help. Giving makes us happy, so don't cut that off once you're retired.

On the opposite end of the spectrum, many retirees have an overabundance of wealth and want to maximize their charitable dollars through some of the strategies we've discussed. One of the ways they can do this is by transforming the required minimum distributions (RMDs) into qualified charitable distributions.

Make sense?

No? Well, let me explain.

RMDs are the minimum amounts that a retirement plan account owner must withdraw annually. Basically, the IRS requires that you have a certain amount distributed from your retirement account to you every year no matter what. Even if you have millions of dollars at your disposal, you still must pull out the minimum amount every year starting at age of 73. The Secure Act 2.0—signed December 29, 2022—stipulates more details (like how it's age 70½ if you reach 70½ before January 1, 2020.)

A lot of retirees don't need that required minimum distribution to maintain their quality of life in retirement, but since they're required to pull it out, they also have to pay the taxes on that distribution, which is the sole purpose of the IRS's mandate. But if you want to avoid those taxes and maximize your donation, there is an option to put that money toward a higher purpose. For example, if you have an IRA and plan to donate to charity this year, you can direct up to $100,000 of distributions (the 2022 annual IRA limit) into a qualified charitable distribution (QCD) from your IRA. This amount can then be excluded from your reported income and may serve to cover some or all of your RMD.

Generally, this is more advantageous than taking a distribution directly from your IRA, paying the tax, and then getting a deduction for donating to charity. As an example, let's say the required IRA distribution is $1000. Your portion of tax is calculated to be $250, leaving you with $750, which you donate. You get the $750 tax deduction, and your charity got the $750 instead of the $1,000 they would've gotten had you used the QCD. QCDs may also be useful in situations where the charitable deduction could not be fully utilized on your tax filing, either because your itemized deductions (including the charitable contribution) fall below the threshold of the standard deduction or because your charitable contribution is so large that it exceeds IRS contribution limits and must be carried forward.

In addition, certain charities are not eligible to receive QCDs, including donor-advised funds and private foundations. While the rules may be complicated, it is worth exploring this option to determine if it makes sense for you, particularly from a tax perspective. Seek the guidance of a professional tax preparer.

If you want to see how this can work in a real-life situation, let me tell you about how Kjaersti and Tyler used their individual retirement accounts to help their favorite charity. Lifelong dog lovers, Kjaersti and Tyler were thrilled to support their local animal shelter and did so in a big way. In addition to volunteering at the sanctuary a few days a week, the retired IRA owners opted to each transfer $100,000 to the nonprofit shelter through a qualified charitable distribution. Because it was done before satisfying their required minimum distribution, it counted toward part or all of their RMD. They didn't have to pay taxes on the amount and thus gave more to the shelter than they would have been able to if they took the distribution, paid tax, contributed the net amount, and took the tax deduction. Now that alone is worth the price of this guidebook!

Making Your Charitable Donation Work for You

Giving is an act of hope, love, and community service. However, many of us, no matter how confident we are in our financial plan, would like the funds earmarked for philanthropic efforts to also serve another purpose: providing income for ourselves and our beneficiaries. Two specialized vehicles allow you to do just that. An irrevocable charitable remainder trust (CRT), for example, can generate an income stream for donors and other beneficiaries you name, with the remainder (hence the name) of the donated assets going to your designated charity after you pass away. A charitable lead trust (CLT) is similar, but the charity receives the income first for a set period and then your heirs receive the rest.

Put simply, a CRT trust can give you steady income during your lifetime and then provide your designated charity the remainder of the money upon your death. A CRT allows for the donation of an asset—in this case, a portion of your concentrated stock position—to a donor-controlled trust. The trustee can then sell the stock and reinvest the proceeds in a diversified portfolio, and you will continue to receive a stream of income for the duration of your lifetime or a set number of years. When this period expires, the remaining assets in the trust become the property of the selected charity.

Because this charitable trust is itself a tax-exempt entity, donating shares to a CRT enables you to avoid capital gains taxes on the sale of the shares you gift. Plus, the transaction may result in a charitable income and estate tax deduction. Consult your professional tax preparer and attorney about this option.

How this would work in real life is pretty simple. Let's look at the example of Susan. Susan wanted part of her estate to fund research on breast cancer, which unfortunately runs in her family, but she was understandably reluctant to sacrifice her vision for retirement. She also didn't want to forgo a sizable inheritance for her own children. Susan opted to establish charitable trusts that support her philanthropy and her children. The funds in each trust would remain invested while she was alive and grow tax-deferred. The tax savings she experiences from her now smaller estate will help her toward her retirement goal.

Combining Gifting Strategies

It's possible that any one strategy won't be enough to accomplish everything you want to do with your generous gifting. In that case, it may make sense to start a conversation about combining these strategies. A little bit of planning will go a long way toward augmenting the effect on your philanthropic causes as well as lowering your tax obligations. For example, you could finance a donor-advised fund for a period of years to maximize the amount you can use with your five-year carry forward, then switch to gifting to charities using QCDs for a period of time. You could also combine a CRT with a DAF, making the CRT flexible by naming the DAF as the beneficiary. Clear as mud? Seek a professional.

I know all of this sounds complicated, and in truth, it *can* be complicated. Don't be afraid to ask for help from both a trusted financial advisor and a trusted attorney. You don't have to do any of this yourself.

Heavenly Promises

God has gifted the people of the earth with the seasons, soil, seed, sunshine, rain, a rich abundance of natural resources, and the miracle of life. He gave all of this to us to benefit His children while they occupy the earth. It is good and natural for people to use the resources God has gifted, but it comes with a strict command that we remain grateful for that which we have been endowed with. Likewise, we are custodians of these rich resources and must use them prudently and with wisdom, nothing wasted.

Doctrine and Covenants 59: 15–16 lays it out pretty plainly:

> And inasmuch as ye do these things with thanksgiving with cheerful hearts and countenances, not with much laughter, for this is sin, but with a glad heart and a cheerful countenance—
>
> Verily I say, that inasmuch as ye do this, the fullness of the earth is yours, the beasts of the field and the fowls of the air, and that which climbeth upon the trees and walketh upon the earth.

The fullness of the earth—not a small part, but the fullness. What a promise! As we ponder on these blessings, let us look at our current situations, whatever they are, and appreciate the blessings we have right now. Generally speaking, we are more blessed than we give God credit for. Look at those blessings and start to see where you could give to others, either financially, with your time, or in some other way you feel inspired to pursue. Take those opportunities and you will quickly discover the windows of heaven opening and even more blessings pouring down upon your head.

It's a promise, and the Lord always keeps His promises (see Doctrine and Covenants 82:10).

One Last Look

Good: You participate in the law of tithing and add a little extra to a humanitarian aid program.

Better: You volunteer time around the holidays along with money to benefit those less fortunate in addition to your tithing and humanitarian giving.

Best: Understanding the law of the tithe, you participate fully. After researching and properly vetting potential charities, you make a concerted effort to financially support those organizations that make genuine impacts for something you truly believe in. You also volunteer your time with these charities several times a year. Regular contributions are made throughout the year, not just during the holidays.

Awful: You reluctantly give to a charity, and you never look close enough to see if your money is actually going to those you want to help. It seems like too much effort. You give mainly so you can feel good about yourself and show others how charitable you are, not really caring if it has effects beyond that. You pat yourself on the back for your charity, congratulate yourself on your holiness, and move on to more important things in your life.

Something for the Kids

Encourage your children to read from the best authors and the best books. Ask family members and friends about their favorites.

Volunteering is a great way for young people to brighten up their resume and show their qualifications beyond their specific job skills. By using their younger years offering their time to a charitable organization, they'll show their worth in the workplace. This will not only show future employers their initiative but will give them a better understanding of how others live and the challenges they face. I have seen young people volunteer at the local food bank and at the hospital pushing patients in wheelchairs. Simple yet helpful.

11

Retirement Planning

Retirement. For some of us, that word conjures images of travel and leisure. For others, it puts them into a savings panic about whether or not they will have enough money put away to sustain their desired lifestyle. There are even those who can't picture themselves ever retiring.

No matter which of these categories you fit into, retirement should be something you plan for. The future is never set in stone. We have been advised by prophets and apostles for over a century that we should always be prepared. Part of that preparation should include our retirement.

For those who find themselves in their twenties and thirties who are starting on their retirement preparation path, you're setting yourself up for success. For those closer to retirement age who haven't put much thought into saving for their post-work years, it's not too late! Remember Christ's words when he talked about the "lilies of the field" and how they were looked after by the Lord (see Matthew 6:25). If we do our part, God will do the rest. No matter how late you're starting, now is the right moment to begin building momentum. The strategies discussed in this chapter are for everyone, no matter how far along you are on your savings journey.

The idea of a "retirement" is actually a pretty new concept. Otto Von Bismarck was the chancellor of Germany in the late 1800s, and he is often credited with creating the model for what we consider retirement.[63] To help combat the pressure from the socialist party during a period of high unemployment, Otto implemented what was then called the Old Age and Disability Insurance Law. This law provided anyone who reached the age of seventy with a state-sponsored pension. This act freed up some employment positions for younger workers. Oddly enough, the average life expectancy was only 43½ years at that time.[64] Talk about playing the numbers!

In the United States, Social Security was implemented in 1935 and defined age 65 as the retirement age.[65] The average life expectancy in the US at this time was about 59 years for men and 63 for women.[66] Today, people are living much longer, reaching the age of 79 on average. When these programs were implemented, citizens were lucky to reach the age required to receive their benefit. Now most people will likely live twenty years or more into their retirement benefits.

Obviously, retirement is about money. It ranks up there with oxygen in this circumstance. But money isn't everything. On a scale of happiness, your mid-life of between 45 and 55 years of age can be a very difficult time in your financial journey. Career stresses, transitioning families, saving for missions and higher education, aging parents, and health and wellness issues all weigh heavily on this age group. The good news is that life generally gets better beyond the mid-50s. Stress levels drop significantly, regrets have less emotional impact, status and keeping up with the Joneses becomes less important. Your preferred lifestyle comes into better focus after these years, and by this time, you have decades of experience managing your emotions.

The point is, money is needed for retirement, but it isn't the be-all-end-all of happiness during any period of your life. Our focus on having more money is in large part driven by a popular myth that is carefully cultivated by mass marketing. We're taught that the ability to acquire high-end goods and services is the measure of a happy and

63. See "Age 65 Retirement: The German Precedent," Social Security Administration, accessed Dec. 28, 2022, https://www.ssa.gov/history/age65.html.

64. See Aaron O'Neill, "Life Expectancy in the United States, 1860–2020," Statista, June 21, 2022, https://www.statista.com/statistics/1040079/life-expectancy-united-states-all-time/.

65. See "Age 65 Retirement."

66. See O'Neill, "Life Expectancy."

meaningful life. Consider the car commercial that concludes with the message: "Anyone who believes that money can't buy happiness hasn't driven a Lexus."

Surveys and research constantly reiterate that the most important factors determining true happiness continue to be health, friendship, and family. Good health habits and maintaining strong family and friendship bonds boost both mental and physical health.

So as you look toward retirement savings and the plans that go with it, remember why you're doing it. It isn't about the money—it's about setting yourself up so you can maintain the relationships and health that bring real happiness. Don't turn this time of saving and investing into something stressful. Turn it into a time of joyful preparation where you trust in God, serve your fellow men, and look forward to a time when you will have the freedom to do all the things you love more fully.

Sources of Retirement Funding

For most people without a background in financial services or at least a serious hobby of studying investment topics, the world of retirement planning can seem overwhelming. Understanding the basics of how retirement plans work is very important when it comes to successfully accomplishing your financial goals.

In order to understand how the retirement planning process can help you, let's first discuss the common types of saving options and retirement plans available today.

Defined Benefit Plan

A defined benefit plan, commonly known as a pension, is a company-sponsored retirement plan. This means the company pays for your retirement.

Back in 1875, the American Express Company established the first pension fund for their employees.[67] With favorable tax laws, pension plans became more common in the American labor force. In 1940, about 4.1 million private sector workers were covered by pension

67. See Patrick W. Seburn, "Evolution of employer-provided defined benefit pensions," *Monthly Labor Review* (Dec. 1991): 16–23. www.bls.gov/opub/mlr/1991/12/art3full.pdf.

plans. By 1980 those pension plans covered nearly 38 million workers. According to the Bureau of Labor and Statistics, by 2020, 67 percent of private industry employees had access to a retirement plan. Of that 67 percent, the defined benefit plans accounted for only 3 percent.[68]

These types of defined pensions are entirely funded by the employer and are called defined benefit plans because the benefit that the employee receives is predetermined and usually based on a formula that accounts for age, years of service, and salary. This is good for the employee since the employee bears neither the responsibility for contributing to the plan nor the management of the investment performance. The employee's responsibility is helping the company remain profitable. Some pensions allow the employee to select an option to provide income continuation to a spouse in the event that the employee dies first.

While popular many years ago, relatively few full pension plans exist today. The original idea behind these programs was that companies making financial promises to their employees use company-generated profits to fund retirement plans for eligible workers. Over decades, though, company leaders found the pensions to be harder and harder to pay for. Many companies fell behind in their obligations to fund the pensions, and the term "unfunded pension" became more widespread. Due to the heavy financial burden employers face in funding pensions, caused in part by increased life expectancies of retired employees and lower investment returns, many pensions have fallen into financial trouble or insolvency. Some have been resolved by issuing less than originally promised.

Politicians were alerted of the pending problem.[69] Legislation was created to help prop up some pension plans, but more and more companies have abandoned these retirement programs altogether by paying off the retirees with one-time settlements. Many companies have

68. See U.S. Bureau of Labor Statistics, "67 percent of private industry workers had access to retirement plans in 2020," Mar. 1, 2021, https://www.bls.gov/opub/ted/2021/67-percent-of-private-industry-workers-had-access-to-retirement-plans-in-2020.htm.

69. See Denise Appleby, "The Pension Protection Act of 2006–and How it Still Helps Retirement," Investopedia, last modified Jan. 22, 2023, https://www.investopedia.com/articles/retirement/06/ppa2006.asp.

moved to defined contribution plans. This change put the financial retirement burden on the employee rather than on the employer.

Defined Contribution Plan

One of the most commonly known defined contribution plans is the 401k. The birth of the popular 401k plan took place in 1978.[70] IRS section 401 paragraph k describes the rules for the company-sponsored retirement plan. The notable change between the contribution plan and the original full pension plan is that the employee volunteers to place a portion of their salary into the company-sponsored 401k plan. An employee is permitted to contribute a portion of his or her salary toward the plan maximums, set by IRS rules each year. In 2023 the maximum for an employee under fifty is $22,500 per year.[71] Those over fifty may contribute an additional $7,500 under what is known as the "catch-up" provision, which we'll detail more fully a bit later.

In a traditional 401k, the employee contribution is pre-tax, so there is a significant tax benefit to participating. For example, if a person in the 25 percent federal income tax bracket saved $500 every month in the company-sponsored 401k plan, their monthly take-home pay would actually be only $375 less, not the full $500. The money you were spending on taxes goes towards your retirement, to be taxed later in life when taken out. This is due to the effect of contributing before the income is taxed. The 401k contribution, coupled with any company match and growth, develops tax-deferred until the retired employee takes cash distributions from the account to live on. At that time, the distributions are taxed as ordinary income.

If you earn $50,000 and elect to have 10 percent of your pay ($5,000) contributed to your 401k plan, you essentially lower your taxable income from $50,000 to $45,000. Similarly, if you make an IRA contribution, you may receive a tax deduction at the time you file your tax forms. The contribution is subject to certain limits and restrictions on your earnings for that tax year. You will pay taxes on

70. See "History of 401(k) Plans: An Update," Employee Benefit Research Institute, Nov. 5, 2018, https://www.ebri.org/docs/default-source/fast-facts/ff-318-k-40year-5nov18.pdf.

71. See "Taxpayers Should Review the 401(k) and IRA limit increases for 2023," Internal Revenue Service, Nov. 21, 2022, https://www.irs.gov/newsroom/taxpayers-should-review-the-401k-and-ira-limit-increases-for-2023.

the entire amount (contributions, company matches, and earnings) when you take a distribution of your money later in life, preferably at retirement age.

Let's look at an example of why these types of 401k accounts are so popular. Say you invested $100,000 in a non-retirement (taxable) account for twenty years. Say that money was compounding interest at 10 percent each year, and you paid 25 percent taxes each year on the earnings. At the end of twenty years, you would have almost $425,000. Not bad. If, however, you invested that same $100,000 for twenty years in a retirement (tax-deferred) account, earning the same compounded 10 percent return where you did not have to pay taxes each year, you would end up with almost $675,000! Keep in mind that typically with traditional IRAs and most retirement plans, the money withdrawn is taxable at that time. The government gets their share eventually.

If the money is taken out prior to age 59½, the money is taxed and penalized by an additional tax for early removal or withdrawal.[72] The government feels the need to punish you financially for taking money out that was meant for retirement.

Now, you may ask yourself, why does the government care whether I save, retire, or pull my money out early?[73] Why does the IRS want to support my choice to save at all? The answer is simple: the government doesn't want you to be a financial burden on society when you are too old to work for your own living expenses. Because of this thought, the government has a vested interest in you keeping your money in your own 401k up to retirement age.

There are some ways around this tax penalty, but none of them are very good ideas. A popular provision in many company-sponsored contribution plans is to allow access to your money prior to retirement for borrowing purposes. There are usually limits, fees, and restrictions, so you will need to contact your human resources representative. Not all company-sponsored plans offer these types of loan programs either.

72. See "Topic No. 558 Additional Tax on Early Distributions From Retirement Plans Other Than IRAs," Internal Revenue Service, last modified Apr. 6, 2023, https://www.irs.gov/taxtopics/tc558.

73. See "Why Were 401(k) Plans Created?," Investopedia, last modified Aug. 10, 2021, https://www.investopedia.com/ask/answers/100314/why-were-401k-plans-created.asp.

Despite the tax penalties and loan fee provisions and upon sponsor plan approval, you can remove money from your 401k at any time. It's your money. But I want to show you an example of why this is a terrible idea. Be disciplined and leave your money in your 401k until retirement. Here's why.

Let's say your 401k balance is now just over $134,000. Against good advice, you pursue a $25,000 loan through the company-sponsored retirement plan. The proper forms are submitted and the loan is approved. You are now obligated to repay the loan by having $200 each month taken from your paycheck until the loan is repaid with interest for the defined term. That $200 is going back into your 401k account over time . . . time that the money could have been in the market growing.

Some people have said that if you have to borrow money, pay yourself by taking a loan against your 401k account. I disagree. The whole point of retirement saving is saving for retirement. If you need financing, yes, a commercial loan will sting more when it comes to interest and such, but that sting will hopefully make you think twice before taking the loan and perhaps pay it off faster if you do take it. There are no perceived advantages with a commercial loan, which hopefully will act as a deterrent for you getting into more debt in the first place.

Lastly, what if you separate from your employer? The loan balance is now due. Are you prepared to pay it off immediately? Chances are high that you will not, and the remaining balance could be taxed and (if you are under 59½) likely to incur the early withdrawal tax penalty if other arrangements are not made to service the debt.

ROTH 401K

Another type of retirement account that is growing in popularity is the ROTH 401k. This type of savings plan is similar to a traditional 401k, but the tax treatment is reversed. Tax is taken immediately from your paycheck. The funds accumulate over your working years, and when you retire, they have grown tax-free. Tax-free means that the principal money used from each paycheck was already taxed at current rates. Having paid tax in the beginning, you are eligible to take your money and its growth and any applicable match without further taxation after certain IRS criteria are met.

The question often arises over which is better, the ROTH 401k or the standard 401k. The answer first depends on your age. If you consider yourself young with a lot of years ahead of you to earn a living and pay taxes along the way, then the ROTH 401k may be a better fit. To pay taxes first, you need the very valuable ingredient of time to work in your favor. Time is money, and your time continues to run out. If you're older with only a few years ahead of you to earn a living and pay taxes, the traditional 401k may be the better fit. A trusted financial advisor can assist you here.

Retirement Spending Priorities

When it comes to pre-taxed savings and monies that still need to be taxed, what should your spending priority be in retirement? I'm glad you asked!

First, let me give you the answer. Put off paying taxes for as long as you can. Use taxed money to support your retirement before anything else. That means money in your checking account, savings account, certificates of deposit, and stocks/bonds in taxable brokerage accounts. Next, use up your ROTH 401k or Roth IRAs. The taxes on these have already been paid. Last of all, you'll want to spend your traditional IRA, 401k plans, or equivalents. It's typically a good idea to put off paying taxes until the end of your life. Each time you use money from the first two sources, you are free from paying income taxes because you paid them the first time through. The money from the traditional IRA, 401k, or equivalent plans were not taxed when you put the money into the account, so those taxes then must be paid when you pull the funds out during retirement, later in life.

This is how that taxation looks in a practical example. Let's say you have a tax-deferred account, and you want to pull $10,000 out and have it in your checking account for the month. Well, approximately 20 percent of that amount will be needed to pay taxes on the withdrawal from your retirement account. Your actual withdrawal would need to be closer to $12,500 in order for you to get $10,000 into your checking. Plus, the longer you keep those tax-deferred dollars in your retirement account, the longer those funds can work for you and continue earning, receiving dividends, and hopefully enjoying market growth.

Individual Retirement Accounts

If someone is not employed by a company with a pension or retirement plan, that employee can still save for retirement on their own. There are a few types of personal retirement savings vehicles available for accruing wealth earmarked for your retirement.

Individual Retirement Accounts (IRAs) are special types of custodial accounts that house investment products like mutual funds or stocks. Like the 401k, federal regulations set a maximum annual contribution limit to IRAs for individuals under age fifty and an additional "catch-up" amount for those who are age fifty and older.

IRAs offer more investment flexibility than a company-sponsored 401k by permitting an account owner to choose from all eligible investment products rather than being limited to a smaller 401k menu of offerings that are approved by the company. Contributions to IRAs, however, are limited to a smaller annual amount and obviously receive no company match. IRAs are also used to accept rollovers from company retirement plans when an employee retires or separates from their employer.

There are two main categories of IRAs, just like with 401ks: traditional and ROTH. The distinction between the two is exactly the same as with a 401k in that the traditional is tax-deferred, meaning you don't pay taxes until you use the money in retirement, and with the Roth IRA, you pay taxes before you save it away and thus pay no taxes when you use the money in retirement.

The decision to contribute to a traditional IRA or Roth IRA involves an assessment of several factors. If you calculate your tax rate and think that your taxable income will be higher in your future, and you want to have lower taxable income in retirement, the ROTH might make sense now. If, on the other hand, you anticipate having less taxable income in retirement than you currently have while working, you might want to consider making a traditional contribution to receive the tax deduction now and pay the tax at a later date, when you anticipate being in a lower tax bracket.

Why Designate a Beneficiary

Your retirement savings can be a fundamental part of your estate plan as well as your retirement funding. To help with the estate plan portion, you need to identify your beneficiary. (Note that you can choose more than one beneficiary.)

Any retirement assets that you have not withdrawn when you die will be passed directly to the beneficiaries you select. Often, the beneficiary is a surviving spouse or your children, but it could be another family member or friend as well. It's your choice, but know this: a spouse must sign off if the beneficiary is someone other than the spouse. This law is now in place to protect spouses from being "surprised" at the death of the retirement owner.

When you open a retirement savings vehicle, you fill out a form to name your beneficiary—the person(s) who will inherit your account after you die. This form is more important than many people realize. If you leave it blank, the account may not go to the person(s) you intended and some of the tax benefits could be lost.

To avoid problems, be sure you name a beneficiary and keep it up to date following events like marriage, divorce, death, or the birth of a child.

If you have ever been divorced and remarried, review all your accounts that allow for beneficiaries. It has happened more than once that someone divorced and never changed the beneficiary to the new spouse. Upon death, the account went to the ex-spouse. Don't be that person!

If you have a retirement savings account and do not designate a beneficiary, it could get lumped into your total estate and divided according to the laws in your state. Your spouse or children may ultimately end up with your money, but they will not have access to the same tax benefits as if you had named them as beneficiaries.

For the Roth IRA only, open one as soon as you can to avoid the five-year rule restrictions. The Roth IRA five-year rule says you cannot withdraw earnings tax free until it's been at least five years since you first contributed to a Roth IRA account. That becomes true for your beneficiaries as well. After five years, everything will function the way you want.

Converting from Traditional to ROTH

Let's say you started with a traditional IRA and you want to convert to a Roth IRA and start paying taxes on your retirement savings now. It is possible, but there are a few things to know first.

Since 2010, anyone can convert a traditional IRA to a Roth IRA, but you have to pay the taxes on those monies converted first. Converting is not an "all or nothing" decision either. You can convert a portion of your account to the Roth IRA and leave the remainder. You might consider converting if you wish to completely eliminate federal income tax on future withdrawals and allow your Roth IRA to grow tax-free. Conversion might also be a viable estate strategy if you have other sources of retirement income and you do not anticipate needing to draw from your Roth IRA. Consider it a tax-free bequest to your heirs. This is a powerful idea to employ

To realize the potential future advantages of converting to a Roth IRA, you must be willing to accept the current tax consequences. Converting a traditional IRA to a Roth IRA triggers a taxable event just like any distribution from an IRA. This amount is added to your taxable income for the current year. Because of this, some people choose to convert slowly over a number of years to lessen the tax burden.

For example, a person converts $100,000 traditional IRA equally over four years, so they are realizing $25,000 worth of additional taxable income each year instead of $100,000 all at once. The taxes must be paid at the filing of the year the conversion took place. You have the option of paying the taxes from outside money (highly recommended) or with some of the traditional IRA itself, but that lowers the amount of the conversion total. Be aware that if you pay the taxes out of the traditional IRA, and you are under 59½ years of age, you also face a 10 percent early withdrawal penalty. Conversion itself is an allowable exception, but using traditional IRA money to pay the taxes is not.

In addition to the five-year rule discussed previously with respect to contributions, there is a second five-year rule that governs whether the withdrawal of principal will be tax-free after a conversion. Traditional IRA principal that was converted to a Roth IRA cannot be withdrawn tax-free for five years. Unlike the "contribution five-year rule," which looks at the oldest contribution for measuring purposes, the "conversion five-year rule" starts a new five-year period for each conversion. So multiple conversions made during different years will have different measuring points and each must satisfy the five-year rule before money can be withdrawn tax-free.

For those diligent retirement savers who may earn too much income to contribute to a Roth IRA, conversion of their traditional IRAs may be a viable option. Some investors (especially those with incomes above the contribution limits) have also opted to make non-deductible annual contributions to a traditional IRA. They then convert those contributions to a Roth IRA immediately before the non-deductible contribution has the opportunity to earn taxable income (same day). This is done to build the Roth IRA. This procedure is referred to as a "backdoor ROTH contribution" since it is a way to have a Roth IRA without the normal procedures. Some tax experts have speculated that this may go against the IRA rule "step transactions," which generally prohibits transactions made using a series of steps that could not otherwise be made. However, the "backdoor ROTH" is common practice, as the IRS has not expressly ruled that this procedure is prohibited.

Keep in mind that when making a conversion of any kind, the IRS does have limits. Even though the traditional IRA account owner is free to convert a partial amount of the IRA assets, he or she cannot cherry-pick certain assets to convert to avoid taxation.

For example, suppose an investor has a $90,000 traditional IRA made up entirely of pre-tax contributions and a second traditional IRA with $10,000 of non-deductible contributions. Converting the $10,000 non-deductible traditional IRA to a Roth IRA would normally be a tax-free event because the $10,000 is comprised of non-deductible contributions. But since the investor has $100,000 in total traditional IRA assets, the amount converted will be taxable in a pro rata manner. In this example, because 90 percent of the traditional IRA assets ($90,000) are taxable and 10 percent ($10,000) are non-taxable, converting $10,000 will be considered 90 percent taxable and 10 percent tax-free.

Ouch. Seek professional help if you find yourself in a similar situation.

Note that when converting traditional IRA assets, the pro rata rule only applies to traditional IRA assets and not 401k assets. So an investor with only non-deductible IRA assets and a $1,000,000 pre-tax 401k would still be able to convert the traditional IRA assets to a Roth IRA without regard to the pro rata requirement.

In most cases, you want to maximize contributions to tax-advantaged retirement savings accounts before saving for your retirement goals in a non-retirement account. Remember, what you save is more important than how much you earn.

The Final Lap Before Retirement

Let's discuss the decade before you plan to retire. What should you do when you're entering the final lap of your working years?

Remember watching the Olympic hurdle races? Runners are rounding the last turn and the finish line is in sight. Everything those hurdlers prepared for up to this point is on the line. They begin to pick up speed and enter a hard sprint. They concentrate on each hurdle, leaping with skill and confidence. The last thing any of these runners want is to stumble before the finish line.

As you enter the last years of your earning power, you don't want to stumble either.

Like the runners passing over the hurdles, let's examine several areas where you might face obstacles. Just remember, those difficulties don't have to take you down. You can leap over them and continue with the same speed toward your finish line.

The first thing you need to do is determine where that finish line is going to be. When is the right time for you to retire? Some people want to retire at sixty-five, others in their seventies, some in their fifties. All of these are fine times to retire, so long as the individual is prepared for them. You need to be prepared for your retirement date too, and that means picking a date that feels right. This date may change as circumstances unfold, of course, but you need to start with a date nonetheless.

Dial in your target nest egg. How much money do you need? Start with a number big enough to replace 70 to 90 percent of your current income. Income needs are so widely different that it's better to overshoot this estimate rather than fall short. Some people need less because they paid off their mortgage. Some people are in excellent health and have the insurances and finances in place to support them in their later years. While these preparations are wonderful, costs for other areas of advancing age can go up, so plan for travel budgets, medical premiums, bucket list items, higher education, new hobbies, philanthropy opportunities, and any other things that are important to you.

Each individual investing for retirement is unique. You must remember that during this entire process. You are unique, so don't compare yourself to someone else. Your needs and wants aren't the same as someone else's needs and wants. There are so many articles, reports, surveys, and talking heads producing numerous books and news stories on how to withdraw your money to meet future financial needs. Can they all be right and wrong at the same time? Yes! So many opinions exist because each investor is so unique. For this reason, seek out a qualified financial advisor who can create a plan for you.

We've talked about financial planning before, and I want to reiterate how helpful the process can be. You don't need to go through all of this yourself. Having an advocate who has your best interests at heart will go a long way alleviating any stresses and fears that crop up.

In the meantime, here is a stab at what you might think about when withdrawing money for retirement. This example is to get your mental juices flowing.

Perhaps you're looking for an annual income of $100,000 from your retirement assets each year. Should you have a large enough savings retirement account, accumulating over $2,181,000 during your working years, you may choose a conservative investment approach that tends to provide about 1.5 percent return, accounting for all fees. Perhaps you aren't saving at quite that rate, say in the range of $1,564,000 over the span of your career. In that case, your portfolio will need to reach for a higher moderate investment approach that returns more than 5 percent, accounting for all fees.

This hypothetical assumes an annual income increase of at least 2.5 percent to keep up with inflation, and the money is distributed monthly. This also assumes such things as a constant rate of return and a depletion of the retirement savings funds by the end of the twentieth year. Your situation has a myriad of moving parts, so again, find a qualified financial advisor who will take the time to listen to your situation and goals.

Social Security

One common myth in the twenty-first century is that Social Security won't be there when you retire.

That's very unlikely to happen, in my opinion, and here's why.

Elected officials want your vote, and they risk losing elections if they tamper with Social Security benefits. That doesn't mean the benefits will be there for everyone though. The government has begun "means" testing, which means some earners will be deemed too rich, and those individuals will find their Social Security benefits taxed away. The politicians will live up to their campaign promises by not removing your benefits, but on the other hand, they allow the Internal Revenue Service to tax wealthier citizens to the point that the benefit is taxed away. That being the case, it's better to prepare for the possibility that you will not receive the monies you placed in the care of the Social Security system. That doesn't mean for certain you won't have them when you retire. Control your own finances and leave the politicians to spin their wheels as they always have.

Don't discount Social Security though. Create a plan to access your Social Security payments, but know that you may not receive those benefits based on your income sources beyond Social Security.

I recommend taking Social Security as soon as you qualify, without sacrificing any to early retirement, unless there is a medical or longevity concern. This usually translates into taking your benefit at full retirement age (FRA). Keep in mind that once you begin receiving your benefit, it becomes a reliable income stream, though a taxable one. The retirement accounts like a 401k, IRA, or similar can provide monies on demand, and with the new IRS rule signed on December 29, 2022, do not force a distribution until age 73.[74] Any distribution from a retirement account becomes taxable in the year it is taken (except for the ROTH 401k or Roth IRA since taxes were paid upfront). With this in mind, you can have some control over your total taxable income because you can withdraw what you need on demand.

It's very important to view and understand your Social Security report. You can find it online at www.ssa.gov. After verification, a simple search will provide your personal benefit information. Verify that everything is correct and that you understand the details provided. Use this information with a qualified financial advisor to develop a plan for your upcoming retirement.

74. See "Retirement Plan and IRA Required Minimum Distributions FAQs," Internal Revenue Service, last modified Mar. 14, 2023, https://www.irs.gov/retirement-plans/retirement-plan-and-ira-required-minimum-distributions-faqs.

You paid into Social Security. It is your money, not a gift from the government. My mother retired at age sixty-five and passed away from leukemia at age seventy. She worked at a hospital for over thirty years. Social Security never paid out anywhere near what she put in. I recommend taking your benefit at full retirement age. There are all sorts of reports out there to maximize your Social Security, and any one of these strategies may benefit you. If you delay your payout in order to get a higher monthly rate, you may die without seeing the benefit. No one but God controls your longevity.

Saving Strategies

Since retirement planning is a long-term savings program, the same principles apply if you want to maximize your nest egg. Find areas in your spending habits that could be curbed or removed completely. Add those savings to your retirement fund. Are you taking advantage of retirement accounts offered by your employer? Can you add a Roth IRA to your household of accounts? Personally, I was able to join my company-sponsored Health Savings Account (HSA). This account allows me to put away more money each year without taxation for medical expenses now or while I am in my retirement years.

If you are over fifty years of age, you can use the "catch-up" provision. Catch-up contributions allow workers aged fifty and older to save more for retirement in a 401k plan. You can make catch-up contributions at any time during the calendar year in which you will turn fifty, even if you have not yet reached your fiftieth birthday. If you maximize all these tax-deferred options, you can always put money away in an investment account or annuity as well.

Also, keep track of your different 401k accounts. You likely have more than one. In today's working world, the average worker will switch jobs several times before retirement. A majority of employers offer 401k or similar plans, which means there are a lot of retirement accounts that may be neglected or forgotten altogether. One client of mine came in with 5 different 401k statements. For her, it was like herding cats. Together we took the time to gather them into one traditional IRA. Now her retirement accounts are consolidated, her investments are focused, and she can breathe easier because it is found in one place and working together. She has a clear picture of her overall asset allocation. The "cats" are now dancing to the same tune in the same IRA.

With all of this, adaptability is a necessity. Although you have a retirement date in mind, remain flexible. You don't know what circumstances are going to come your way. It's always best to retire when the economy is good so your investments are maximized, but that may not be an option. Pay attention to economic forecasts, avoid drawing on your retirement too early or unnecessarily, and don't panic if things in the macro-economy are shifting uncomfortably. We never make good decisions when we panic. Again, seek a trusted financial advisor. Talk, listen, act, repeat.

Lastly, update your beneficiaries in these plans. Beneficiaries listed on your retirement accounts take precedence over the beneficiaries listed in your will or trust (if you have one). Check in with your trusted attorney on this matter of importance.

Retirement Lifestyle

When reaching the age of retirement, for most people, everything comes down to lifestyle. Will you be able to live in the same way you are accustomed to living? If you currently have the means to travel around the world twice a year, and then suddenly in retirement you no longer have the means to continue that travel, retirement won't be as enjoyable as you assumed.

Now is the time to think about all of these "bucket list" items.

Determine what you want to do in retirement. Maybe you don't want to stop working altogether but would rather work part-time, return to school, serve a senior mission, or volunteer somewhere and give back to the community. Consider ways to keep your mind and body active through physical exercise and hobbies. Determine how to stay connected to friends and family.

Most importantly, right now is the time to continue (or start) saving! Contribute as much as you can financially toward your retirement savings. This is always important. Remember, if you are behind on your retirement savings, at age fifty you can take advantage of the catch-up provision and make larger contributions to your 401k and other qualified retirement plans.

Develop a retirement income strategy. Identify sources of income in retirement. Determine how much the sources will generate and when to use them. Manage your debt. Eliminate financial obligations that keep you from adding more money monthly to your retirement fund, like memberships you no longer use that automatically debit your account.

Review your retirement plan, as you still have time to make changes and close any gaps. Make sure all beneficiary designations are in place and that your will is up to date in the state you reside in. Each time you reread your will, sign and date the last page. This exercise will help you remember when you last reviewed this important document.

As retirement nears, you will want to continue planning for this next phase of your life. Remain focused on saving for retirement while beginning to envision and organize how you plan to enjoy these future years.

I hear from some retired clients that it is not easy to be of the mindset to save your whole working life, then withdraw from those savings for the rest of your life. I get it. This is why a plan in place will help you visualize the rest of your life.

Consider Serving as a Senior Missionary

To learn more about serving as a senior missionary, visit the Church website. Currently, in the drop-down menu, there's a section that says SERVE and a button in that menu that says "Volunteer and Serve." On the left side, find the words "Senior Missionary" and click on the hyperlink. Learn more there, and then talk to your bishop.

Ask a question using the interactive site. Your question will be answered through email. Simple. Read through some of the thirty meaningful senior missionary experiences. You can use the filters to sort through many domestic and international serving opportunities. Lastly, look at this list and you may find, as I did, hundreds of service opportunities containing many details. Speak with your family members about your considerations, take your righteous desires to the Lord in prayer, and then consult with your local bishop.

Retirement Twenty Questions

Before we wrap up, I want to pose twenty retirement questions to you. Answer these as best you can, and then you can check you answers in the appendix in the back of the book. We've gone over many of these questions in this chapter and previous ones. Other questions will come as a fresh surprise. Study them, retake the quiz as necessary, and I promise that they will help you better prepare for your retirement.[75]

- A good score is between 7 and 12 correct.
- A better score is between 13 and 16 correct.
- The best score is between 17 and 20 correct.
- An awful score is between 1 and 6 correct.

1. For someone currently retiring at sixty-five years old, how long do their retirement funds need to last based on average life expectancy?

   A) 7 to 10 years
   B) 11 to 14 years
   C) 15 to 18 years
   D) 19 to 22 years

2. At what age can you normally begin taking distributions from a traditional IRA without incurring penalties imposed by the IRS?

   A) 55
   B) 59½
   C) 67
   D) 72½

3. What is the largest source of income for most retirees?

   A) Social Security
   B) Personal retirement accounts (401k, IRA, etc)

75. This quiz and the explanations that follow are general in nature and should not be considered or relied upon as legal, tax, or investment advice, or an investment recommendation, or as a substitute for legal or tax advice. This quiz and the explanations are for educational use only. Seek out your professional tax and legal experts for your personal situation.

C) Part-time work
D) Pensions

4. The Lord has provided the Church members with the law of tithing for what purpose?

A) So He can bless us
B) The Church needs money to pay its bills
C) To expand the Church educational programs
D) More money keeps the Church from debtors

5. Being prepared for unforeseen emergencies includes one of the following:

A) Having all bills paid and up to date
B) Having a line of credit established
C) Having a three-month food supply
D) Holding an additional job

6. What percentage will your monthly social security benefit check be reduced if you start withdrawing at age sixty-two instead of waiting until your full retirement age (FRA)?

A) 5 to 10%
B) 11 to 15%
C) 25 to 30%
D) 45 to 50%

7. Distributions from a traditional 401k or IRA are taxable.

A) True
B) False
C) Never
D) Not prior to 59½

8. A valid sequence of withdrawals is represented in which order:

A) Roth IRA, liquid cash sources, 401k
B) Liquid cash sources, Roth IRA, 401k

C) Social Security, 401k, Roth IRA
D) 401k, Roth IRA, liquid cash sources

9. What is the median number of years a homeowner keeps their home before they sell it to move somewhere else?

A) 7 years
B) 13 years
C) 19 years
D) 5 years

10. Earning 8 percent on your investments each year until you retire will nearly guarantee hitting all retirement goals.

A) True
B) False
C) Nearly
D) Only when you don't have any

11. At what age do you qualify for Medicare?

A) The same age you file for Social Security benefits
B) 59½
C) 62
D) 65

12. What was the average monthly Social Security benefit paid to retirees in 2023?

A) $910
B) $1,827
C) $1,954
D) $2,601

13. Approximately what percentage of individuals are forced to retire early due to circumstances beyond their control?

A) 9%
B) 16%

C) 22%
D) 48%

14. From the following four, what is a major theme found in the Book of Mormon?

A) The brass plates contained the fullness of the gospel
B) The message of the prophet Abinadi changed the hearts of the Lamanite people
C) Keep God's commandments and prosper in the land
D) Temple attendance is key to salvation

15. What is the main purpose for a 529 plan?

A) To save for future college expenses
B) To have an additional savings program for retirement
C) To have a rainy day fund
D) To have a generation-skipping account to save on taxes

16. What is the Rule of 72?

A) The average age retirees begin to take Social Security
B) The tax-free amount expected on the sale of stocks
C) The required minimum distribution (RMD) age
D) Time in years to double an investment

17. What is the average interest percentage rate charged for the typical credit card?

A) 22
B) 25
C) 27
D) 15

18. What are the Activities of Daily Living (ADLs) as it relates to long-term care?

A) Transferring, memory care, toileting, dressing, eating, and grooming

B) Transferring, ambulation, bathing, dressing, and grooming
C) Continence, transferring, toileting, bathing, dressing, and eating
D) Continence, ambulation, transferring, bathing, toileting, and eating

19. What is typically the biggest expense category for retired people?

A) Housing
B) Health care
C) Travel
D) Food

20. What percentage do many financial professionals recommend as a rule of thumb for taking out of your retirement account each year?

A) 2%
B) 4%
C) 8%
D) 10%

When it comes to retirement, again, now is the time to begin. If you wish you had started twenty years ago, it's twenty years too late. You can't go back in time. You can, however, begin right now and do your best from here. John Greenleaf Whittier said, "Of all sad words of tongue or pen, the saddest are these: 'It might have been!'"[76]

Don't let your retirement become a succession of "might-have-beens." Start now and look to the future with faith. Die with experiences, not dreams.

One Last Look

Good: Although you are not participating in saving for your retirement, your employer is forced to contribute to your retirement

76. John Greenleaf Whittier, "Maud Muller," *The Complete Poetical Works of John Greenleaf Whittier* (Boston, MA: James R. Osgood and Company, 1873), 204–206.

account due to the Safe Harbor provisions the company elected. The employer plan is a benefit provided to you. The cost of administering the plan is carried by the employer.

Better: Whether your employer contributes or not, you choose to save through payroll deduction and contribute the most you can afford while working. Your employer offers to match a percentage, and you contribute enough to qualify for the full match offered. The company match is free money to you. Take all you can.

Best: You contribute the maximum allowable amount to your retirement fund, whether 401k or ROTH 401k, and your employer is matching your contribution.

Awful: Your employer has no retirement plan, and you are not consistently saving in an IRA. Retirement is in the distant future, and you don't think about it. Eventually you might take a closer look, but who has time for that sort of thing?

If you find yourself in this circumstance and you want to do something about it to escape the "awful" category, you may think seriously about lobbying your business owners or management team to have a retirement plan adopted. If they aren't willing to entertain that possibility, you should seriously consider changing employers. It matters that much!

As of 2023, the maximum for an employee under fifty to contribute is $22,500 per year.[77] For someone over fifty, the "catch-up" provision is an additional $7,500 per year for a total of $30,000. If a person were to work another ten to fifteen years, contribute the most possible, collect a company match, and invest wisely, that annual amount may provide you with about $40,000 a year at retirement. Add social security to that and you may be retiring with around $70,000 a year in today's dollars. That's how beneficial it can be to participate in your employer-sponsored retirement savings plan.

Something for the Kids

Teach your children that when looking for a job, do not simply look at the hourly wage. Retirement may seem far away and unimportant,

77. See "Taxpayers Should Review the 401(k) and IRA limit increases for 2023," Internal Revenue Service, Nov. 21, 2022, https://www.irs.gov/newsroom/taxpayers-should-review-the-401k-and-ira-limit-increases-for-2023.

but retirement contributions from your company become a crucial part of your overall compensation.

Whether you are thirty and have $40,000 in a retirement plan, or you are forty with a retirement plan balance of $130,000, this can help you obtain financing for a home mortgage because lenders will recognize the asset.

12

Life Insurances, Long-Term Care, and Other Considerations

When we think about our finances, retirement, and long-term well-being, life insurance must enter that conversation. It's another of those seemingly boring, decades-away necessities, but having the right policy can create peace of mind, and our lives improve when we are at peace. It's written in 2 Corinthians 13:11, "Finally, brothers, rejoice. Aim for restoration, comfort one another, agree with one another, live in peace; and the God of love and peace will be with you" (English Standard Version).

Living in peace is possible. One of the ways we make that happen is by removing worries about our potential future. In truth, life insurance helps with that.

A truly complete financial plan takes into account every aspect of your financial future, including considerations of those who depend on you for their financial support. Life insurance can be an integral component of that plan because it helps protect your loved ones should the unthinkable occur.

Life involves risk. That's why risk management is a crucial part of a long-term financial plan. When it comes to investments, that would mean diversification. When it comes to your family, health, property, and income, it means having proper insurance.

Life insurance was created to protect families from financial loss should one or both income-earners pass through the veil prematurely. We've all known people who have been taken from this life too soon and left behind spouses and dependents. There is no balm that will take away the sting of such a loss, but in the case of life insurance, it can at least remove further hassles, worry, and despair for those remaining here in mortality.

Purchasing life insurance requires you to enter into a contract with an insurance company. The annual cost of your life insurance policy is called a premium. This premium is the same flat fee each year. As the policy holder, you can expect to pay premiums on a monthly or annual basis in exchange for a lump sum payment at claim time, also known as a death benefit. When you pass away, this benefit is paid to your beneficiaries to help cover living expenses, outstanding debt, or other costs.

Young married couples usually start out living poor as to worldly possessions. Over the years, based on their earning power, one or both may enter into a long-term mortgage obligation to buy a home. The mortgage will likely be the largest debt the family will accrue. At this point in life, a life insurance policy may be a way to protect the family should one earner tragically die. Additionally, once children enter the family, it is common to plan for some sort of college and mission savings program. This too can be a larger future expense that may need a form of life insurance on the earners to cover potential costs of higher education or a mission should a parent pass prematurely.

There are two types of life insurance to be aware of: term and permanent. Both have advantages and disadvantages and, depending on your stage of life, will give you the peace you require. Remember, the purpose of life insurance is to help the family recover financially after an untimely death. It has the potential to bring peace to the survivors at that sorrowful moment *and* peace to the person who bought the policy during their lifetime.

Term life insurance is the simplest and usually the most affordable option. Policies can be purchased for a specified length of time, such as ten, twenty, or thirty years. If you die within that defined time period, the insurance company will pay your beneficiaries the full amount of your policy—the death benefit. Once that policy time expires, however, the policy as-is terminates. The life insurance company creates the policy in hopes that the term will end before the insured dies, at which point the insurance company profits. Should the insured die prior to the term's end, then the beneficiary would be paid the death benefit.

These term policies are often purchased solely for time periods when the loss of a parent or spouse would have a large negative impact on family finances, such as when children are young. That's why these contracts have expiration dates, because after your chosen date, it is assumed the family will be in a better financial position since children will have grown and no longer be dependent on their parents' income.

Term life insurance is useful if you want life insurance but can't afford a continual life policy.

The other major category is permanent life insurance. This one is pretty self-explanatory. You pay a premium for as long as you live. Once you pass away, your beneficiaries receive the full amount of the death benefit. Permanent life insurance typically comes with a "cash value" savings element, which means you can overpay the life premium. This excess can build up value to continue premiums well into the future. You can also borrow against the value of the policy once you've reached certain thresholds. There are three main types of permanent life insurance: whole, universal, and variable.

Whole life insurance has a premium that never changes, no matter how long you own the policy. These policies generally have higher premiums than term life, but over the decades they are guaranteed never to have premiums go up. Insurance companies look at a number of different factors before they issue a permanent policy to someone. Health is always the top consideration. Obviously, the insurance company only wants to accept healthy clients so that their risk of paying out prematurely is mitigated as much as possible, all the while collecting the annual premium payments from the insured.

Most whole life policies allow for borrowing against their value, which is in essence taking a loan from yourself. Borrowing against the policy will of course reduce how much money your family will get when you die and may open your estate up to tax liabilities, so proceed with caution if you're thinking about taking out this type of loan against your policy.

Universal life coverage offers a bit more flexibility than a whole life policy. Once money has accumulated in your account, you may be able to vary the frequency, as well as the amount, of your premiums. You may even be able to adjust the policy so the invested earnings cover the cost of the entire premium. Again, any change to a policy like this brings with it the risk of lower death benefit claims, tax liabilities, and more fees, so look before you leap. Some conveniences just aren't worth it in the long run.

In the case of variable life insurance, the third permanent option, your policy covers the same death benefits as with other two types, but you have control over how your cash value is invested. With whole life and universal life, you may not have a say in where your money is invested. With most variable life policies, you can choose to invest in the sub-accounts, bonds, or money market funds of your choice. This allows you to potentially grow your policy's cash value more quickly, or not. Just like with all investing, though, it also brings with it more risk. If your investments underperform, your death benefit will likely be affected, and your family will receive less money when you die.

Permanent life insurance is fine, but for most needs, term life will be sufficient to cover you. Term life insurance usually has term lengths of ten, fifteen, twenty, or thirty years. The younger and healthier you are, the lower the annual cost, and that cost remains for the life of the policy.

Here's a quick example of how all this works. Rich and Carissa are married at age twenty-four. They both have good-paying jobs. Some years later, they decide to purchase a home for $500,000. The mortgage payment is about $2,700 each month. They get term life insurance and plan for children. They choose a $700,000, twenty-year term life insurance policy on Rich, as Carissa plans to stay at home while raising their small children. Should Rich die within that term, Carissa would collect a $700,000 death benefit. She would have the cash to pay off the mortgage and have some money for higher education and missionary savings for the children.

As another example of a good place to be, consider Matthew and Ashlyn, who are fifty-two and forty-eight respectively. Their children are in college on scholarship. Their assets well exceed their only debt, which is a mortgage. They do not need life insurance of any sort. They are what I call self-insured.

Planning for Long-Term Care

As we've already mentioned, people are living longer than they did a century ago; for many, thirty years longer. This is wonderful, but it does change the dynamics of our retirement and life insurance needs. Because of this, a person aged sixty-five has a higher chance of needing some type of long-term care (LTC) during retirement.

This isn't something we generally want to talk about around family gatherings, but when we're creating a financial plan and talking about LTC insurance policies, you can't avoid the subjects that make you uncomfortable. Face them head-on. That means you need to look at the possibility of needing long-term care insurance and know the cost associated with that care.

We assume that the risk of long-term disability is too minimal to worry about, but sadly, the Social Security Administration estimates that more than 25 percent of twenty-year-old workers will become disabled before reaching retirement age.[78] According to the US Department of Health and Human Services, unfortunately only one out of ten has planned ahead to pay for disability.[79]

Help with the tasks of daily living, similar to care provided in a nursing home, isn't covered by Medicare.[80] Securing private long-term care insurance allows you control over the situation, making sure your future needs will be met without creating an undue financial burden for your loved ones. Though coverage can be expensive at first, there are federal and state tax breaks available for qualified plans.

Today, more than half of all long-term care services are being provided in the home.[81] The most common form of long-term care is

78. See "The Faces and Facts of Disability," Social Security Administration, accessed Dec. 29, 2022, https://www.ssa.gov/disabilityfacts/facts.html.

79. See "Social Security Disability Insurance Benefits," Benefits.gov, accessed May 29, 2023, https://www.benefits.gov/benefit/4382.

80. See Priya Chidambaram and Alice Burns, "10 Things About Long-Term Services and Supports (LTSS)," Kaiser Family Foundation, Sept. 15, 2022, https://www.kff.org/medicaid/issue-brief/10-things-about-long-term-services-and-supports-ltss/.

81. See "How Much Care Will You Need?," Administration for Community Living, last modified Feb. 18, 2020, https://acl.gov/ltc/basic-needs/how-much-care-will-you-need.

informal and home-based. Even if your spouse or children provide the care, that care will still have costs associated with it. Caregivers have significant out-of-pocket expenses: about $7,000 annually for in-home caregivers and $12,000 annually for out-of-home caregivers.[82]

Here are a few more statistics. Over 34 million Americans provided unpaid care to an adult age fifty or older in the past twelve months. Caregivers spend an average of 24.4 hours a week providing care to their loved one. The time commitment increases to 44.6 hours per week for those caring for a spouse or partner. One in five caregivers reports a high level of physical strain resulting from caregiving, while two in five consider their caregiving situation to be emotionally stressful. Six in ten caregivers report having to make a workplace accommodation as a result of caregiving.[83]

And that's just for in-home caregiving. Once you take into account the possible need for extensive long-term care, things ratchet up significantly. Long-term care is expensive and could be significantly more costly in the future when you consider that an insurance claim for these types of needs tends to last, on average, just shy of four years.[84] Here are some current annual average costs of long-term care:[85]

- Adult day care: $20,280
- Assisted living facility: $54,000
- Home health aide services: $61,776
- Nursing home (semi-private): $94,900
- Nursing home (private): $108,405

All of these possibilities need to be talked about and planned for. LTC insurance policies exist that cover the cost of the six common activities of daily living (ADLs): continence, transferring, toileting,

82. See Chuck Rainville, Laura Skufca, and Laura Mehegan, "Family Caregiving and Out-of-Pocket Costs: 2016 Report," American Association of Retired Persons, Nov. 2016, http://tffc.usc.edu/wp-content/uploads/2017/09/caregiving_and_oop_costs.pdf.

83. See "Caregiver Statistics: Demographics," Family Caregiver Alliance, accessed Dec. 29, 2022, https://www.caregiver.org/resource/caregiver-statistics-demographics/.

84. See "Caregiver Statistics: Demographics."

85. See "Cost of Care Survey," Genworth Financial, accessed Dec. 29, 2022, https://www.genworth.com/aging-and-you/finances/cost-of-care.html.

bathing, dressing, and feeding.[86] If this is something that you worry about, insurance may bring you the peace you need. Pray about it, seek counsel, but don't discount it just because it would be something you're paying for today that you might not need for twenty to thirty years or ever.

Here is a simple way to remember the six ADLs. When you are in bed after a restful sleep, you wake up and hope you did not wet the bed (continence). You get out of bed (transferring) and head to the bathroom (toileting). Then you draw water for your bath (bathing), get your clothes on for the day (dressing), and go to the kitchen to eat your breakfast (feeding) Today you perform those six active daily living exercises without thinking.

Obviously, none of us knows the future, but understanding there is always a chance that the need for these expenditures could occur helps us make decisions now that will mitigate their potential financial impact. A little more saved in your retirement fund each month could make all the difference if you or your spouse are eventually faced with these expenses. An insurance policy specifically geared toward this need could also offer the peace of mind you're seeking.

How Can You Benefit from Life Insurance?

If you are unsure whether life insurance is a good fit for your needs, consider how it can help protect the people you value most. Life insurance can provide your family members the resources to maintain their lifestyle. It can replace some or all of your income, pay off debts, cover funeral costs, and help fund future expenses such as mission service and higher education costs. Life insurance can also provide a legacy for your children and grandchildren. When properly structured, life insurance proceeds are tax-free. This will help ensure that your estate is passed down in a tax-efficient manner.

Today, many insurance companies encourage an additional person of contact in the event a premium payment is missed. You do not want to carelessly let your policy lapse. Having a family member listed on the policy may help keep the policy in order.

86. See "What is Long-Term Care?," Administration for Community Living, Feb. 18, 2020, https://acl.gov/ltc/basic-needs/what-is-long-term-care.

Since we just covered retirement in our last chapter, this is a good time to bring up how life insurance can help protect your retirement goals as well. For example, you can use life insurance to shield any dependents you may have, such as disabled adult children, or to fulfill financial obligations, such as the mortgage on a vacation property. Since retirement can last several decades, life insurance also helps protect your spouse from the loss of an income stream.

Depending on your financial situation, you can also get what is known as an umbrella insurance policy that acts as an extra layer of liability coverage above the limits on your home, auto, and other policies—protection just in case you or a family member causes harm to someone else. For example, if your dog attacks a visitor and your home insurance covers up to $300,000 of liability, then you are on the hook for anything above that amount if the injured party wins a suit against you above your coverage. Or, even worse, let's say a wrongful death happens. If you do not have the money, your wages could be garnished. The right umbrella insurance can cover you.

Again, none of this is fun to talk about, but we can't shy away from asking the hard questions and finding the equally hard answers. Facing risk isn't easy, but the protection you can gain for yourself and your loved ones can make it all worth it. That's why you should review your insurance needs once a year and after each big milestone in life. You can always call on your trusted financial advisor to coordinate with other professionals to determine the proper policies and coverage for you.

It's all about peace of mind. When you're at peace, it's easier to feel the Spirit, easier to serve, and easier to make wise life-affecting decisions.

Single adults with no dependents generally do not need life insurance.

One Last Look

Good: You have a large, close family and everyone agrees to help each other out in case of disability or untimely death. Even so, you purchase a term life policy with your auto insurance company because it is easy and convenient.

Better: You pay for all the insurances offered by your employer, which includes a small life insurance and disability policy, knowing from the start that it is not portable once you leave the company. You shop around and ask your family and friends where they purchased their life insurance policy. The death benefit is up to date with enough coverage for the appropriate loss should you pass through the veil prematurely.

Best: You shop around and discover life insurance, disability insurance, long-term care, and an umbrella policy that fits your needs. Between the ages of about twenty and fifty, you have term life insurance that covers one year of salary, the mortgage balance, and extra for additional expenses that are important to your family. In your fifties, you purchase a permanent life insurance policy with a long-term care rider. You have kept yourself healthy and thus qualify with the insurance company of your choice for the best premium cost available.

Awful: You rely on the government disability safety net and have a very difficult time finding a way to afford the care you need. Many of your needs go unmet as you struggle to afford the basic expenses of life. You had insurance policies once but stopped paying the premiums because they didn't seem necessary, and you spent the premium money elsewhere.

This is an unfortunately common scenario. After a series of unfortunate events, a friend of mine had to place her mom in an adult care facility. While sorting through her mother's important papers, she discovered twelve life insurance policies. The death benefits were between five and ten thousand dollars each. Some had been terminated because the premium payments stopped. The policy contracts still in force would soon require the contracted premium payments. My friend couldn't afford to keep up with the premiums needed to continue the life insurance policies. None of the policies covered long-term care benefits either. My friend and her siblings are still scrambling to cover the monthly care expenses for their mother.

Something for the Kids

Make sure your children know that the younger they are when they begin their life insurance policy, the less expensive their premiums will be and the more likely they are to qualify for life insurance. Encourage them to be proactive and get covered as soon as they can qualify after becoming a responsible earning adult with a family.

Tragedy strikes randomly, and those who are prepared are better off and feel greater peace. Life insurance, disability insurance, and long-term care insurance can help bridge a gap in life that helps heal wounds caused by random misfortunes.

13

Wills and Trusts

Everything we've covered up to this point has been to help you become financially free during your lifetime. Now we're shifting gears. This chapter is about what happens after you pass through the veil . . . and not in a "you go to spirit paradise or spirit prison before the Final Judgment" sort of "pass through the veil." We're talking about legacy and what you leave behind for those you love and perhaps people who haven't been born yet.

After all, we are commanded to do good in this life, right? Prophets, scriptures, missionaries, and our Savior have all pointed us toward doing good. Well, with the right planning, the good you do in life doesn't have to end when you leave this life. You'll have work to do on the other side of the veil, I am told, but your assets here in mortality can continue to do good too!

We hear about wills and trusts quite a bit, but let's start with the basics and then go into how they can add to your financial well-being.

A will is a legal document that spells out how you want your affairs handled and assets distributed after you die. A trust is a monetary arrangement where a grantor (also called a trustor) gives a trustee (the person overseeing your assets) the right to hold and manage property or monetary wealth for the benefit of a specific family, person, or organization.

Both wills and trusts have to do with legacy and what you leave behind to the world at large. It could be just for your family, or it could be to an organization that helps people all over the world. Your assets, your choice.

Is a will or trust better for your situation? You're going to need to ask an attorney if you want an answer to that question. I'm not an attorney, but for the purposes of this guide, I will at least go through and give you the knowledge you need to make an informed decision when the time comes for you to meet with that attorney.

So let's dive in, shall we?

When it comes to a will, the key thing to remember is to create one early and update it regularly. Having a living will allows you to dictate where you want your assets to go when you die. Do you want your children to have a certain percentage and the rest go to charity? Do you want one of your grandchildren to have an inheritance that matures when they come of age? All of these types of things can be clearly listed in your last will and testament.

Innumerable families have been torn apart fighting over the assets of a deceased parent. We all hope our children will work things out amicably once we're gone, but even the best of relationships can be strained in these types of situations. Satan will use money to divide your family. Having a clear will makes the dividing of assets far easier and can save familial bonds from being frayed by the experience.

Your Will Executor (Male) or Executrix (Female)

Every will has an executor/executrix, or simply the person you name to carry out your wishes after you pass. When you die with a legally valid last will and testament, a judge will approve the person you've named and allow that person to execute your desires. This person will act as your personal representative, verifying that your wishes are implemented.

When selecting your personal representative, consider the role's many responsibilities. While it is an honor to be chosen as a personal representative, it's also a demanding commitment consisting of more than two dozen responsibilities and liabilities. For instance, a representative can be held personally liable for improperly spending estate or trust assets or for allowing insurance coverage on the assets to lapse.

Considering the many responsibilities, it's important to take several factors into account when determining who is right for the role. The Berl Group presents the following for your consideration:

> **Trust is key.** It might seem obvious, but it is essential that your executor/executrix be someone you trust. Not only will they be held legally liable for any corrupt behavior, but you will also be putting your legacy intentions in their hands and relying on them to handle important legal documents, such as annual tax returns, honestly and appropriately.
>
> **Responsible parties only.** Yours should be a responsible individual who is able to fulfill the time commitment and duties of their role, as well as manage the inherent legal liabilities. For example, if your representative fails to pay taxes or file tax returns in a timely manner, it can throw a wrench in tax-minimization strategies and expose your estate to interest charges and penalties. That is why it is crucial to choose someone you can rely on.
>
> **Ban biases.** Your first choice may be a family member or friend. Keep in mind, however, that the person you choose should be able to act in an impartial way. If the beneficiaries of your estate believe that yours has ulterior motives and do not consider them a neutral party, it can cause unnecessary tensions and maybe legal battles.[87]

You'll want to set yourself and your representative up for success by establishing realistic expectations. Once you decide, it's important to sit down with them and explain why you consider them the best person for the position. You will want to relay the level of commitment involved and give them time to decide whether they can accept the responsibility. You will also want to have a second person in mind in case your first choice is unable to accept your offer.

Another important aspect of your representative and wills is our growing digital footprint in the twenty-first century. You likely have numerous online accounts with various usernames and passwords. You will need to determine what digital access your personal representative needs. We're talking about email, online bank accounts, social media profiles, websites—whatever you use to transact and communicate.

87. The Berl Group, "Who should you choose to execute your estate?," Alex Brown, Aug. 18, 2022, https://www.alexbrown.com/berlgroup/resources/2022/08/18/who-should-you-choose-to-execute-your-estate.

Without the right passwords or credentials, it can be highly challenging to access your digital assets. For instance, Google may provide the contents of a deceased user's account if the family produces proof of death, but Yahoo accounts require a court order to access accounts without a password. You can imagine how stressful this could be for your family and representative. Add this component to your will planning so your representative is able to finalize everything quickly and seamlessly.

Living Your Legacy

We often think of legacy planning as merely the financial assets we'll someday leave behind. But building a legacy goes beyond money; it's about aligning day-to-day actions with the difference you want to make in the world and the values, experiences, and memories you want to share. Let's explore six meaningful ways to live your legacy at home, at work, and within your community right now.[88]

Make Time for Happiness

It's easy to get stuck on cruise control in your everyday life. Family, work, church callings, and other obligations often take up so much of our time that we leave out the close relationships that matter most in mortality. It's easy to forget to plan that family outing or spend quality time with our spouse, children, siblings, or parents. If you want to build strong family ties, it's time to start taking tangible steps now that will bear fruit in the months and years to come. If you feel like you're behind on this, or that those opportunities are now gone, don't lament past mistakes. Take action today. There's an old saying: "When's the best time to plant a tree? Twenty years ago. When's the second-best time? Today."[89]

Maybe you could begin simply with a family game night. Free up time for bonding with the family by outsourcing some everyday tasks. Perhaps invest in a vacation home or partial ownership in a property

88. These six points are taken from "6 ways to live your legacy," Raymond James Financial Center, Spring 2020, https://www.raymondjames.com/-/media/rj/advisor-sites/sites/g/u/gunterfinancialservices/files/financial-perspectives-newsletter-q1-2020.pdf.

89. Dieter F. Uchtdorf, "The Best Time to Plant a Tree," *Ensign*, Jan. 2014, 6.

where generations can gather for the next few decades. The point is to create space for the moments that make mortal life worth living.

A person I got to know in my office shared with me that her living parents gifted her a sizable amount of money when she was fifty years old. The parents wanted to see their daughter enjoy a portion of the potential inheritance while they were living. She said she knew it was a test to see what she'd do with this sizable amount of money. She also said she had her living parents as a resource to her when she did deploy the inheritance. She purchased a mountain cabin for the family to gather at. For the years I knew her, the cabin brought the family together and was a rewarding experiment for all. Smart.

Plan for the Unexpected

The very nature of the unexpected is that it's unexpected. Even so, it's possible to create space for the unknown. One of the ways you can do this is through an estate plan where you arrange in advance for the management and disposal of your assets once you pass away. This includes properties, liquid wealth, stocks, bonds, and insurance policies. Consider the following:

> More than 40% of U.S. adults don't have life insurance, according to a 2018 study conducted in part by the trade group LIMRA.[90] This and other conventional estate planning concerns are part of living your legacy, knowing your preparation sets a good example for your loved ones to follow. An estate plan is also your opportunity to make a deliberate choice about the future, rather than settling for whatever may come. For example, you can use it as a learning tool for money management, structuring a trust that specifies exactly how an inheritance should be used, whether for retirement, education or some other purpose. When you create such a plan, it allows your voice—and your values—to be heard even when you're not there.[91]

90. See "2021 Insurance Barometer Study Reveals Common Misconceptions That Prevent Americans from Getting Life Insurance They Know They Need," Life Insurance Marketing and Research Association, Apr. 12, 2021, https://www.limra.com/en/newsroom/news-releases/2021/2021-insurance-barometer-study-reveals-common-misconceptions-that-prevent-americans-from-getting-life-insurance-they-know-they-need/.

91. "6 ways to live your legacy."

Pay It Forward by Mentoring

It's very likely that someone has helped you get to where you are today. Likewise, you can be that same sort of lifeline for a colleague, friend, or family member. Mentoring is an incredibly fulfilling endeavor where you can pass along your knowledge and experience with no motives beyond helping someone else succeed.

There are plenty of resources that will allow you to be matched with someone who needs your precise experience. If you are a business owner, you can help other entrepreneurs as a volunteer mentor with the Network for Teaching Entrepreneurship. Also, websites like mentoring.org can match you with a child who needs a caring adult in their lives. In the words of the legendary NFL coach Vince Lombardi, "People who work together will win, whether it be against complex football defenses, or the problems of modern society."[92]

Build a Successful Team

Similarly, a well-rounded team of professionals working in harmony can be a game changer for your legacy planning. Since we were just quoting Vince Lombardi, we'll stick with the football team example. Humor me on this. It's far more fun to think of your tax professional as a burly lineman taking down the opponent's defense than just a person sitting in front of their computer.

In this example, think of yourself as the coach. It's your financial game plan, and you're in charge. If you're married, your spouse shares this role. You will vet and hire the team of professionals and define the goals you are trying to achieve while keeping each player updated on any changes in your situation.

Your financial advisor is your quarterback. They have a big-picture perspective on your finances and will act as the leader of your money team, coordinating with your tax and legal specialists to guide you through your interactions with each. Your financial advisor may help during tax time and provide updates throughout the year on events that could affect your tax plan. They also can work with your estate attorney to suggest any necessary changes to your will or trusts.

92. "Famous Quotes by Vince Lombardi," Vince Lombardi, accessed Dec. 30, 2022, https://www.vincelombardi.com/quotes.html.

When estate planning, your tax situation might become more complex than tax filing software can handle. At this point, you'll need a good defensive tackle in the form of your tax professional. Begin by asking your financial advisor for a referral, since it's important that these two professionals communicate well when working toward your financial goals. You may want to look for someone who has a CPA license or is an Enrolled Agent (EA). After all, you don't want weak tackles on the line of scrimmage.

Finally, when you're in the estate-planning phase, you'll want to think of your estate attorney as your wide receiver. Planning for the future of your estate and how you will provide for loved ones is no small task. You want someone with demonstrated expertise in your area of concern. If you do not know an estate attorney, ask your financial advisor or your state and local bar association for a referral.

The more complex your situation, the more important it is to seek professionals who specialize in the issues you face. This team will guide you through the process of setting up your will, inform you if a trust is a better option for your situation, and allow you to look into the future to see what good your assets can do once you've passed on.

Create a Succession Plan

If you are a business owner, picking your successor is a crucial yet often overlooked task. According to the Deloitte's Family Business Center, nearly 59 percent of family-owned businesses surveyed in 2019 did not have a succession plan. The statistics are similar for selling a successful business—67 percent of owners selling a business did not do any in-depth planning before putting the business on the market, according to a 2018 Market Pulse Survey. A succession plan allows you to avoid unexpected problems, such as you passing away without an heir groomed to continue in your stead, forcing your family to sell the business because no one is in place to take the reins.

Nurture a Philanthropic Family Tradition

Habits don't just spontaneously form overnight. They take time, effort, and endurance. The same goes for traditions. It takes years for them to become part of a family culture. If you want to create a legacy of giving that goes well beyond your own lifespan, you need to instill that habit in your own family. For example, note the following:

> Inviting family members to join in charitable giving discussions and volunteer efforts can amplify your impact. If you're interested in serving the community as a family, sites like generationOn.org make it easy to find volunteer opportunities welcoming to people of all ages. If you like the idea of giving your family members a vote in which charities you should donate to, charitable accounts such as a DAF [see chapter 10] can be named after a family or cause, helping inspire regular family discussions about how to make a difference.[93]

If you do each of these six things now—make time for happiness, plan for the unexpected, mentor people in your community, build a team, create a succession plan, and nurture a philanthropic family tradition—you'll be well on your way to designing a legacy that will outlive you.

Charitable Remainder Trust (CRT)

Having a last will and testament is a necessary starting point for any estate plan, but if you want to go further and create something perpetual that can last for decades, you'll want to look at forming a trust.

Let's use a fictional example of an ultra-high net worth client whose great-grandfather was one of the original investors in the ABC Company. My client inherited $15 million and, being philanthropically inclined, was looking for a way to invest it so that he could methodically give it all away.

Using a financial advisor, the client set up a charitable remainder trust (CRT). You'll remember from chapter 10 that a CRT can generate an income stream for donors and other beneficiaries you name, with the remainder of the donated assets going to your designated charity after you pass away. In the case of this client and his $15 million, the trust sold inherited stocks with no tax consequences and was then able to diversify the proceeds to other investments while giving the client a lifetime income stream and seven years of tax deductions. The client then opened another trust and bought a life insurance policy inside it to replace the money they had given to the CRT.

A few years later, the client inherited the remaining $20 million and did the exact same thing with that inheritance, thus creating

93. "6 ways to live your legacy."

current income and a large donation to be dispersed upon his death, and the life insurance replenished the money for his family tax-free.

The Importance of a Trustee

A trustee is the person or entity who will manage the assets within your trust. This duty involves similar responsibilities and liabilities as an executor/executrix but tends to be more long-term. It can be a challenge to find a loved one who is able and willing to do the job. This is one reason many investors use a corporate trustee.

Whichever type of trustee you choose—individual or corporate—you will want to keep a keen eye out for a few particular characteristics. You want a trustee who fits the "three Ts: time, temperament, and tenure."[94] Here's why:

Managing a trust requires a notable *time commitment.* Your trustee will need the availability to manage a multitude of tasks and liabilities like disbursing income to beneficiaries, filing the trust's income tax return, maintaining records of all transactions, and performing countless other responsibilities. Consider whether their current schedule allows for these additional responsibilities. Time also refers to their long-term ability to hold this important position. Will they still have the capacity and ability to serve as your trustee in years to come?

The second T is *temperament.* Your trustee needs to display the right degree of impartiality. Family dynamics can add an emotional layer of complexity to estate planning, and your trustee will need to make decisions without exhibiting bias or bending to external influence. In fact, your trustee has a legal duty to manage the trust in the best interests of both its current and future beneficiaries. They will be held liable for a number of duties, like ensuring all beneficiaries are informed of the trust and its administration, identifying conflicts of interest, and complying with all specific trust document provisions and governing laws. You will want to confirm that they understand these responsibilities and can carry them out with professionalism.

The third T is *tenure.* What I mean by tenure is experience. Your trustee should have the knowledge, background, and skill set

94. "The three T's of effective trustees," Raymond James, accessed Dec. 30, 2022, https://www.raymondjames.com/crossbridgewealthstrategies/news-and-resources/2023/01/31/the-three-ts-of-effective-trustees.

to efficiently manage a trust account. Not every family member or friend will have experience with the financial and administrative responsibilities involved. These can include principal and income trust accounting, investing, and tax reporting. Be sure your selected trustee is familiar with the tasks they will need to handle—and that you are confident in their ability to complete them correctly.

So who is the most appropriate person to appoint as a trustee? A digital sleuth with accounting acumen and the skills of a diplomat? Most of us don't have that person on speed dial. Thankfully, there are several ways to help ensure that your estate is settled properly.

If it's impartiality and expertise you're looking for, a corporate personal representative might be an appropriate choice. For instance, a corporate executor/executrix can offer their guidance and experience to help ensure that assets are distributed according to your wishes, reduce unnecessary expenses, and achieve the most efficient and accurate settlement of your estate with the lowest costs possible. Alternatively, you could appoint both a corporation and an individual to serve as co-executors, or name a corporation as agent for the personal representative, offering an assist to this important role.

Being named a personal representative is an honor, but there's a reason that it's often a paid position: it's a job unto itself. If you want to choose the best fit for the role, it's important to understand the realities of the position and know the steps you can take to help ensure your legacy ends up in the right hands.

One Last Look

Good: You have chosen a family member or friend you trust as the executor of your estate. You have a will that outlines your wishes after death.

Better: You have chosen a non-family member as executrix of your estate—someone who is not likely to get pressured in any family drama when it comes time to execute the wishes in your will.

Best: After putting a team together, including a financial advisor, tax professional, and estate attorney, you finalize your will and may create a trust. You select a skilled corporate representative who understands your desires and has all necessary documents, both physical and digital. Your family is aware of your plans and has participated in choosing charities that will receive some of your financial assets once you pass beyond the veil.

Awful: You never took the time to create a will since you figured there would be time for that later. You die unexpectedly, leaving your family members to fight bitterly over what becomes of your estate. Any tax advantages are lost because the family member who is appointed by the court is unfamiliar with finances and taxation. No money goes to your preferred charities.

Something for the Kids

Friends come in all shapes and sizes. Teach your children to surround themselves with good people and be a good friend in return. This will help in all aspects of their life but especially during difficult times when they need trusted individuals to advise them, officiate duties, and execute their needs.

Something More for the Kids

Many people don't believe in God because of all the bad things that happen in life. Unexpected tragedies take innocents far too young, and war destroys lives indiscriminately. We ask ourselves, "Why?" Why were so many Jews slaughtered during World War II? Why did Stalin order the murders of so many millions of his own population? Why did the Romans execute Christians?

Answers to these questions are hard to come by and can be exacerbated when dealing with the death of a loved one or having to manage wills and fights over trust money. When I think about this, I'm reminded of Alma and Amulek's experience in Alma 14:8–11. Alma and Amulek are imprisoned and beaten. They suffer greatly. Those who they taught, and who subsequently believed their testimonies, were burned alive along with their scriptures. Amulek, no doubt moved by the horrific scene before him, cries out to Alma to use the power of God to stop the appalling scene. Alma is constrained and says that the Lord is taking the victims unto Himself.

Wow! The Lord is there taking each one unto Himself at that very moment.

I imagine the victims of atrocities across world history being received by a loving Father in Heaven. Believing in this helps me understand that God allows the agency of men and women, but He will keep every promise ever made. After all, He has eternity to make good on His word.

There is more to our existence than just this mortal life. Faith plays an important role. Hope plays a role. When dealing with the death of a loved one, particularly a parent, sibling, or grandparent, we must remember there is a Father in Heaven and that He is in control of everything, always. He is just, and His justice will prevail. The Father sent His Son to atone—to die to be resurrected—so that all of God's children will be resurrected. You will be with loved ones again. Believe.

14

ADULTING: TAXES AND HOME OWNERSHIP

AH, BUYING A HOME AND PAYING TAXES—THE TWO MOST ADULT things any of us can do. We all want to buy a nice house at a good price with a great interest rate and pay as little in taxes as is legally possible. All of those things can happen, but you need to know what you're doing if you want to take advantage of any of them.

Let's start with buying and paying for a home.

We want to avoid needless debt at all costs, right? The answer is "right." When it comes to going into debt, your home is one of the few things that is actually considered responsible debt.

Clients often ask me the question of whether they should pay off their mortgage as fast as possible or over the contracted time of fifteen to thirty years. To address that question, I ask two more questions. First, how old are you? And second, do you plan to be in that home for the rest of your life? The answer I hear to the first question varies of course, but the answer to the second question is pretty much always the same: no. A little search on the internet tells me that, according to current research, the median duration of homeownership is thirteen years as of 2021.[95]

I believe more in cash flow than I do in paying off your mortgage early, if this is not your final home. Why give a banker more of your hard-earned cash so you can see the black ink on your white paper statement show a number that decreases almost infinitesimally each month? Unless you plan to be in the home for the rest of your life, I believe you should retain your cash, invest it, and keep it accessible. Most middle-class folks like you and me find ourselves with little extra cash at the end of the month. Cash is king. In business, this is especially true. So, in business and your monthly budget, you need cash to last. Do not give this liquidity away to the banker so that the banker can lend it out and make the bank more money while you are strapped for cash. Keep sufficient cash, as it is the financial blood you need to avoid peril during economic turmoil that occurs fairly regularly in our society. Since the year 2000, we've been through several recessions (and one even called the Great Recession) when many banks failed. Want to hear about another "once-in-a-lifetime" financial collapse during your local TV show broadcast? Wait six months. These stories are recycled. Remain liquid.

Consider two different fictional families. Family ABC has a $100,000 mortgage on a typical 30-year term. Their monthly payment is $1,000 each month, which they pay on time. The extra they could use to pay down the mortgage is another $200 each month. Family ABC invests that $200 each month instead of paying down the mortgage. Across the street lives Family XYZ, with a similar mortgage and terms. They choose to pay $1,200 each month, with the extra $200 going towards principal. When disaster strikes, Family ABC accesses their liquid reserves, while Family XYZ has no cash reserves to weather the financial storm and uses credit cards or goes to the bank to apply for a short-term loan to get by.

Family XYZ has made extra payments for years, and their mortgage balance is lower than their neighbors. If the bank needs to foreclose on either of the two homes, which will the bank foreclosure on

95. See Dana Anderson, "The Typical U.S. Home Changes Hands Every 13.2 Years," Redfin, Mar. 2, 2022, https://www.redfin.com/news/2021-homeowner-tenure/.

first? The home of family XYZ—because there is so much equity in their home compared to ABC. The banker has a greater chance of making the bank whole by foreclosing on those fabulous clients who always gave more to the bank each month and continually reduced the bank's risk. Foreclosing on family ABC could still happen, but the bank might take a greater loss when trying to resell that home.

I am only saying to not give away all your cash reserves to pay off a mortgage early.

Cash keeps businesses and families out of financial trouble when the winds of misfortune and volatile markets hit. I know we talk about recessions like they are this rare occurrence that catches us all off guard, but in truth, recessions happen about every four and a half years. Some economists argue that recessions are good and natural for an economy, yet a recession could take your job away or impact your family in some unforeseen way. Keeping liquidity helps your family avoid a lot of turmoil. Cash is king. Unrealized profits in a real estate property or highly appreciated stocks are a prince.

Reverse Mortgage

Reverse mortgages have gained popularity over the past decade, and I believe the trend will continue for several good reasons. For those of you who are unfamiliar, a reverse mortgage is a type of loan. A homeowner who is sixty-two or older and has significant home equity can borrow against the worth of their property and receive funds as either a lump sum, fixed monthly payment, or line of credit. Unlike a standard mortgage (the type used to buy a home), a reverse mortgage doesn't require the homeowner to make any loan payments. Instead, the loan balance becomes due when the borrower dies or sells the house.

In 1989, 20 percent of homeowners in their senior years (age sixty-two and up) still carried a mortgage on their home.[96] By 2018 this number more than doubled to 41 percent. The median amount of equity seniors have in their homes is $160,000 for married couples,

96. See "Housing America's Older Adults, 2018," Joint Center for Housing Studies of Harvard University, accessed Dec. 30, 2022, https://www.jchs.harvard.edu/sites/default/files/reports/files/Harvard_JCHS_Housing_Americas_Older_Adults_2018_1%20%281%29.pdf.

$107,000 for single males, and $120,000 for single females. Their loan-to-value ratio is between 45 and 56 percent, which has more than tripled since 1989.

One reason reverse mortgages will continue to be popular is that the owners may have a bucket list of items they still want to experience, and they do not have the liquidity to fulfill those dreams. These may be vacations, educational pursuits, recreational vehicles—whatever the owner wants. A reverse mortgage unlocks money to fulfill those desires that would otherwise be left undone. Another reason is that a reverse mortgage can take a lot of stress off the owner by selling their house slowly to a financial institution. During that time, they can enjoy the benefits of selling while still living in the home. The reverse mortgage can also help the owner lower their overall monthly living expenses.

The loan does not generally need to be repaid until the last legal owner no longer occupies the home as their primary residence. After that time, the estate has six months to repay the loan or sell the property to settle the balance. Any remaining funds go to the estate. Should the home sell for less than the mortgage balance owed, the estate is not liable because of the mortgage insurance involved in reverse mortgages.

There are positives and negatives of a reverse mortgage. The top positive is that the homeowners can remain in the home until the last person on the title passes away. The owner also receives money under flexible terms. The interest rates may be lower than traditional mortgages, so shop around since everything is negotiable and each comes with a price. And if the family wants to keep the house once the parents or grandparents pass away, they can pay off the reverse mortgage and keep the property.

Now, just like with any loan, there are concerns you will want to be aware of as well. Reverse mortgage programs are still relatively new, and most people are not familiar with the working parts. While reverse mortgages don't usually affect Supplemental Social Security or Medicaid benefits, they can under the wrong circumstances, so you need to know beforehand to avoid any potential problems. Lastly, as the loan amount against the home grows with time, there may be less of an inheritance later for children and grandchildren. If you're looking to leave behind as much as you can, a reverse mortgage might not be for you.

If you are real estate equity rich and cash flow poor, the reverse mortgage may be your ticket to realize your desired lifestyle. Die with experiences, not dreams.

Taxes

We are born free and then taxed to death.

Uninformed working-class citizens pay the most taxes by percentage of income than any other demographic.[97] People who understand tax law and how to use the system to their advantage pay far less. Billionaires like Warren Buffett reduce their tax burden by making key financial maneuvers that allow them to keep their money and use it however they wish.[98] Those tax maneuvers are not illegal, and they are open to everyone who understands the tax system.

That includes you.

The most recent studies show that the average family earning $51,661 annually might pay about $5,828 in federal tax and $2,634 in state tax. Sales tax at 6 percent could be more or less than $600, and depending on where you live, there may be around $2,500 in property tax. Add those numbers up and it comes out to be about 22.4 percent. Almost one quarter of the average household's earnings goes to one government entity or another. Could there be more taxes paid? Yes! See the list I compiled below. Shaving off even a few percentage points through smart tax practices can save thousands and allow families more control over their money.

Let's look at one of the ways Mr. Buffett goes about holding on to his earnings each year. The first thing to realize is that income from an employer is taxed at a higher rate than a long-term capital gains tax.[99]

97. Christopher Ingraham, "For the first time in history, U.S. billionaires paid a lower tax rate than the working class last year," *Washington Post*, Oct. 8, 2019, https://www.washingtonpost.com/business/2019/10/08/first-time-history-us-billionaires-paid-lower-tax-rate-than-working-class-last-year/.

98. Tom Wheelwright, "5 Ways That Billionaire Warren Buffett Pays a Lower Tax Rate Than His Secretary," Entrepreneur, Aug. 30, 2019, https://www.entrepreneur.com/money-finance/5-ways-that-billionaire-warren-buffett-pays-a-lower-tax/338189.

99. See Wheelwright, "5 Ways That Billionaire Warren Buffett."

Mr. Buffett purposefully takes a lower cash salary in exchange for other company-sponsored benefits. His capital gains are offset when donating cash and securities to recognized nonprofit organizations to lower (or completely offset) the income earned. He then donates sizable sums of cash and securities to various nonprofit organizations each year. He's a charitable man. He overproduces and shares, and many people follow his example.

In this way, people like Warren Buffett are able to hold on to their money, use it efficiently, and help those around them. Are there men and women who use the tax code to simply enrich themselves? Of course. Even so, at the end of the day it is their money to spend. As long as each of us is paying taxes legally, we are under no obligation to pay more than that amount, no matter what anyone says. The Savior taught, "Render unto Caesar the things that are Caesar's, and unto God the things that are God's" (Mark 12:17). If we render to Caesar only that which is required of us, we have more to render to God and our fellow men, if that is what we choose.

You may be thinking at this point that the tax code is too complicated to figure out on your own. Unfortunately, you and I are aligned in thinking that. The tax code is a crazy mishmash of laws that undergo changes regularly. This is one of those circumstances where hiring a skilled tax advisor to legally steer your wealth in the right direction is a smart investment. Not only does Mr. Buffett have top-notch attorneys on staff, but he also takes advantage of all the current tax laws too. The only way he can do that is by using the professionals around him.

Consider this example. A wealthy woman is currently unemployed but has inherited a sizable stock portfolio. There is nothing wrong with an inheritance, and there is nothing wrong with people who receive inheritances. It is money earned and money gifted. In this case, most of the portfolio stocks happen to pay periodic qualified dividends. Current tax laws allow qualified dividends to be taxed at a 15 percent flat tax rate. Imagine taking in over $90,000 a year and paying just 15 percent in taxes. The income tax for an employed single person making at least $41,775 or more each year falls into the 22 percent tax bracket. Every dollar earned over this amount of $41,775 is taxed at 22 percent. Of course there is an effective tax rate, and I am all in favor of a flat tax as low as 10 percent. The point I wish to make is that the working class gets crushed with taxes, and it never gets better.

This is not equitable. It gets worse too.

Make over $89,075 and every dollar earned over this amount is taxed at 24 percent. I believe everyone should pay their fair share of taxes to keep the schools, police, fire departments, and other essential government offices open. Even so, our current tax laws are so skewed that all fairness is thrown out the window. In my opinion, a more equitable tax system would be unbiased toward everyone, with a flat tax of 10 percent regardless of income level. (Sound familiar? The law of tithing.) Everyone would pay the same percentage. No more freeloaders, no more high-priced tax accountants finding loopholes for the rich to avoid paying taxes. This would also make everyone's tax obligation very clear. We would all see that amount and understand exactly how much we pay to our government. This would likely make us pay more attention to how our taxes are being spent and hold our elected officials more accountable for wasteful expenditures. Currently it's very rare we know how much we've actually paid in taxes, which makes us less likely to worry about public wastefulness beyond the occasional complaint about "fat cats in Washington."

Taxes can be used and misused, but it is up to us to pay attention, pay only what we are required to pay, and hold governments accountable for corruption and bad policy. When bad issues get out of hand, governments can end up taking far more from their citizens than is their right.

Here is a real-world example of how when we don't pay attention to spending and money matters at a government level, it can have huge effects on the general public. This is regarding the toll road on the 405 freeway in King County, Washington State.[100] Traffic was bad on the 405. Government lobbyists pushed for a solution for their rich, high-class clients so they could skip the congestion. A toll road system was put in place with high-cost tolls in effect during peak hours of congestion, becoming less of a cost during the slower times of the day. The cost of the tolls range from $10.00 at peak times to

100. See "I-405 Express Toll Lanes," Washington State Department of Transportation, accessed Dec. 30, 2022, https://wsdot.wa.gov/travel/roads-bridges/toll-roads-bridges-tunnels/i-405-express-toll-lanes.

$0.75 during times of low demand. The local government collects the tolls and makes an enormous sum of money every year to maintain roads they were already maintaining through their tax base on local citizens. So, after this toll was enacted, did they lower the taxes on their citizens? No, they did not.

This toll system created an imbalance favoring the wealthy that didn't exist before its creation. The high-paid business executive can afford hundreds of $10 tolls and move freely along the 405 freeway. It isn't a cost burden to the high-salaried executive. The congested right lanes, however, are full of cars that barely move through traffic because those commuters are unable to afford the $10 toll. Keep in mind that those drivers in the right lanes not being "tolled" are still paying for the very lanes the rich are driving on through existing taxes. The wealthy, with government approval, confiscated the people's state highway in Washington State, and no one does anything about it.

We see examples of this in the scriptures as well. In the Book of Mosiah, it talks about how King Limhi and his people were in a difficult bind (see Mosiah 19:22–26). Because of their bad policies and rejection of the word of God, they had been conquered by their enemies. To save themselves from destruction, they entered into an agreement with the Lamanite king to "pay tribute unto him, even one half of all they possessed" (Mosiah 19:26). At times I feel like *I'm* paying one-half of all I possess to the government through various taxes. While I get certain things in return for those taxes, I have a right to pay only what is required and nothing more. Yet the government is requiring more and more each year on everything possible. Have you heard that in some states, they want to tax the miles you drive each year? If the government could tax air, they would.

If you want to take a closer look at how many different taxes each of us pays, here is a partial list of the known taxes the government imposes upon me and my friends, some of their best-paying citizens:

- Federal Income Tax
- State Income Tax
- County Tax
- Excise Tax
- Sales Tax
- Family Leave Payroll Tax

- Unemployment Payroll Tax
- Long-Term Care Payroll Tax
- Medicare Tax
- Social Security Tax
- Property Tax
- Vehicle Registration Tax
- Concession Recovery Fee
- Customer Facility Charge
- US Domestic Flight Segment Tax
- US PSGR Facility Charge Tax
- US September 11 Security Fee Tax
- US Transportation Tax
- Emergency Medical Tax
- County Highway Tax
- School District #1 Tax
- Library Tax
- City Cemetery Tax
- Mosquito Abatement Tax
- Western County Recreation Tax
- College State Tax
- Fuel Surcharge Tax
- Vehicle License Cost Recovery Fee
- State Parks Tax
- Hunting/Fishing License Tax
- Foul Stamp Tax
- 911 Tax
- Driver's License Tax
- Toll Roads/Bridges Tax
- Gasoline Tax
- Regional Transit Tax
- Capital Gains Tax
- Inheritance Tax
- Utility User Tax
- City Utility Tax
- State Refuse Tax
- Health Insurance Tax
- Federal Universal Service Fund Tax
- Regulatory Programs & Telco Recovery Fee Tax

If you started feeling light-headed after reading that list, it's completely understandable. There are a lot of taxes that hit US tax-paying citizens every year. When it's laid out plainly, it becomes easier to realize why having a tax professional is a good idea. Would it be great to have a simple flat tax? Yes. Until that time, however, take advantage of the professionals in your life. Allow them to help you pay what you need to pay and use the rest in whatever way is best for you and your family.

Inflation

When looking at taxes and home ownership, there is one other financial aspect we should discuss: inflation. Inflation can be good, it can be bad, and it can be confusing, but it's important to understand since it's a natural aspect of any macro-economy. Depending on inflation rates, your chances of buying a home could increase substantially due to inflation.

Here is a simple example of inflation. The market consists of ten apples, each apple being worth one dollar. The government prints more dollars for the market to spark the economy, making each dollar worth slightly less. Now each apple is valued at $1.30. The worth of the apples hasn't really changed, but the value of the money being used to purchase them has dropped. This is inflation. The apples cost more, even though more money exists. Now take five apples away due to supply problems. At that point, you have a financial market worth $13 but only five apples. Each apple is then valued at $2.60. Some people will pay an inflated price for the apple. Others will choose to go without. Once supply problems are resolved and all ten apples return to the market, the apples are again valued at $1.30 each.

The apple is not going to return to $1.00 until either the supply of money is reduced by the government or society increases production and produces more apples. Say something new is invented and thirteen apples are produced. Now each apple is valued at $1.00. Should the invention prove to be near miraculous and produce twenty apples, then society values each apple at $0.65 each. This is the preferred economic situation since more apples feeds more people for less money. For the same dollar as mentioned in the beginning, perhaps society can purchase an apple and an orange. That is economic expansion.

Expansion is generally good for society. Thankfully, in our present time, technological advances have curbed inflation for many years.

Simply put, more cash in circulation means there is more cash to buy the same number of products or services. Everything then becomes like a kind of bidding war. As prices rise, you may be outbid for the products and services you want by someone willing to pay a higher price. That makes the prices of those products or services go up. You may find yourself choosing one product and forgoing another product with the limited cash you have for items costing more.

Inflation is a natural part of any economy and plays a role in economic growth. If it gets out of hand, though, it can cause long-term problems for everyone.

Inflation takes away buying power. If I put $100 in my mattress when a gallon of milk costs $3, and I take my $100 to the store to purchase a gallon of milk a year later, I may be surprised that a gallon of milk now costs $5. Your $100 hidden away in the mattress for a year lost some buying power to inflationary effects.

Inflation hurts mostly the poor and middle class. The rich do not care if milk is $3 or $5 or $10 since they can afford to pay these higher prices. Families on the lower end of the economic spectrum cannot.

Two of my favorite economists are Brian Wesbury and Bob Stein from First Trust. From their blog and in their own words, they wrote:

> Just so we get our facts straight, here are the consumer price inflation rates per decade looking backward [over the last 70 years]. The 1950s – 2.2%, 1960s – 2.5%, 1970s – 7.4%, 1980s – 5.1%, 1990s – 2.9%, 2000s – 2.6% and 2010s – 1.7%. So, while the US in the 1970s and early 1980s was not Zimbabwe [which had an inflation rate of 50% in 2020], it was the worst sustained inflation in US history. Prices were doubling every 10 years and the Fed had to push interest rates up to 20% to stop the inflationary damage.
>
> Nonetheless, the "revisionists" say that the inflation of the 1970s was good for many people. They argue that home ownership rose, student debt got wiped out, and inflation reduced the value of the national debt. In other words, if you can see these benefits, why don't we do it again?
>
> First, it is true that home ownership rose in the 1970s, but it was rising even faster in the second half of the 1960s. Moreover, Savings & Loans provided assumable mortgages in the 1970s,

> which allowed buyers to assume a lower, pre-inflation mortgage rate. Eventually, this led to the collapse of the Savings & Loan Industry.
>
> Second, because student debt has fixed interest rates, of course it would disappear faster with higher inflation. In addition, people with student debt tend to have higher lifetime incomes than people without that debt. [This means that wealthier sections of the population are more likely to benefit substantially from this inflation paradigm.]
>
> Third, the national debt did fall as a share of GDP after World War II. But almost all the decline happened between 1946, when debt was 118% of GDP, and 1969 when it fell to 36%. It only fell by another 4 percentage points of GDP, to 32%, by 1981. And from 1946 through 1969, inflation averaged 2.5% per year. In other words, the inflation of the 1970s was not the key behind reducing the national debt.
>
> The primary problem with 1970s-style inflation is that everyone involved in the economy—every business owner, every worker, every investor, every manager, and every entrepreneur—would have to spend time trying to forecast it . . . .
>
> Ultimately, inflation is a "hidden" tax that doesn't stay hidden. People adapt by redirecting resources away from production and toward inflation-hedging, which doesn't raise standards of living over time.[101]

People of all classes worried over the Great Inflation of the 1970s and 1980s. Commodity prices shot up, and oil in particular soared, causing shortages and price gouging. Others were concerned about the end result of aggressive government monetary and fiscal policy.

The pandemic of 2020 had a similar effect, disrupting supply chains and forcing governments all over the world to flood more cash into their economies. Some companies were fearful that future demands may be low, so products have been held back rather than making excessive inventories to sit on shelves. Companies waited for confirmed orders before calling back a workforce to begin production. This situation made manufacturing any product clunky. The result

101. Brian Wesbury and Bob Stein, "Inflation Revisionism," First Trust, June 1, 2021, https://www.ftportfolios.com/blogs/EconBlog/2021/6/1/inflation-revisionism.

was higher prices for what was available, and inflation grew. There were fewer products and services but many more consumers flush with cash willing to bid up prices for what they wanted.

With strong demand for housing and continued disrupted supply constraints among suppliers and builders, home prices jumped during the pandemic. I built a backyard tool shed in 2020. The two-by-fours were about $3.50 each. In 2021, the same two-by-four lumber was $9 each. In 2022, that two-by-four was about $6 each. That is an incredible increase for a limited supply going up against strong demand. I paid $9 per piece for a small project in 2021 but redesigned my project to use fewer two-by-fours.

All these economic aspects, from taxes to inflation, accumulate to create the marketplace in which we buy, sell, and raise our families. Everyone will be affected by shifts and depressions in the macro-economy, but as long as we are following sound principles, paying attention to the world around us, voting, and listening to the admonition of prophets both modern and ancient, we will end up in a far better place than we could have hoped for if we merely closed our eyes and hoped for the best.

I believe the best and quickest way to reduce inflation is supply-side economics. Innovate and produce more to meet demand. Remember the apple example introduced earlier. New inventions keep prices down. If gasoline prices are $6.00 a gallon, then producing more oil and refining more gasoline for consumption will reduce the price of gasoline. Engineers will figure out better ways to get the oil. If lumber is expensive, thus driving up home prices, harvest more trees and have the lumber mills increase production of two-by-fours. Engineers and others will create innovative ways to produce. The government can also reduce regulations that can strangle a business sector from producing more.

One Last Look

Good: You are living a good life. Your mortgage is nearly paid off as you get close to retirement. You may tap into a reverse mortgage, but for now you stick to the plan of paying the current house payment while still working toward a retirement of your own. Your career choice is paying you enough money each year to surpass the negative effects of inflation.

Better: Your mortgage is fully paid off. You have a small retirement fund, but you know that you will require more money to support your lifestyle. Inheritance for any younger family is not a concern, and so you find that a reverse mortgage will supplement the cash flow you need while going into your retirement years. Your current job offers raises, allowing you and your family to prepare well for the future.

Best: Your career choice continues to grow beyond inflationary fears of 5 percent or more. You have qualified yourself to be compensated well in the marketplace. Also, your investments are well-allocated and are also growing. No more than 10 percent of your investments are in precious metals like gold or silver. You have some ambitious retirement goals that will require a lot of money. You have assets.

Awful: For years, you have used your home as a piggy bank. Too many second mortgages means it looks like you will be paying for your house for the rest of your life. No option exists for a reverse mortgage since there is little equity in the home. You realize that the company salary has not kept up with inflation, and your raises are well below the standard cost of living. You can no longer afford the products you desire. You are being left behind in the economic world.

Something for the Kids

Here is my advice to young people considering buying a home and growing assets.

When the time comes to buy a house, start with a home you can afford and work up as your income grows with your family size. One very important life lesson is to purchase in the best location possible. Think about schools, parks, community centers, shopping centers, and all the amenities that make your community a safe place for your family. Pay extra for location. Remember these words: location, location, location.

Here are a few things that tend to increase in value over time: vacant land near enough to amenities, a home, quality stocks, gold, and gems. Here is a short list of items that people hope will retain value but usually do not: cosmetic jewelry, cars, boats, hobby collections, and many other items. Once I heard of a widow who sold her deceased husband's gun collection for an outstanding $20,000 cash. Later she learned that the collection would have easily sold for more than $100,000 in the right gun market. She did not know the market value and took the first offer.

15

Financial Advisors and Planning

I've mentioned financial advisors throughout this book, but I wanted to go a bit deeper on the subject. We tend to think we can handle everything on our own and that asking for help makes us somehow less worthy. Many falsely think that paying someone to help them is even worse! However, this kind of mindset is counterintuitive to the plan of salvation. We ask for help from God and our Savior all the time. God expects us to ask for help. He *tells* us to ask for help. He also admonishes us to seek the aid of our neighbors and family as well. There is nothing wrong with asking someone for help, and there is nothing wrong with paying a respected professional for their expertise on a subject. You do this frequently when visiting your doctor.

If you want to build a house from the ground up, you'll want to contact a building contractor. If you want to build your financial house from the ground up, you'll want to consult a trusted financial advisor.

There are a few things you should know about a financial advisor, or FA. Some are sole practitioners and others belong to a team. Just like all doctors are different in their approach to healing, so too are all FAs different in their methods and what they see as important. Each FA has their own likes and dislikes of investment vehicles. Because of this natural difference in financial advisors, you owe it to yourself to interview several and find one that fits your personality, style, and investment philosophy. Search for an FA like you would a doctor. Your financial life depends on it.

The first important job of the FA is to understand what their client hopes to accomplish and discover a solution that will match their risk tolerance and objectives. The FA has the modern tools at their disposal to create a financial plan that can be adjusted as time wears on. That person should be your partner in all of this, not a dictator.

For me, though, the number one reason to have a financial advisor is to protect you from yourself. I'm being completely serious here.

I've worked in the financial field for decades and know my way around the block pretty darn well. But none of us can separate our emotions from our financial decisions. This unfortunate truth will cost you dearly when markets turn on their heads. Most "do-it-yourselfers" will get extremely emotional and make the wrong investment decisions at the wrong times. This is one of the primary reasons to have a financial advisor you know and trust. At the very least, the FA acts as a sounding board for you to discuss anything with a dollar sign next to it. My clients call me directly and we talk about money and family too. Oftentimes I'm able to talk clients off a fiscal ledge and convince them that better days are ahead and not to panic.

Here's how that can look in a real-world situation. In 2020, a client of mine was worried about the November elections. He wanted me to sell his highly appreciated stocks in his taxable account and go to cash. I reasoned with him, and we found a few areas to sell where the sale would limit tax obligations. If he were in charge of his own portfolio, I am 100 percent sure he would have sold out in July and transitioned to cash only. Liquidating his highly appreciated stocks would have brought about a severe tax obligation, taking between 25 and 35 percent. He had some of the best US company stocks, and his portfolio was not speculative at all. This would have been a bad, emotional move that would have needlessly cost him hundreds of thousands of dollars in capital gains taxes.

After the election, he thanked me for talking him down from the financial ledge. Not only did he still have his stocks that generated cash, but they also appreciated further. After the election, he continued to collect the dividends and tax-free income from his municipal bonds. In addition, he avoided a needless but potentially serious tax bill.

This is what I mean when I say that most individuals cannot separate their emotions from their financial decisions. When we're angry or scared, we tend to have very poor judgment. Only someone from the outside helping us to see our failing logic can keep us from damaging our long-term finances. This is where the financial advisor is worth more to the client than the client pays to have their portfolio managed.

Those who manage their own investments believe they are saving money when times are relatively calm, and that may be true. But once the markets turn down, the right professional at the helm will guide your portfolio through the economic hazards. They won't panic, they won't freak out—they will remain steadfast and knowledgeable. If you discovered a large cancerous growth on your back, you wouldn't turn to the internet to solve the problem. Even if you were a doctor, you wouldn't be able to properly diagnose yourself. You would be too close to the problem, too worried to see effectively. Instead, you would go to a trusted physician and get checked out. Trust a professional in medical situations *and* in finances. Things will turn out better in both circumstances, I promise.

Many people avoid financial advisors simply because they don't want to pay someone to give them monetary and investment advice. It always comes down to money, doesn't it?

Some things are worth the peace of mind. When I look at my insurance premiums, I wish I didn't have to pay for insurance. That doesn't mean I'm going to cancel my policies though. I know the insurance is there when I need it, and it gives me peace of mind. A financial advisor is the same way. The FA should be adding value to your life, not taking it away. The professional should be growing your investments more than they charge. If so, it's a win-win and you avoid a lot of needless stress, regretful decisions, sleepless nights, and wasted time. If you have an FA now and you do not feel this is your experience, change now.

If investing is not your expertise, find someone to help and don't feel bad about it. You may find a new friend.

The Importance of Vetting Your Financial Advisor

There is one other reason people avoid financial advisors, and it has nothing to do with the fees they charge. We've all heard stories and read news articles about investment managers who swindled millions from their clients. Currently the news carries the FTX cryptocurrency scandal.[102] Risks are real, but there are things you can do, and paying attention will keep you from working with charlatans and cheaters.

Let's talk about the media's old friend Bernard L. Madoff.[103] He started his Investment Securities firm in 1960 when he was just twenty-two years old. His business was up and down until the late 1980s. At that time, he started bringing in larger profits than seemed reasonable for the times. Madoff claims he turned to illegitimate ways to keep those returns high in the early 1990s, but evidence suggests he began long before that. He ended up running the largest Ponzi scheme in history for more than forty years.

Here is the first thing to look out for: Madoff was claiming returns that seemed too good to be true. If that is the case for you, those returns likely *are* untrue, and you should run the other way. People invested billions of dollars in Madoff's management because he was a skilled salesman and promised clients impossible growth on their securities. When the market tanked in 2008, Madoff could no longer support his scheme and came clean. He had cheated people all over the world out of $65 billion! In the end, Madoff lost everything as well. His supportive wife divorced him. His oldest son, Mark, committed suicide in 2010 at the age of forty-six. And Bernie himself spent the rest of his life in prison, where he died in 2021.

102. See MacKenzie Sigalos and Rohan Goswami, "Crypto firm BlockFi files for bankruptcy as FTX fallout spreads," CNBC, Nov. 28, 2022, https://www.cnbc.com/2022/11/28/blockfi-files-for-bankruptcy-as-ftx-fallout-spreads.html.

103. See Adam Hayes, "Bernie Madoff: Who He Was, How His Ponzi Scheme Worked," Investopedia, last modified Mar. 29, 2023, https://www.investopedia.com/terms/b/bernard-madoff.asp.

Looking back, there were many warning signs for investors. Madoff was very much a people person.[104] He had charisma. His clients loved him and raved about him. He could connect with someone on a personal level while always avoiding talking about unpleasant business. A good FA will never shy away from discussing the nitty gritty of your portfolio. When asked directly about how his investing worked, Madoff would tell clients that the investing process was too complicated and they wouldn't understand it—that's why they needed to hire a professional. A good FA should be transparent with fees and returns and be able to explain it all clearly to you. Madoff did not have transparency on his investments either. Even when a client tried to do their due diligence, they could not get a clear picture of what was going on. A good FA should be 100 percent transparent. It's your money, and you are entitled to see what it's doing.

Seek out references from trusted people when choosing a financial advisor. Ask discerning questions to be sure they are a good fit for you, not just a charismatic personality. Do they take the time to explain your investments in a way you can understand? Can they show you what is going on with your money?

A little advanced work, some realistic expectations, and a bit of due diligence will keep you from being taken by shady advisors. And always remember—if the deal sounds too good to be true, it is.

A Story of Church Finances and Foul Play

Even the elect may be deceived sometimes. We're told this clearly in Matthew 24:24. In fact, Doctrine and Covenants 10:37 reads, "But as you cannot always judge the righteous, or as you cannot always tell the wicked from the righteous, therefore I say unto you, hold your peace until I shall see fit to make all things known unto the world concerning the matter."

This brings us to the story of Mark Hofmann. Mark Hofmann was a forger who sold fake historical documents to the leaders of The

104. See Julie Creswell and Landon Thomas Jr., "The Talented Mr. Madoff," *The New York Times*, Jan. 24, 2009, https://www.nytimes.com/2009/01/25/business/25bernie.html.

Church of Jesus Christ of Latter-day Saints in the 1980s.[105] About thirty different seemingly authentic documents were purchased by Church leaders or people on behalf of Church leaders during this time, which led to Hofmann creating even more forgeries. The Church leadership created a market for Mark Hofmann, and he was motivated by the fame and money to keep producing even more fraudulent papers. All of this ultimately led to the murder of two innocent people and the arrest and incarceration of Mark Hofmann.

The leadership of the Church was deceived—the very elect.[106] The world produced a man bent on deceiving anyone he could: his wife, his friends, the public, and the leadership of The Church of Jesus Christ of Latter-day Saints. The scripture was fulfilled about how even the elect may be deceived. I suspect the leadership repented and moved on.

Here is what Elder Dallin H. Oaks said back in 1987 during a BYU address when asked how the leaders of the Church had been deceived:

> As everyone now knows, Hofmann succeeded in deceiving many: experienced church historians, sophisticated collectors, businessmen-investors, national experts who administered a lie detector test to Hofmann, and professional document examiners, including the expert credited with breaking the Hitler diary forgery. But why, some still ask, were his deceits not detected by the several church leaders with whom he met?
>
> In order to perform their personal ministries, church leaders cannot be suspicious and questioning of each of the hundreds of people they meet each year. Ministers of the gospel function best in an atmosphere of trust and love.
>
> In that kind of atmosphere, they fail to detect a few deceivers, but that is the price they pay to increase their effectiveness in counseling, comforting, and blessing the hundreds of honest and sincere

105. See Dennis Romboy, "Who is Mark Hofmann and what did he do?," *Deseret News*, Mar. 1, 2021, https://www.deseret.com/utah/2021/3/1/22307305/who-is-mark-hofmann-what-did-he-do-forgery-murder-among-mormons-lds-church-netflix-documentary.

106. Church History Topics, "Hofmann Forgeries," ChurchofJesusChrist.org/study/history/topics.

> people they see. It is better for a church leader to be occasionally disappointed than to be constantly suspicious.[107]

This sequence of events and consequences does not unsettle my testimony in the least degree. These imperfect men are like you and me, susceptible to the deceivers of the world. Heavenly Father has provided each of us with agency. If God interfered with our decisions immediately, He would violate our agency. Keep in mind that only one person was perfect, and His name is Jesus Christ. Do not fool yourself thinking that anyone else is perfect and avoids making mistakes. We all are in need of repentance and forgiveness. After all, it is by the grace of God we are saved, after all we can do (see 2 Nephi 25:23).

At a young age, I remember being ridiculed at school for my belief in the First Vision story that was under criticism because of the plot that Mark Hofmann and his salamander letter had created. The deception was widespread and hurt a lot of people. Yet think about how shallow some testimonies turned out to be. A forgery knocked many people off their covenant path. Those foundations were made of sand. I hope yours and mine contain a bit more mortar.

My Rookie Beginnings

Now that the bad example of trusting people is out of the way, I wanted to focus on some good examples. Luckily for all of us, the good examples dwarf the bad by a magnitude of much. I wanted to take a minute and talk about why people become financial advisors and what they get out of it. I'll use my own story so you can see why these types of advisors can be so helpful, and why, more often than not, they are excited to support you!

My journey in the profession isn't a common one, but it shows that believing in yourself, despite the crushing weight of defeat that looms heavy, can lead to great success if you're doing something you love and are not trying to hurt people.

I've always sought to understand the workings of money and its purpose in investments. As I learned more, it made sense to me. I enjoyed the intricacies of the market and getting involved with stocks as a teenager. I was that kid who went to the grocery store to buy *The*

107. Dallin H. Oaks, "Recent Events Involving Church History and Forged Documents," *Ensign*, Oct. 1987, 63.

Wall Street Journal as early as fourteen years of age. In April 1999 I chose to accept the "golden parachute" my employer offered, and after six months of sabbatical, I accepted a career change. I was hired at Prudential Securities in November of that year. After passing all the licensing tests and certifications needed in order to work in the investment world, I furthered my qualifications. I became a candidate for more serious training in La Jolla, California, near the Navy base that trains fighter pilots.

I was one of seventeen recruits, and I was honored to be included. After three weeks of intense training, our instructors presented the coveted "Top Gun Award" to one of my fellow classmates. Unexpectedly, the instructor then produced a simple one-page employment application for the McDonald's fast food restaurant chain and announced that I, Scott Carter, was the recipient of this embarrassing award. Everyone laughed and I took it in stride.

You can imagine how I felt. I loved investments! I loved talking to people about their investments. I wanted to help people achieve their investment objectives, retire, and live life to the fullest. And yet here I was, in front of all my peers from the West Coast, being told specifically that I wasn't going to make it here and that McDonald's was hiring.

I was already committed 100 percent to this career. This phony award only emboldened me.

This was a crossroads moment in my life. Would I step away, accept that I failed, and move on to other opportunities? Or would I use this experience to propel me toward my dream career? How could a negative be turned into a positive? I was determined to win.

I knuckled down to succeed at nearly all costs. There was no plan B. I came home from La Jolla and pinned that employment application to my office wall to remind me of what a mistake those three instructors had made.

During this time, everything felt stacked against me despite my best efforts to create a successful advisory business. I found myself twice in the hiring manager's office with an official letter of dismissal warning me that if I fell off target, I would be terminated within thirty days. There were ups and downs. I went sideways for a spell. I had to rework my strategy more than once. Sometimes I felt completely hopeless, but I did not stop. The manager I worked for had his own agenda, and it was this: turn the recruits often and confiscate their accounts. Even so, day after day, week after week, month after month, and year after year, I worked my plan. The journey was rough and exciting, and in the end, I did reach my goal. My plan ultimately worked. I qualified myself.

Against all odds—and with some help from supporters and a lot of prayers cast heavenward—I clawed my way to success. Though there were those who opposed me, I believed in myself. Believing in yourself no matter what others believe is truly all that matters in this mortal life. No one will believe in you more than yourself. (Your mother is usually second.) Reach for the stars and pray to God for strength, relief, and help.

That is how I qualified myself into the career choice that drives me. I love every minute of it.

The only way to succeed at something is to make a good plan and begin the journey. Hold out faith that if it is a good plan that bears good fruit and God is by your side, you have a high probability of success. The journey may surprise you if you don't give up.

By the way, I know of only one other person from that elite training class in La Jolla, California, who is still in this profession. Everyone else was fired for not hitting the strenuous goals. The classmate who received the "Top Gun Award" washed out less than a year after that ceremony.

Later in life I found my way back to the La Jolla area, which reminded me of that day when I was presented the "Least Likely to Succeed" award. That day I toured the USS Midway, docked there in the San Diego harbor. I toured that magnificent aircraft carrier, a piece of history, and in the gift shop I found and purchased a black cap. In gold stitching it reads *Top Gun*. I wear it occasionally. It reminds me of my little life story. What's *your* story?

I share all of this with you so you can gain an appreciation of dedication, smart work, and belief in oneself, and also so you can see the love that most financial advisors have for their work and their clients. We get up in the morning excited for our day to begin. We work hard to stay where we are. This is the type of advisor you want to find: someone who will smile, listen to you, work with you, and be as committed to your financial success as they are to their own. And in truth, they are far easier to find than you may think.

How Advisors Can Help

If you're still on the fence regarding whether you should hire a financial advisor, here are a few things an FA can help with that will make your life easier.

Taxes—The outright sale of a low cost-basis position can lead to a large tax liability. However, taxes are only one consideration when making a financial decision and should be weighed alongside the risk of volatility and significant losses in a stock. Try not to "let the tax tail wag the investment dog." Seek the advice of a professional tax preparer too. Financial advisors can help offset gains with losses or vice versa when opportunities are presented.

Dividend income—When the dividends from a large stock position provide a significant source of income for a family, it can be difficult to look past that fact and consider selling the stock for other opportunities. GE was an example like this. The dividend yield on a stock, however, is only one component of its total return and risk profile. The dividend is not guaranteed and can be cut with no advance notice by the board of directors. You may be able to position your portfolio to provide the same level of income for your family without taking on the risk associated with a highly concentrated single stock position.

Behavioral finance biases—Individual investors often make investment decisions based on emotional biases and misconceptions that can lead to unfounded behaviors and actions. Once you better understand these biases, you may be more willing to realign your risk-return balance. Informed, objective counsel can help clarify your choices and help you devise more suitable solutions.

Overconfidence—If you hold a concentrated stock that has appreciated over time, you may expect this pattern of appreciation to continue. This sense of confidence may cause you to focus solely on the stock's positive return and underestimate or ignore the risks.

Anchoring—You may target a price above where the stock is currently trading as the point at which you are determined to reduce your concentration risk. However, that limit price may represent a recent high for the stock, and there may be no fundamental reason for the stock to trade back up to that high price again. Should the stock trade down further, you will continue to participate in downside price movements.

Mental accounting—If you are like many investors, you may categorize various parts of your personal wealth into different buckets. Single-stock concentrations may be viewed separately from other investments, and you may also segregate retirement plans, bank accounts, insurance policies, and so on. You should actually incorporate all of these assets into a comprehensive review of your risk-return profile. This is especially true if you are employed by the company in which you own a stock concentration.

Retirement planning—When I ask couples how much they think they need to save for retirement to maintain their desired lifestyle, half say, "I have no idea," and the other half disagree on how much they will need. Advisors provide data that allows you to see where you want to be and what it's going to take to get there.

Unknowns—"Expect the unexpected" applies all the way along your financial journey. While you obviously can't plan precisely for an unknown, financial advisors have a lot of experience and have seen plenty of situations that will help you make decisions. Experience is everything, and that helps when staring into the unknown.

Thorough preparation—Financial advisors will help you make plans for investing and saving. A well-structured financial plan will also include appropriate cash reserves, which will prove especially important should your personal economy be threatened due to the loss of a job or some other struggle.

Helping with Your Financial Plan

While we've touched on financial plans before, let's take a closer look here and see what they can do for you and why you'll want professional help in creating one.

First and foremost, a financial plan will help you get your balance sheet in order. Update your personal balance sheet (assets versus liabilities, broadly speaking). If you are retired, make note of the income you receive from Social Security, pensions, retirement plan assets, or other sources. Everything proceeds from this first step, so take the time to bring these numbers up to date.

From there you'll want to review your budget and spending. How closely did last year's spending match what you'd planned? Were unexpected increases one-time items or ongoing costs? Where can you trim expenses?

Although some budget items are fixed, a sharp pencil and some slashing can produce significant savings on other costs. Start with what you realistically expect to have as income, then assign those dollars to your various expense categories while also maintaining flexibility to account for things like health care that can't be pinned down precisely. Then evaluate your cash holdings. A certain amount of assets should be set aside in cash accounts that can be readily accessed—talk with your advisor about whether your current allocation strikes the right balance. Note that the cash portions of your brokerage and retirement accounts serve a different purpose and shouldn't be counted as emergency reserves. This is also a good time to revisit your asset allocation and investments.

Another key component to your financial plan is evaluating your retirement income foundations. Most retirees have several income sources, such as Social Security, pensions, retirement portfolios, rental properties, notes receivable, inheritances, and so on. Think about how secure each source is. Can you count on that inheritance? Would rental property vacancies interrupt your cash flow? Are the notes receivable backed by collateral? If too much of your retirement income is from less-than-solid sources, it may be time to reposition your assets.

Do It Yourself?

Like with everything, you *can* do all of this yourself. It won't cost you money upfront, but it will cost you time, and time is money. Which of those is a more valuable resource to you: time or money? Most of us wouldn't try to build our own house without professional help, and we shouldn't try to build our financial house without a professional either. It's your choice, but in the end, I can assure you that you'll be in a much better position if you simply ask for help and follow the advice of your financial advisor.

One Last Look

Good: You've met with an advisor who came highly recommended, and that person helped you build a financial plan. You feel that is as far as you need to go, and you implement the plan going forward without any other ongoing help.

Better: You meet with your financial advisor annually and listen to their advice on retirement planning. You have implemented their advice but handle all the details yourself in order to save money.

Best: You meet with your financial planner semi-annually, going over details of your investments and retirement. You allow them to manage your investments because they have gained your trust. You pay attention to your portfolio and understand where your money is being invested. You trust their advice and listen to your advisor when making changes to your plan.

Awful: A financial advisor is too expensive, so you do it all yourself. You handle a few investments but find yourself trading whenever the wind changes. You pull out of stocks too soon and pay heavy tax penalties each time. The process is too complex to master, so you give up and decide that investing and retirement saving is too much for you to handle. You throw everything into a savings account and call it good.

Something for the Kids

Technology has brought everything to young people quicker than their parents or grandparents ever imagined. In the past, companies researched and held their findings close to them in order to give themselves a competitive advantage over their competition. Today, information is so grossly over-available that it is hard to know what truth is, what opinion is, or what an outright lie is.

There is a lot of misinformation everywhere. Call it what you will, but the state of our society is a state of confusion. Because of this, teach your children to locate sources of truth and hang on to them. Search the scriptures. Understand the life your Heavenly Father intended His children to tread. Find someone you trust to help you learn good money management skills. Earn your money, participate in the law of tithing, live gospel principles, and strive to follow good counsel.

Conclusion

Well, it's been quite a ride, but we're just about done. I wanted to end with a few extra thoughts to help you begin (or continue) your financial journey. I prepared my message to encourage you to overproduce, invest, and share, and may I also suggest here and now to never compare yourself to anyone else. I hope you have learned from the examples of others throughout this experience as well. When it comes to finances, there are always plenty of good *and* bad examples. Learn from the best people you can find. A popular saying goes like this: "When the student is ready, the teacher appears." Get ready for the best life by qualifying yourself for your financial future right now.

I trust that you will acknowledge the five talents or two talents or one talent that God has given you. Return more to Him. Your environment is similar to everyone else around you. We each benefit from God's gifts of seasons, soil, seed, sunshine, and rain. What we do with God's gifts is up to each of us individually. Some people can acquire a plot of land, work, reap, and harvest while another allows weeds to overtake their parcel and ends up producing very little. Why would two similar plots of land yield different results? Each received the same seasons, soil, seed, sunshine, and rain—the difference was in what was done with them.

This can be best illustrated with a story I heard once as a child. One afternoon, a farmer had a guest come by to admire his beautiful fields. The guest said, "What a great-looking farm you have here. God sure has created something wonderful for you." The farmer looked around the land and said, "Yes, but you should have seen this place when God had it all to Himself."

That story always makes me smile, and it teaches an important principle. The farmer acknowledged God's blessings of seasons, soil, seed, sunshine, rain, and what God and the farmer can accomplish together. Granted, sometimes it can rain too much or too little. Some seasons are harsher than others. Yet what we accomplish with what God sends us will define who we are. Will we grow in wisdom and stature, or will we complain like Laman and Lemuel because they felt their lot in life was too difficult? Their circumstances were exactly the same as the rest of the family traveling in the wilderness. What will you make of the blessings and trials that await you in your life?

I believe that if you listen to those around you, you can pick up on some very wise words and unexpected counsel. I heard one person share with me the phrase, "God sends some experiences in life to try us, and some trials we bring upon ourselves. It's our responsibility to know the difference." Isn't that interesting? If I break the civil law, I find myself punished or fined. If a tree falls on my car during a storm, do I curse God, complain, and throw a fit, or do I just realize that such is life and do my best to move forward? Perhaps someone swindles funds from my employer, and because of their dishonest actions, many people are laid off, including me. Perhaps I rejoice because I had sufficient money saved for just such a disruption, and my family will be fine because I learned to follow the counsel of the prophet by being prepared. I could just as easily curse God for my circumstances and allow my testimony to grow cold as I become bitter because of my afflictions.

Similar seasons, soil, seed, sunshine, and rain, but it's how we *respond* that dictates the harvest. We will all face storms and drought at different times in our lives. No one goes through mortality without facing stiff headwinds. Reread Helaman 5:12 and focus on the phrase "when the devil shall send forth his mighty winds." The phrase does not say "*if* the devil shall send forth his mighty winds" but "*when* the devil shall send forth his mighty winds."

People succeed because they understand where the challenges of life are coming from, and they persevere. Some start with more, some less, but as we've discussed extensively in this book, it isn't how much you possess that creates a happy existence—it's what you do with it.

And yes, at times the world just doesn't seem fair. But I have a revelation for you—mortal life is *not* fair. I remind my kids of this routinely when they begin to feel injustice. I simply agree with them and remind them that, as their father, it is not my job to make life fair for them. I try to teach them this truth so that their happiness and productivity are never bound to their circumstances. You can be poor and happy, and you can be rich and miserable. If you can feel the joy of life even when facing struggles, you will be open to blessings beyond what you believe possible. That's how the Lord works His miracles.

Life isn't fair, but Heavenly Father is just. Life will throw curves every day—you'll be lucky one moment and unlucky the next—but if you keep your mind fixed on the eternities and the covenant path, you're going to be just fine.

The Card Game of Life

There is actually a fun way to mimic life's cycle of success, failure, talent, skill, and luck to teach yourself and your kids how to manage the emotions involved in winning and losing in mortality: play a card game.

I'm serious—card games are more representative of our earthly experience than we give them credit.

I love playing card games. They require strategy and luck combined. I enjoy playing skilled opponents who bring their proficiencies to the table. We match wits while always adapting to the randomness of the deal. I love all types of strategy games. In fact, I actually placed second in the Dartmouth Junior High School chess tournament as a youth. Wow, right?!

Anyway, back to my card-playing analogy. I am dealt cards. My opponent is also dealt cards. We share small talk as we arrange our hands. Play begins. I must be careful to play the proper card at the right time to beat my opponent. If I make a mistake, that hand may be lost. Each hand brings with it a new shuffle and cards dealt—a new chance to win or lose. As I apply my skill to the random cards and play with thoughtfulness, I may come out the winner. I may capitalize on my opponent's mistakes too. The game is fun, and the conversation is warming. Put down your phone and play a game of skill and luck with your family.

Here is the underlying principle: if I did not have an opponent, I would not have a game. I would not sharpen my skills. I would not grow. In life as well as card games, I win some and I lose some. Either way I can grow.

The trick to winning at cards—and winning at life—is to get very good at executing your skills no matter what cards you draw. This sharpens your mind and thus improves your game.

This plays out in real life all the time. Sometimes we go into a job interview with our set of skills where we are matched against other applicants. There are variables in the game of job hunting. Some work for you and some against you. Perhaps the interviewer reviewed your social media posts to get a feel of how you might fit within the organization and decided you're not a good fit. Perhaps you are competing with someone already in the company looking for a change within. Perhaps your skills and personality are exactly what the corporation wants and they hire you on the spot.

You can't control any of these scenarios or their outcomes. All you can control is your qualifications, your expectations, and how you respond.

Eternal Royalty

We began this book talking about how blessed we all are, and that we live better than kings and queens of old. This is completely true. But even so, we will face challenges of all types—lost jobs, broken-down cars, lost love, stubbed toes, and bent fingers. We may even encounter a true heartache and despair in mortality, such as a painful divorce, wayward children, the unexpected death of a cherished loved one, or perhaps the floundering of our own faith.

These challenges and painful moments don't define us. Our Savior offers us rest from the storm and the comfort of His forgiveness. The Lord has promised us peace.

Spiritual peace.

Mental peace.

Physical peace.

And yes . . . financial peace.

We are called to "go and do." With our finances in order, we are better able to *do* just that. Set your sights on the life you want, knowing it can be achieved. And know that through your affluence, you can help your brothers and sisters in mortality accomplish the same and more.

We are all blessed with essentially the same seasons, soil, seed, sunshine, and rain. What are you going to do with your allotment?

I invite you to find out and share. This book gave me that opportunity, and I am grateful for that.

One Last Look

Good: You apply the principles in this guide and begin your family's financial journey today.

Better: You apply the principles in this guide, pray every day, read the scriptures, and serve in your community so you can teach others what you have learned. You give back.

Best: "Swifter, higher, stronger."[108] You apply these lessons, pray, serve, and work with a financial advisor. You plan as best you can for the storms of life, always knowing that you will have to adapt. You trust in the Lord, share your testimony, and use your wealth to make this world a better place.

Awful: You give in to despair, listening to the whispers of the adversary that nothing you do matters. Every failure, real or perceived, cuts you a little deeper. You allow your finances and your entire life to stagnate, doing no evil but no good either.

Learn from the example of John Kennedy Toole, who wrote the book *A Confederacy of Dunces*.[109] What is so unfortunate about John's example is that the talented young author committed suicide before his book was ever published, based primarily on his belief that he would never find success as a writer.

After his 1969 suicide at age 31, John's mother, Thelma Toole, found a smeared carbon copy of the manuscript. Thelma was persistent

108. See Robert L. Backman, "Swifter, Higher, Stronger," *Liahona*, July 1982.

109. Sam Jordison, "John Kennedy Toole's A Confederacy of Dunces is June's reading group book," *The Guardian*, June 6, 2017, https://www.theguardian.com/books/booksblog/2017/jun/06/john-kennedy-tooles-a-confederacy-of-dunces-is-junes-reading-group-book.

in having the manuscript published as a memorial to her son. She tried many different publishers but to no avail.

Walker Percy, an author and college instructor at Loyola University New Orleans, recounts how Thelma worked tirelessly to have him read the manuscript:

> [The] lady was persistent, and it somehow came to pass that she stood in my office handing me the hefty manuscript. There was no getting out of it; only one hope remained—that I could read a few pages and that they would be bad enough for me, in good conscience, to read no farther. Usually, I can do just that. Indeed, the first paragraph often suffices. My only fear was that this one might not be bad enough, or might be just good enough, so that I would have to keep reading.
>
> In this case I read on. And on. First with the sinking feeling that it was not bad enough to quit, then with a prickle of interest, then a growing excitement, and finally an incredulity: surely it was not possible that it was so good.[110]

The book was published by LSU Press in 1980. It won the Pulitzer Prize for fiction in 1981. If John had shown the same faith in himself that his mother had, perhaps he could have accepted his award himself and gone on to create more works of art that would have enamored and inspired millions.

None of us know what tomorrow will bring. God has promised us that the storm clouds of life will pass. We must trust His word. No matter where you are now, your life is just as likely to improve as it is to get worse. It's actually more likely to get better according to statistics. Keep your spirit focused on the good, and good will enter your life.

Something for the Kids

For kids and for everyone, my advice is this: know your worth. You are first a child of God. Second, you can be on the covenant path. And third, be a disciple of Jesus Christ. Follow good examples. Allow yourself to feel joy and share that joy with others. Learn how to use your finances for good. Learn of Christ and the prophets. Remember

110. Sam Jordison, "John Kennedy Toole's A Confederacy of Dunces"

all the simple "Primary answers" to gospel and life questions. They are more correct than all the volumes ever written.

My Final Words

Obedience to God's laws are the keys to success, whether financial or spiritual. God created all things (see Doctrine and Covenants 104:13–15). All of nature obeys God's laws perfectly. The birds migrate. They don't decide one year to weather the storms—they migrate. Water obeys gravity. Water doesn't decide to move upward—it always follows the course of least resistance. The oak tree produces acorns—it doesn't decide to produce peaches instead. The horse acts like a horse and not an alligator. The sun rises and sets according to God's laws. Every living creature obey God's laws . . . except the human family. God granted you and me agency, which is not "free" because our choices have consequences, both good and bad.

God wants us to return to Him and live eternally in a kingdom He is willing to share with us, should we choose to obey His laws. Heavenly Father will not force our decisions, only reward us for obeying His commandments.

This guidebook and others like it provide you with the information to make better financial choices, all based on sound principles and truth to eternal laws. What will you do with this knowledge and agency to act?

As Paul McCartney once sang, "And in the end, the love you take is equal to the love you make."[111]

111. The Beatles, "The End," track 16 on *Abbey Road*, Apple Records, 1969, compact disc.

Appendix A: Extra Resources

Talks and books worth reading:

- Marvin J. Ashton, "It's No Fun Being Poor" (Brigham Young University devotional, Mar. 30, 1982), speeches.byu.edu.
- Robert L. Backman, "Swifter, Higher, Stronger," *Liahona*, July 1982.
- Ezra Taft Benson, "Prepare for the Days of Tribulation," *Ensign*, Nov. 1980, 32–34.
- George S. Clayton, *The Richest Man in Babylon* (New York: Penguin Books, 1988).
- Lawrence E. Corbridge, "The Way," *Ensign* or *Liahona*, Nov. 2008, 34–36.
- Jeffrey R. Holland, "Safety for the Soul," *Ensign* or *Liahona*, Nov. 2009, 88–90.
- Harvey B. Mackay, *Swim with the Sharks Without Being Eaten Alive: Outsell, Outmanage, Outmotivate, and Outnegotiate Your Competition* (New York: Harper, 2005).
- Thomas S. Monson, "Guideposts for Life's Journey" (Brigham Young University devotional, Nov. 13, 2007), speeches.byu.edu.
- Dallin. H. Oaks, "Good, Better, Best," *Ensign* or *Liahona*, Nov. 2007, 104–8.
- Dallin H. Oaks, "Preparation for the Second Coming," *Ensign* or *Liahona*, May 2004, 7–10.
- Boyd K. Packer, "The Choice," *Ensign*, Nov. 1980, 20–22.
- Boyd K. Packer, "Self Reliance" (Brigham Young University devotional, Mar. 2, 1975), speeches.byu.edu.
- Nathaniel Popper, *Digital Gold: Bitcoin and the Inside Story of the Misfits and Millionaires Trying to Reinvent Money* (New York: Harper, 2016).
- Ayn Rand, *Atlas Shrugged* (New York: Random House, 1957).
- Jim Rohn, "Living an Exceptional Life," audiobook or video, https://www.youtube.com/watch?v=TYtv3s8x8gg.
- Brad Wilcox, "His Grace Is Sufficient" (Brigham Young University devotional, July 12, 2011), speeches.byu.edu.
- Daniel Yergin, *The Prize: The Epic Quest for Oil, Money & Power* (New York: Free Press, 2008).

Appendix B: Answers to "Retirement Twenty Questions"

Let's go over the answers to the "Retirement Twenty Questions" quiz found in chapter 11.

1. D) 19 to 22 years[112]

According to data from the Social Security Administration, men and women retiring at age 65 today can expect to live, on average, 19 to 22 years in retirement. But those are just averages. About one out of every four 65-year-olds today will live past age 90, and one out of ten will live past age 95.

2. B) 59½[113]

Money in a traditional Individual Retirement Account (IRA) cannot typically be withdrawn without penalty before the age of 59½. Any withdrawals taken before this age will need to pay a 10 percent penalty plus regular income taxes. Ouch!

3. A) Social Security[114]

Social Security provides at least 50 percent of household income for more than 50 percent of people age 65 or older. For about one in four seniors, it provides at least 90 percent of their income.

---

112. See "Retirement & Survivors Benefits: Life Expectancy Calculator," Social Security Administration, accessed Dec. 31, 2022, https://www.ssa.gov/OACT/population/longevity.html.

113. See "What if I withdraw money from my IRA?," Internal Revenue Service, Nov. 21, 2022, https://www.irs.gov/newsroom/what-if-i-withdraw-money-from-my-ira.

114. See Irena Dushi, Howard M. Iams, and Brad Trenkamp, "The Importance of Social Security Benefits to the Income of the Aged Population," *Social Security Bulletin* 77, no. 2 (2017). https://www.ssa.gov/policy/docs/ssb/v77n2/v77n2p1.html.

4. A) So He can bless us.[115]

Search the scriptures. Read Numbers 18:26; Proverbs 3:9–10; 2 Chronicles 31:4–5; Genesis 14:19–20; Malachi 3:10; Doctrine and Covenants 64:23; and Doctrine and Covenants sections 119 and 120.

5. C) Having a three-month food supply[116]

Most people I know have never used it but have moved it more than once! At least it is no longer one year. When I grew up in the 1960s, a two-year supply was recommended.

6. C) 25% to 30%[117]

If you were born between 1943 and 1954, your full retirement age is 66. Starting your monthly benefits at age 62 will result in a 25 percent reduction. If you were born after 1954, your full retirement age is 67, and benefits started at age 62 would be reduced by 30 percent.

7. A) True[118]

Distributions from traditional 401ks and IRAs are generally taxable because investments are made using pre-tax income. With ROTH 401ks and Roth IRAs, investments are made using after-tax income, so qualified withdrawals are tax free.

8. B) Liquid cash sources, Roth IRA, 401k

Some believe this, and I also support this sequence. Liquid cash in a checking account is already taxed, a Roth IRA is tax-free, and finally the 401k because you put off paying taxes for as long into your life as you can.

115. See "Food Storage for One Year," *Ensign*, Mar. 2006.

116. See "Longer-Term Food Storage," The Church of Jesus Christ of Latter-day Saints, accessed May 29, 2023, https://www.churchofjesuschrist.org/topics/food-storage/longer-term-food-supply.

117. See "If you were born between 1943 and 1954 your full retirement age is 66," Social Security Administration, accessed Dec. 31, 2022, https://www.ssa.gov/benefits/retirement/planner/1943.html.

118. See Denise Appleby, "Roth IRA vs. Traditional IRA: Key Differences," Investopedia, last modified Mar. 30, 2023, https://www.investopedia.com/retirement/roth-vs-traditional-ira-which-is-right-for-you/.

9. B) 13 years[119]

It seems that people on the West Coast keep their homes longer than people on the East Coast, some studies show. The point is that people move several times in their life.

10. B) False[120]

First, hitting any consistent return will never happen in the stock market or any free market. For this reason, professionals turn to a Monte Carlo tool that provides a more realistic probability of reaching your financial goals.

11. D) 65[121]

You are eligible for Medicare on your 65th birthday. If you retire before age 65, you will need to purchase your own health insurance plan until Medicare kicks in. If you plan to delay receiving Medicare benefits until after age 65 because you are still working, it is generally advisable to still register at age 65 to avoid any delays or late enrollment penalties.

12. B) $1,827[122]

While getting a monthly check for $1,827 may sound nice, that equates to only $21,924 per year in income in January 2023. The maximum at FRA is $3,627/mo.

119. See Dana Anderson, "The Typical U.S. Home Changes Hands Every 13.2 Years," Redfin, Mar. 2, 2022, https://www.redfin.com/news/2021-homeowner-tenure/.

120. See Will Kenton, "Monte Carlo Simulation: History, How it Works, and 4 Key Steps," Investopedia, last modified Mar. 26, 2023, https://www.investopedia.com/terms/m/montecarlosimulation.asp.

121. See "Who's eligible for Medicare?," Department of Health and Human Services, last modified Dec. 8, 2022, https://www.hhs.gov/answers/medicare-and-medicaid/who-is-eligible-for-medicare/index.html.

122. See Emily Brandon, "How Much You Will Get From Social Security," U.S. News, May 8, 2023, https://money.usnews.com/money/retirement/social-security/articles/how-much-you-will-get-from-social-security.

13. D) 48%[123]

Recent studies show that 48 percent of retirees are surprised by an unexpected early retirement, so being prepared is a good idea. The most common reason for early retirement is health problems or disability. The second most common reason for early retirement is company downsizing or closure.

14. C) Keep God's commandments and prosper in the land

See 2 Nephi 1:20 for one of many examples.

15. A) To save for future college expenses[124]

For tax reasons alone, this has been a popular way to save for higher educational needs. When these funds are used for the costs associated with higher education, then the capital gains will go untaxed.

16. D) Time in years to double an investment[125]

The Rule of 72 gives an estimation of the doubling time for an investment. The formula is useful for understanding the effect of compounding interest. If a certificate of deposit paid 9 percent interest each year in compounded interest, then in 8 years, your original investment will double its value (9 x 8 = 72).

17. A) 22[126]

The average credit card interest rate is now at 22.37 percent at the time this was written, according to recent data. Regardless of the

123. See Lisa Greenwald and Craig Copeland, "The 2017 Retirement Confidence Survey: Many Workers Lack Retirement Confidence and Feel Stressed About Retirement Preparations," Employee Benefit Research Institute, Mar. 21, 2017, https://www.ebri.org/docs/default-source/ebri-issue-brief/ebri_ib_431_rcs.pdf.

124. "Topic No. 313 Qualified Tuition Programs (QTPs)," Internal Revenue Service, last modified Apr. 4, 2023, https://www.irs.gov/taxtopics/tc313.

125. See Will Kenton, "The Rule of 72: Definition, Usefulness, and How to Use It," Investopedia, May 31, 2022, https://www.investopedia.com/terms/r/ruleof72.asp.

126. See Sienna Wrenn and Lars Peterson, "Average Credit Card Interest Rate is 22.37%," The Balance, last modified Jan. 10, 2023, https://www.thebalancemoney.com/average-credit-card-interest-rate-4772408.

slight variation, you and I are outnumbered by the deep budgets and well-funded marketing groups that financial institutions have to keep their clients in debt when using revolving debt credit cards.

18. C) Continence, transferring, toileting, bathing, dressing, and eating[127]

Any two or more of these will trigger a claim for long-term care benefits with your doctor's authorization.

19. A) Housing[128]

On average, housing is still the biggest expense in retirement. Even if you have your mortgage paid off, or close to it, costs such as insurance, property taxes, utilities, maintenance, and general household items still add up.

20. B) 4%[129]

Withdrawing 4 percent of your retirement account each year is often viewed as the "Goldilocks" amount. Taking out less may not generate enough income to support your lifestyle, but taking out more runs the risk of depleting the account too early.

127. See "What is Long-Term Care?," Administration for Community Living, Feb. 18, 2020, https://acl.gov/ltc/basic-needs/what-is-long-term-care.

128. See "Housing Expenditures," U.S. Bureau of Labor Statistics, Mar. 2002, https://www.bls.gov/opub/btn/archive/housing-expenditures.pdf.

129. See Julia Kagan, "What Is the 4% Rule for Withdrawals in Retirement and How Much Can You Spend?," Investopedia, last modified Jan. 20, 2022, https://www.investopedia.com/terms/f/four-percent-rule.asp.

Appendix C: Disclaimers

While the author has used his best efforts in preparing this book, he makes no representation or warranties with respect to the accuracy or completeness of the contents of this book and specifically disclaims any implied warranties of merchant's ability or fitness for a particular purpose. The advice and strategies contained herein may not be suitable for your situation. You should consult with a legal advisor, a financial advisor, a tax advisor, and any other professional where appropriate. Neither the publisher nor the author shall be held liable for any loss of profit or any other commercial damages, including but not limited to special, incidental, consequential, or any other damage. This guide is for educational purposes only. The views expressed are of the author alone and should not be taken as expert instruction or commands. The reader is responsible for his or her own actions. Adherence to all applicable laws and regulations—including international, federal, state, and local laws governing professional licensing, business practices, advertising, and all other aspects of doing business in the United States and abroad—is the sole responsibility of the purchaser. Neither the author nor the publisher assumes any responsibility or liability whatsoever on behalf of the purchaser of this guide.

Any perceived slight of any person or organization is purely unintentional. Past performance is not necessarily indicative of future performance. Stock and option trading is not appropriate for everyone. There is a substantial risk of loss associated with trading these markets. Losses can and will occur. No system or methodology has ever been developed that can guarantee profit or ensure freedom from losses, nor will it ever likely be. No representation or application is being made that using the methodology or systems or information contained within this book will generate profits or ensure freedom from losses. The information contained in this guide is for educational purposes only and should not be taken as investment advice. Examples presented here are not solicitations to buy or sell. The author and publisher and all affiliates assume no responsibility for your trading results. There is always a high risk in trading. Hypothetical or simulated performance results have certain limitations. Unlike an actual performance record, simulated results do not represent actual trading. Also, since the trades have not been executed, the results may have under- or over-compensated for the impact, if any, of certain market factors such as the lack of liquidity. Simulated trading programs in general are also subject to the fact that they are designed with the benefit of hindsight. No representation is being made that any account will or is likely to achieve profit or losses similar to those shown.

The information contained in this book does not purport to be a complete description of the securities, markets, or developments referred to in this material. The information has been obtained from sources considered to be reliable, but we do not guarantee that the foregoing material is accurate or complete. Any information is not a complete summary or statement of all available data necessary for making an investment decision and does not constitute a recommendation. Any opinions of the chapter authors are those of the chapter author and not necessarily those of RJFS or Raymond James. Expressions of opinion are as of the initial book publishing date and are subject to change without notice.

Raymond James Financial Services, Inc. is not responsible for the consequences of any particular transaction or investment decision based on the content of this book. All financial, retirement, and estate planning should be individualized since each person's situation is unique.

This information is not intended as a solicitation or an offer to buy or sell any security referred to herein. Keep in mind that there is no assurance that our recommendations or strategies will ultimately be successful or profitable, nor protect against a loss. There may also be the potential for missed growth opportunities that may occur after the sale of an investment. Recommendations, specific investments, or strategies discussed may not be suitable for all investors. Past performance may not be indicative of future results. You should discuss any tax or legal matters with the appropriate professional.

The Dow Jones Industrial Average (DJIA), commonly known as "The Dow," is an index representing thirty stocks of companies maintained and reviewed by the editors of *The Wall Street Journal*.

The S&P 500 is an unmanaged index of 500 widely held stocks that is generally considered representative of the US stock market.

Index returns do not reflect the deductions of fees, trading costs, or other expenses. The Index is referred to for informational purposes only: the composition of each Index is different from the composition of the accounts managed by the investment manager. Investors may not make direct investments into any index. Past performance may not be indicative of future results.

401k plans are long-term retirement savings vehicles. Withdrawal of pre-tax contributions and/or earnings will be subject to ordinary income tax and, if taken prior to age 59½, may be subject to a 10 percent federal tax penalty.

Roth 401k plans are long-term retirement savings vehicles. Contributions to a Roth 401k are never tax deductible, but if certain conditions are met, distributions will be completely income tax free. Unlike Roth IRAs, Roth 401k participants are subject to required minimum distributions at age 72 (or 70½ if you reach 70½ before January 1, 2020).

Matching contributions from your employer may be subject to a vesting schedule. Please consult with your financial advisor for more information.

Traditional IRAs: Contributions to a traditional IRA may be tax-deductible depending on the taxpayer's income, tax-filing status, and other factors. Withdrawal of pre-tax contributions and/or earnings will be subject to ordinary income tax and, if taken prior to age 59½, may be subject to a 10 percent federal tax penalty.

Roth IRAs: Earnings withdrawn prior to 59½ would be subject to income taxes. Roth IRA owners must be 59½ or older and have held the IRA for five years before tax-free withdrawals are permitted.

Like traditional IRAs, contribution limits apply to Roth IRAs. In addition, with a Roth IRA, your allowable contribution may be reduced or eliminated if your annual income exceeds certain limits. Contributions to a Roth IRA are never tax deductible, but if certain conditions are met, distributions will be completely income tax free.

Unless certain criteria are met, Roth IRA owners must be 59½ or older and have held the IRA for five years before tax-free withdrawals are permitted. Additionally, each converted amount may be subject to its own five-year holding period. Converting a traditional IRA into a

Roth IRA has tax implications. Investors should consult a tax advisor before deciding to do a conversion. IRA tax deductibility and contribution eligibility may be restricted if your income exceeds certain limits. Please consult with a financial professional for more information.

RMDs are generally subject to federal income tax and may be subject to state taxes. Consult your tax advisor to assess your situation.

Dollar-cost averaging cannot guarantee a profit or protect against a loss, and you should consider your financial ability to continue purchases through periods of low price levels.

Diversification does not ensure a profit or guarantee against a loss. Diversification and asset allocation do not ensure a profit or protect against a loss. Holding investments for the long-term does not ensure a profitable outcome. Investing involves risk, and you may incur a profit or loss regardless of strategy selected. Keep in mind that there is no assurance that any strategy will ultimately be successful or profitable nor protect against a loss. Dividends are not guaranteed and must be authorized by the company's board of directors.

Please be aware that there may be substantial fees, charges, and costs associated with establishing a charitable remainder trust.

Options: Investing involves risk, and you may incur a profit or loss regardless of strategy selected. Options involve unique risks, tax consequences, and commission charges and are not suitable for all investors. When appropriate, options should comprise a modest portion of an investor's portfolio. No statement within this document should be construed as a recommendation to buy or sell a security or to provide investment advice. Prior to making any options transactions, investors must receive a copy of the Options Disclosure Document, which may be obtained from your financial advisor, from cboedirect.com/resources/intro.aspx or by contacting Raymond James at 880 Carillon Parkway, St. Petersburg, FL 33716. Supporting documentation for any claims (including any claims made on behalf of options programs or the options expertise of salespersons), comparison, recommendations, statistics, or other technical data will be supplied upon request.

Raymond James and its advisors do not offer tax or legal advice. Please note that changes in tax laws may occur at any time and could have a substantial impact upon each person's situation. While we are familiar with the tax provisions of the issues presented herein, as financial advisors of RJFS, we are not qualified to render advice on tax or legal matters. You should discuss tax or legal matters with the appropriate professional.

Crypto: Prior to making an investment decision, please consult with your financial advisor about your individual situation. The prominent underlying risk of using Bitcoin as a medium of exchange is that it is not authorized or regulated by any central bank. Bitcoin issuers are not registered with the SEC, and the Bitcoin marketplace is currently unregulated. Bitcoin and other cryptocurrencies are a very speculative investment and involve a high degree of risk. Investors must have the financial ability, sophistication, experience, and willingness to bear the risks of an investment and a potential total loss of their investment.

Life insurance: These policies have exclusions and/or limitations. The cost and availability of life insurance depend on factors such as age, health, and the type and amount of insurance purchased. As with most financial decisions, there are expenses associated with the purchase of life insurance. Policies commonly have mortality and expense charges. In addition, if a policy is surrendered prematurely, there may be surrender charges and income tax implications. Guarantees are based on the claims paying ability of the insurance company.

With variable annuities, any withdrawals may be subject to income taxes and, prior to age 59½, a 10% federal penalty tax may apply. Withdrawals from annuities will affect both the account value and the death benefit. The investment return and principal value will fluctuate so that an investor's shares, when redeemed, may be worth more or less than their original cost. An annual contingent deferred sales charge (CDSC) may apply.

Long-term care: These policies have exclusions and/or limitations. The cost and availability of long-term care insurance depends on factors such as age, health, and the type and amount of insurance purchased. As with most financial decisions, there are expenses associated with the purchase of long-term care insurance. Guarantees are based on the claims paying ability of the insurance company.

529s: As with other investments, there are generally fees and expenses associated with participation in a 529 plan. There is also a risk that these plans may lose money or not perform well enough to cover education costs as anticipated. Most states offer their own 529 programs, which may provide advantages and benefits exclusively for their residents. The tax implications can vary significantly from state to state.

Favorable state tax treatment for investing in Section 529 college savings plans may be limited to investments made in plans offered by your home state. Investors should consult a tax advisor about any state tax consequences of an investment in a 529 plan.

—Raymond James & Associates, Inc., member New York Stock Exchange/SIPC

About the Author

Scott Carter grew up in San Jose, California, and has been involved in investments since his teenage years. Passionate about his career, he now has over twenty-three years of professional experience as a financial advisor. He combines his knowledge of numbers with his interest in the investment markets to assist clients in the following five areas: equity investments, 529 college savings plans, insurance needs, taxation, and estate planning.

Scott is a dedicated father of eight and a grandfather to a growing number of grandkids. His family is his number one interest, and he and his wife Cristie invest most of their time with their immediate family, extended family, friends, church family, and community at large. His four life pursuits are inscribed on a ring he wears constantly: "Financially Free, Large Property, Christian Family, Good Health."

In his spare time, Scott enjoys playing golf, riding his bicycle, swimming, building unique projects, playing card games (and playing to win!), and watching *The Waltons* with his family on Sunday evenings. His motto is "Work smart, play often," and he believes fully in the phrase, "Die with experiences, not dreams."

Scan to visit

www.carterinvestmentadvisory.com